Christina E. Metz

Information Dissemination in Currency Crises

Springer

Author

Dr. Christina E. Metz
Goethe-University Frankfurt
Finance Department
Mertonstr. 17–21
60325 Frankfurt
Germany

Cataloging-in-Publication Data applied for

A catalog record for this book is available from the Library of Congress.

Bibliographic information published by Die Deutsche Bibliothek
Die Deutsche Bibliothek lists this publication in the Deutsche Nationalbibliografie; detailed bibliographic data is available in the Internet at http://dnb.ddb.de

ISSN 0075-8450
ISBN 3-540-00656-7 Springer-Verlag Berlin Heidelberg New York

Springer-Verlag Berlin Heidelberg New York
a member of BertelsmannSpringer Science+Business Media GmbH

http://www.springer.de

Typesetting: Camera ready by author
Cover design: *Erich Kirchner*, Heidelberg

Printed on acid-free paper SPIN: 10917336 41/3143/du 5 4 3 2 1 0

Lecture Notes in Economics and Mathematical Systems 527

Springer
Berlin
Heidelberg
New York
Hong Kong
London
Milan
Paris
Tokyo

To Stephan

Preface

Of course, this book cannot go without many thanks to my family, friends and colleagues, who all had their part in the completion of it. Without their constant encouragement, constructive comments and also critique, my research work would most probably have never led to the book you are holding in your hands. Here, now, is my chance to thank them all.

First of all, my dearest thanks go to Prof. Jochen Michaelis, the supervisor of my doctoral thesis. He was the one who guided me through the process of finding my personal approach to economic research. By providing me with constant support and undivided interest, I benefited tremendously from the time we were working together. I cannot thank him enough for opening up the world of science to me.

To Prof. Peter Weise I am indebted for very constructive comments throughout my work and for refereeing my thesis together with Profs. Frank Beckenbach and Rainer Stöttner. Also, I would like to thank Prof. Hans Nutzinger for always giving me advice and cheering-up words while we shared the same floor at Kassel university.

This book would be unthinkable without the support by Hyun Song Shin, Stephen Morris and Frank Heinemann. The whole idea of conducting theoretical work on currency crises was sparked off by the paper of Stephen and Hyun. Together with Frank they also kept the spark alive. In many discussions they gave me new ideas of research questions still to be dealt with and interesting insights into their own work. I will never be able to fully express my thanks to Hyun for inviting me to work in the congenial atmosphere of the London School of Economics. Also, I very much benefited from discussions in various of the London seminars with Heski Bar-Isaac, Margaret Bray, Max Bruche, Jon Danielsson and Charles Goodhart.

Special thanks go to my co-author Frank Heinemann. He is one of the very rare kind of economists who take a real interest in other people's work and, above all, take the time for a serious and detailed comment. Working together with him was a pleasure and taught me how to derive theoretical results in the most thorough way.

With hindsight, I have to admit that the most exhausting part of my dissertation's completion has been borne by my colleague Jörg Lingens. He had to suffer from all my throwbacks and complaints, which inevitably made their way to his office. Thanks, Jörg, for putting up with me during these times.

The largest part of my gratitude is due to my family and friends. My parents supported me in my scientific career in any possible way and never lost their confidence in the course of life that I had chosen. Melanie Apel, my friend of many years, had the difficult task of discussing all the non-scientific aspects of my dissertation – a task that she mastered very well. Thank you all for the effort you took in me.

My deepest thanks, however, are to my fiancé, Stephan Bannier. He lightened up my life in a way that I had never believed to be possible. Never before have I experienced such an unfaltering confidence in my work and in myself. He also had an eye on the linguistic style of this book, even from overseas. Many thanks, Sid, for sending me the "Economical Writing" and for introducing me to the mystic world of Power Point.

Finally, I want to express my gratitude towards the Center for Financial Studies, Frankfurt. Apart from providing me with a constructive audience for discussing my research results, I very much appreciate the generous support that made this book possible.

Frankfurt,
January 2003

Christina E. Metz

Contents

Introduction

Following the currency crises of the last decade in Europe, Mexico and Asia, a growing literature has appeared trying to explain and formalize financial turmoil. In today's world of fast-changing and complex markets with large numbers of interacting speculators of different sizes and market power, the so-called first- and second-generation currency crisis models no longer seemed to be able to explain the observed collapses of fixed exchange rate regimes. Many countries thought to have learned better and returned to flexible exchange rate systems or introduced currency boards (with problems of themselves). Yet, it is important to understand the reasons for the observed crises in order to prevent future ones, since there are still reasons that call for fixed exchange rate pegs. In contrast to the first- and second-generation models, the newer "third-generation" models analyze a large number of different aspects of currency crises. There is, however, one issue to which not only many of the newer currency crisis models but also a growing number of models concerned with financial markets in general ascribe a central role in explaining turmoil: information. Actions of financial market participants are mostly led by incoming "news" as well as already processed "past" information, i.e. elaborate knowledge about the market, its participants and the underlying fundamentals. In this respect, the following work is aimed at two aspects: first, we want to give an overview of the existing literature on currency crises with special regard to the influence of information. Second, we want to go into more detail concerning the effects of information dissemination in foreign exchange markets, and present own research results on this context. Whereas the first parts of this book analyze the role of information in currency crises on a purely theoretical level, the last part is dedicated to giving evidence for the theoretical predictions from "real-life" observations.

Starting point of our work is a revision of the "classical" currency crisis models by Krugman (1979) and Obstfeld (1994, 1996). These two types of models are still the basis for the more recent work, which usually chooses either of the two approaches to start from. In the first-generation models of currency crises, developed by Krugman (1979) and Flood and Garber (1984), crises are triggered by the deterioration of economic fundamentals. The underlying reason for the eventual collapse of the fixed parity is mainly a seigniorage driven aspect: a country excessively monetizing its budget deficit will most certainly face a crisis, since this strategy will eventually collide with the target of keeping the exchange rate fixed. This explanation has been seen fit for the observed currency crises in several Latin American countries during the 1980s, where large debt burdens and high inflation rates led to the breakdown of the fixed-rate regimes. However, for most of the speculative attacks of the 1990s these arguments no longer held, since the crises were not so much justified by a worsening of fundamentals, but were rather seen to have been increasingly triggered by a change in market sentiment. Obstfeld (1986, 1994, 1996) therefore proposed a completely different approach of explaining the collapse of fixed exchange rate systems. His classical second-generation model (Obstfeld, 1994) blamed the crisis on the trade-off between different policy targets pursued by a government that is engaged in a fixed exchange rate regime. On the one hand the government is committed to keeping the fixed parity, on the other hand the defence of the peg against attacking speculators leads to costs, which prevent achieving several other targets like reducing the fiscal burden or stimulating economic growth. Since the costs of defending the peg typically increase in the number of attacking speculators, speculators' actions become reinforcing, so that this model is prone to self-fulfilling beliefs: if speculators expect the government to abandon the peg, all rational speculators will attack the peg in order to profit from the anticipated devaluation. This raises the costs of maintaining the peg, so that the government indeed has to abandon the parity. Speculators' actions in anticipation of an attack thus precipitate the crisis itself. In contrast, if speculators believe the peg not to be in danger, they will refrain from attacking, thereby again vindicating their initial beliefs. Second-generation currency crisis models are therefore characterized by the fact that the same state of fundamentals may be consistent with both a crisis and a situation of stability. Although sudden switches between crisis and non-crisis situations without major changes of the underlying fundamentals have been observed in the past, and second-generation models have been praised for being able to explain this feature, the major drawback of these models is the lack of predictability of outcome. Only for extremely good or extremely bad economic states is it possible to predict whether or not a speculative attack will take place and be successful. For a rather large intermediate range of economic fundamentals, however, the outcome is completely ambiguous: there may be speculative attacks as well as financial stability. During the last years, second-generation currency crisis models, their explanatory power notwithstanding, have more and more often been criticized for displaying multiple equilibria in the relevant range of fundamentals: a feature, which does not allow the derivation of policy advice that is urgently called for in order to prevent future crises.

Most of the "newer" currency crisis models therefore try to explain the probability of a crisis as being dependent on both the fundamental state of the economy and on speculators' expectations. One strand of literature in this respect concentrates on the importance of coordinated behavior among speculators for the question whether a potential attack will be successful or not. Starting with the Obstfeld-model,[1] where aspects of coordination were taken into account for the first time in currency crisis models, this topic has gained importance. Quite unsurprisingly, coordination aspects are strongly linked to the issues of information and knowledge of traders. When deciding on whether to coordinate their actions or not, agents have to know their opponents' "optimal" actions as well as the fundamental state underlying the economy. Changing the structure of knowledge by disseminating different forms of information with varying precisions, will very strongly influence the possibility and profitability of a coordinated attack on the fixed parity. In one of the most recent currency crisis models as proposed by Morris and Shin (1998), it is shown that restricting the possibility of coordinated behavior on the part of the speculators by providing them with noisy instead of complete information, will help to solve the multiple equilibria problem. In later models, Morris and Shin (1999a,b, 2000, 2001), demonstrate how coordinated behavior can be influenced by changing the precision and structure of speculators' information about the fundamental state of the economy. Following these intriguing findings, a large part of this book concentrates on analyzing the influence of information dissemination on the probability of a currency crisis, respectively on the probability of a speculative attack on the fixed parity. Naturally, investigating into the role of information disclosures in currency crises leads to the question, in which way the central bank or government can use the effects of disseminating fundamental information in trying to prevent currency crises. Giving an answer to this question will be one major aim of this book.

During the last few years, the literature on currency crisis models à la Morris and Shin strongly expanded and took into account a growing number of complex issues. Within the scope of this book, we will concentrate on mainly two of the large number of interesting aspects. In this respect, we will analyze models that allow for traders of heterogeneous size. Since large traders have often been suspected to render markets more volatile, scrutinizing the influence of a large speculator's informational position relative to the rest of the market should be a fruitful exercise. A second, particularly interesting approach of analyzing financial markets is concerned with a dynamic structure of agents' decisions. Since speculators on foreign exchange markets are usually able to observe their predecessors' actions, models which take these aspects into account assign an important role to herding behavior and informational cascades as a consequence of the dynamic sequencing of decisions. In this book, we will delineate the very recent models which try to combine

[1] In the following "the Obstfeld-model" always refers to the model as laid out in Obstfeld (1994), which in a similar form has been taken up again in Obstfeld (1996).

a dynamic approach with the currency crisis models à la Morris and Shin, thereby giving a realistic picture of today's markets.

Apart from the theoretical analyses on the role of information dissemination in currency crises, the last months and years have produced some intriguing work on empirically testing the results from theory. Within this book, we would like to emphasize several of these approaches. Since the theoretical models mostly display game-theoretic structures within a macroeconomic setting, two types of testing procedures seem to be appropriate: whereas evidence for game-theoretic predictions is usually found through experiments in the form of laboratory situations, tests of macroeconomic phenomena are generally conducted through econometric analyses of economic data. We will portray both types of testing procedures in one of the latter parts of this book.

Due to the up-to-datedness of the topic analyzed, there exists a vast amount of literature examining interesting questions related to information dissemination on financial markets. Unfortunately, however, we cannot report and comment on all of these. Within this book, we therefore concentrate only on the most important and influential research approaches concerning aspects of information disclosure in currency crises. In particular, we will neither investigate into questions referring to the microstructure of financial markets, nor into more macroeconomic oriented topics such as e.g. speculative bubbles. A superb overview of models dealing with these issues can be found in Brunnermeier (2001). For a more detailed revision of the market microstructure of foreign exchange markets, see also Lyons (2001) and O'Hara (1997).

The book is structured as follows. Part I critically reviews the first-generation currency crisis model by Krugman (1979) and its extensions in Chap. 1. Chapter 2 follows by depicting the second-generation model with self-fulfilling expectations as introduced by Obstfeld (1994). After pointing out the shortcomings of both approaches, part II concentrates on a solution method on how to overcome the major problems connected with the classical currency crisis models. Since this method is heavily based on game-theoretic concepts, we will lay out the most important theoretical preliminaries in Chap. 4. Chapter 5 proceeds with introducing the currency crisis model by Morris and Shin (1998). It will be demonstrated how they succeed in deriving a unique equilibrium from a currency crisis model with self-fulfilling expectations. In this model the event of a crisis also depends on the fundamental state of the economy, so that it solves the problems of the classical models on currency crises. As we will see, their result strongly relies on the assumption that speculators cannot flawlessly perceive information about economic fundamentals. Instead they receive noisy private, i.e. individual, signals about the fundamental state of the economy. The assumed noisiness of information thus presents an additional condition, which eliminates all but one equilibrium. Extensions of the seminal paper by Morris and Shin (1998) with regard to transparency aspects and expectation formation on the part of the speculators will be presented in Chap. 6.

Part III of this book is concerned with the influence of different types of information on the probability of a currency crisis in the typical setting of a Morris/Shin-model.[2] In accordance with Metz (2002a), we distinguish between two types of information: public and private. Chapter 8 gives a detailed characterization of both forms of information. As will be shown, introducing noisy private and public information into a simple Morris/Shin-model delivers a unique equilibrium, provided that certain conditions for the precision of information are satisfied. Deriving a unique equilibrium in Chap. 9 allows to investigate the influence of the exogenous parameters on the equilibrium in a comparative statics analysis. Apart from the effects of costs and payoffs associated with an attack on the fixed parity, we are foremost interested in the influence of private and public information on the probability of a currency crisis. Surprisingly, increasing the precision of private and public information does not always diminish the danger of a crisis. Rather, it follows that the impact of varying precision of private and public information is contingent on the market sentiment, i.e. the fundamental state that is commonly expected by the speculators. Additionally, it is shown that most of the time the two types of information have opposite influence on the event of a crisis. Naturally, these results lead to the question which information policy a central bank or government should conduct in order to minimize the danger of an attack on the fixed parity. The answer to this question is given in Chap. 10 and follows research results by Heinemann and Metz (2002), who analyze optimal information policy and risk taking for a government to avoid currency crises.

Part IV of this book depicts further theoretical work on currency crises, which uses the basic Morris/Shin framework to analyze additional topics. In this respect, we concentrate on aspects of traders' heterogeneity and dynamic time structures. The influence of a single "large" trader on foreign exchange markets during crisis situations has extensively been examined by Corsetti, Dasgupta, Morris and Shin (2001), as well as Corsetti, Pesenti and Roubini (2001), and will be delineated in Sect. 12.1. Alternatively to these analyses, Sect. 12.2 investigates into the role of a large trader and his informational position in a model with a modified time structure. This approach follows Metz (2002b) and allows to answer even more complex questions concerning the large trader's influence on the probability of a currency crisis. Not surprisingly, it is shown that the large trader may render the market more aggressive, but not necessarily has to do so. Whereas the models by Corsetti, Dasgupta et al. (2001) and Corsetti, Pesenti et al. (2001) demonstrate that the market always becomes more aggressive due to the existence of the large trader whenever he possesses information of superior precision, the model by Metz (2002b) concludes that the large speculator's influence depends on the market sentiment. Whenever the market is sufficiently pessimistic with respect to the maintenance of the fixed parity, it will become even more aggressive, if there

[2] Unless otherwise stated, the notion "Morris/Shin-model" refers to the model as derived in Morris and Shin (1998).

is a single large speculator on the market. A precisely informed large trader on an optimistic market, however, will reduce the market's aggressiveness.

Chapter 13 concentrates on a rather different approach of extending the basic Morris/Shin-model. In contrast to the former, consistently static models, it examines a dynamic sequencing of speculators' decisions, in which traders can observe their predecessors' choices. As one of the few models combining herding behavior with coordination games, we will depict the approach by Dasgupta (2001) and present its results concerning the influence of information, especially of signalling effects, on the event of a crisis. Chapter 13 concludes with combining the effects of traders' heterogeneity with a dynamic time structure and shows that the dynamic sequencing of actions strengthens a large speculator's influence.

Part V finally attempts at finding evidence for the theoretically derived results of the previous chapters. In this respect, Chap. 15 delineates experimental analyses trying to verify whether or not subjects behave according to the predictions of coordination-games theory, especially whether their actions converge towards a unique equilibrium strategy. By describing the results from experimental analysis on the behavior of agents in coordination situations, we refer to the work by Heinemann, Nagel and Ockenfels (2001). They find evidence that subjects in a laboratory, when faced with a crisis-like situation, actually behave in accordance with the theoretical predictions. However, they also conclude that agents do not ascribe as much importance to the specific type and precision of information as expected. The experimental results hence weakly support the theoretical findings. Chapter 16 presents a different approach of giving evidence for the theory on information dissemination in currency crises. Prati and Sbracia (2001) in a very recent paper tested whether the predictions for the influence of information precision as derived in Chap. 9 actually hold for observed currency crises of the past. They use data from six Asian countries for the time of 1995 to 2001 and find that indeed uncertainty among private investors to a large extent can be made responsible for the pressure on the exchange rate. Since their test-hypotheses are taken from the model by Metz (2002a) as delineated in Chap. 9, we will depict their testing procedure and the subsequent results in greater detail. Chapter 16 closes with a brief examination of the Mexican peso crisis in 1994–95, which, according to most of the observers at the time, was characterized by a general lack of information about relevant monetary data. By concluding from the literature at the time of the crisis, we try to find out whether the information policy conducted by the Mexican government has been similar to the policy predicted as optimal in Chap. 10.

Please note that each part of this book has been constructed to be self-explaining, with subsequent chapters not necessarily relying on previous ones. Due to this concept, the shortness of analysis has been sacrificed to repetitions of specific modelling types. In order to keep these reiterations short, however, we will refer to one thorough and detailed description in one of the earlier chapters whenever possible.

Part I

The Classical Currency Crisis Models

1

First-Generation Model – Krugman (1979)

The so-called first-generation research on currency crises presented a response to the observed foreign exchange turmoil in the 1970s in developing countries such as Mexico (1973–1982) and Argentina (1978–1981). These crises were typically preceded by extremely expansive fiscal policies. The aim of the first-generation models therefore was to show how overly expansionary domestic policies combined with a fixed exchange rate eventually lead to a crisis concerning the fixed currency. It was demonstrated that crises were triggered by private market participants trying to profit from uncovering inconsistent policies. Speculators in this approach were therefore seen as rather blameless. Since the currency crisis was the inevitable result of governmental policies inconsistent with a fixed parity, the foreign exchange traders were simply tearing down structures that would have broken down anyway.

The roots of the first-generation currency attack models lay in the work of Salant and Henderson (1978). They showed that pegging the price of gold and using a governmental held stock to keep that peg, eventually leads to a speculative attack which wipes out the stock and hence the fixed peg. Krugman (1979) used this idea to demonstrate that a fixed exchange rate parity cannot be maintained, if the central bank uses monetary policy to finance the governmental budget deficit. He also succeeded in showing that in a world with perfect foresight, the transition between a fixed-rate regime and the successing regime cannot be smooth, but involves a speculative attack. In this attack, speculators purchase all foreign reserves from the central bank which are held to defend the fixed parity. By fixing the exchange rate while at the same time conducting inappropriate domestic policies, the central bank in essence offers speculators a one-sided bet: a successful speculative attack (Obstfeld, 1986).

The following sections portray the classical model, commonly referred to as "the first-generation" model by Krugman (1979), as well as several extensions and modifications of it. A brief overview of empirical approaches trying to test the results of first-generation theory will be given in Sect. 2.2 together with tests of second-generation models, which will be delineated in Chap. 2.

1.1 The Classical First-Generation Model by Krugman (1979)

The currency crisis model by Krugman (1979) considers a small country, which attempts to keep a fixed exchange rate parity (denoted as $\bar{e}$) against the rest of the world. The analysis is conducted in a monetary approach. As such, it is assumed that the purchasing-power parity holds

$$p = p^* + e \,,$$

with p denoting the log of the domestic price level, p^* being the foreign price level in logs, and e the log of the spot exchange rate, quoted as the domestic-currency price of foreign exchange. Moreover, it is assumed that uncovered interest-rate parity holds, so that the domestic interest rate i equals the foreign rate i^* plus the expected rate of exchange rate change $E(\hat{e})$

$$i = i^* + E(\hat{e}) \,.$$

Domestic money market equilibrium is described by

$$m - p = l(y, i) \,,$$

where, again in logs, m denotes the domestic supply of high-powered money, and y the domestic output. In order to simplify the analysis, it can be assumed without loss of generality that domestic output is at its full-employment level, so that the money market equilibrium can be written as

$$m - p = -\,\alpha(i) \,, \quad \alpha > 0 \,.$$

The domestic money supply in log-linear form is given as the sum of domestic credit d and foreign reserves f

$$m = d + f \,.$$

Since fixing the exchange rate is in the responsibility of the domestic monetary authority, we have to analyze private and government respectively central bank actions in the domestic money market. In order to determine the exact timing of a currency crisis, Krugman (1979) additionally had to make certain presumptions concerning the behavior of the government and central bank. First, it is supposed that the central bank allows the stock of domestic credit d to grow with a constant rate. This can be thought of as reflecting the government's need to finance its budget deficit by borrowing money directly from the central bank, since the central bank's claims on the government are part of its domestic assets. Secondly, it is presumed that the central bank fixes the exchange rate at a level of $\bar{e}$ and promises to defend the peg by selling foreign assets f to the bitter end.[1] However, if foreign reserves are ever completely exploited, the central bank is supposed to allow the exchange rate to float freely forever. This latter assumption can be understood as a limit on the central bank's ability to borrow foreign reserves in order to defend the currency peg against a speculative attack. Usually this limit is set to zero, but it is also thinkable that the central bank abandons the peg even at an earlier stage, when she still possesses a positive amount of foreign assets to defend the peg.[2] The last and very important issue in this simple model is the presumption of certainty. Speculators are supposed to have perfect foresight concerning the future, so that arbitrary shifts in expectations are ruled out.

With a fixed exchange rate and certainty, it follows that $E(\hat{e}) = 0$ and $i = i^*$. If the foreign price level p^* and interest rate i^* are constant and domestic credit d grows with a rate of μ, money market equilibrium is characterized by

$$f + d - p^* - \bar{e} = -\alpha(i) \ . \tag{1.1}$$

Whenever d grows with a rate of μ, foreign reserves f have to decline with a rate of μ in order to maintain the equilibrium, since all other parameters in (1.1) are either exogenously fixed $(p^*, \bar{e})$ or endogenously determined as constant (i). Of course, the country will eventually run out of foreign reserves, so that money market equilibrium can no longer be sustained and the fixed exchange rate arrangement will break down.

In order to determine the timing of the collapse, remember that the central bank has been assumed to let the exchange rate float freely afterwards. This is in line with what has generally been observed for the currency crises of the 1980s (Flood and Marion, 1998). To keep the analysis of the collapse timing simple, it is useful to introduce the idea of a "shadow exchange rate" as defined by Flood and Garber (1984). According to their definition, the shadow exchange rate is given as the floating exchange rate that would prevail if the traders purchased all remaining foreign reserves used to defend the peg, and the central bank refrained from foreign market interventions thereafter. The concept of the shadow exchange rate is used to assess the achievable profits for the speculators from a crisis. It gives the price at which traders can sell the foreign assets after the (successful) attack, which they bought from the central bank before.

In the Krugman (1979) model, the shadow exchange rate can be calculated as the rate that balances the money market after all foreign reserves have been depleted. Let the shadow exchange rate at time t be denoted as e_t^s. From the monetary approach we know that if foreign reserves f are completely exploited and domestic credit d still grows at a rate of μ, money supply rises as well. Due to this inflationary process the shadow exchange rate must be increasing.

[1] Since any speculative pressure on the fixed exchange rate will be fended off by a change in official reserves, this type of crisis is also referred to as a balance-of-payments crisis. See also Krugman and Obstfeld (2000).

[2] This issue will be taken up again in Chap. 12.

This can also be seen from the following equations: money market after an attack is consistent with

$$d - e^s = -\alpha(i)$$
$$d - e^s = -\alpha(E(\hat{e})) ,$$

so that the shadow exchange rate is given by

$$e^s = \alpha\mu + d ,$$

which is increasing in d. The upward-trending behavior of e^s can also be seen in the upper panel of Fig. 1.1.

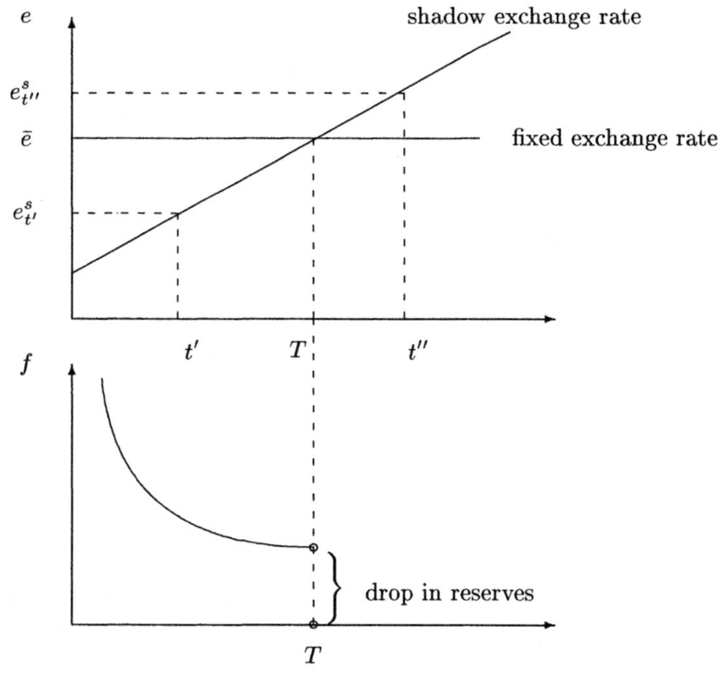

Fig. 1.1. Timing of a speculative attack

Time t is being depicted on the horizontal axis. The vertical axis in the upper panel gives the exchange rate (both fixed and shadow), in the lower panel it presents the foreign reserves. T denotes the point in time when the shadow exchange rate e^s equals the fixed parity $\bar{e}$. The lower part of the panel shows the behavior of foreign reserves over time, when domestic credit steadily increases. Foreign reserves can be seen to follow a declining curve with a sudden drop to zero at $t = T$. Time T thus presents the speculative attack on the fixed exchange rate, when traders buy all the remaining foreign assets from the central bank.

For deriving the exact timing of the attack, it is crucial to keep in mind that speculators are assumed to have perfect foresight. Hence, predictable shifts in the development of the exchange rate are precluded. In order to elaborate on this point, consider the following. Imagine what happens if speculators attack the fixed parity at a time earlier than T, so that reserves hit zero at time $t' < T$. In this case, the formerly fixed exchange rate will be replaced by the shadow exchange rate, which, for $t' < T$, is lower than $\bar{e}$, so that the currency appreciates. Consequently, speculators experience a capital loss following the attack. Due to the assumed ability of perfect foresight on the part of the speculators, therefore, no attack will ever occur at any date before T, since speculators know that an attack will inevitably lead to an appreciation of the exchange rate and hence a capital loss for them.

What happens at time $t'' > T$? In this case, $e^s > \bar{e}$, so that after the attack the exchange rate will be depreciated, leading to a capital gain for every unit of foreign reserves bought from the central bank. Since speculators can foresee this capital gain, they will compete against each other for the largest profit. Each market participant knows that the exchange rate will depreciate sharply the second that the central bank's foreign reserves are depleted. Hence, each of them will try to buy as many foreign assets as possible just an instant earlier. This competition continues until the attack date is driven back to a point in time at which the attack is no longer rewarded by a positive profit, which is the case for time T. Only in T, the fixed exchange rate equals the shadow rate, so that speculators will neither experience a capital gain nor a loss if the attack takes place in $t = T$.

Note that if the attack takes place in T, the money market is continually in equilibrium. The key feature of the equilibrium therefore is that reserves take a discrete jump to zero at T, rather than declining smoothly to zero at a later time. The discrete jump in reserves is necessary to avoid a swift movement of the exchange rate. Instead, e starts to increase steadily from the attack-time T on. Since there is no expected jump in exchange rate behavior, arbitrage opportunities are completely removed, so that equilibrium is stable. Hence, money market is in equilibrium because two effects exactly offset each other in T: first, after the attack the exchange rate increases with a rate of μ; consequently, the domestic interest rate must jump up by μ in order to reflect the prospective currency depreciation, and money demand decreases by $-\alpha\mu$. Secondly, due to the drop in foreign reserves, money supply falls by the size of the attack, denoted by Δf. For money market to be balanced, the drop in money supply must equal the drop in money demand: $\Delta f = -\alpha\mu$. The timing of the speculative attack can then be pinpointed by assuming that domestic credit follows a process given by $d_t = d_0 + \mu t$, so that $f_t = f_0 - \mu t$. At time T, foreign reserves drop to zero, so that $-\Delta f = f_0 - \mu T = \alpha\mu$. The attack time is then given as

$$T = \frac{f_0 - \alpha\mu}{\mu} . \tag{1.2}$$

Equation (1.2) shows, that the collapse of the exchange rate parity will happen the earlier, the lower the initial amount of international reserves, f_0, held by the central bank and the higher the rate of credit expansion μ is.

Note, again, that in this typical first-generation model a crisis must inevitably occur at some point in time, since profligate monetary policies are inconsistent with the target of keeping the exchange rate fixed. Moreover, although the attack happens at a time when the central bank still possesses international reserves to defend the peg, the currency crisis is not the result of a premature panic. Instead, the attack is the only outcome that does not allow any arbitrage opportunities for speculators.

1.2 Modifications of the First-Generation Model

1.2.1 Sterilizing Money-Supply Effects

The first-generation model by Krugman (1979) derives the exact timing of a speculative attack on the fixed parity by equating the drop in domestic money supply due to the speculative attack with the drop in domestic money demand. This is caused by the increase in the domestic interest rate following the expected currency depreciation during the attack. Throughout most of the last decades and also during most of the observed currency crisis (especially those of the 1990s in Europe), however, money-supply effects of reserve losses were sterilized by respective measures concerning domestic credit. One interesting modification of the original Krugman model therefore analyzes the incorporation of sterilization policies into the standard approach (Flood and Marion, 1998; Willman, 1987, 1988). In these models, money supply is held constant throughout the attack: $m = \bar{m}$. With a fixed exchange rate, money market equilibrium is then given as

$$\bar{m} - p^* - \bar{e} = -\alpha(i^*) . \tag{1.3}$$

After the attack, international reserves are exploited, the economy switches to a floating exchange rate and money supply starts to grow at rate μ. The flexible exchange rate will therefore also increase at rate μ, so that the domestic interest rate is given by $i = i^* + E(\hat{e}) = i^* + \mu$. Money market equilibrium just after the attack results in

$$\bar{m} - p^* - e^s = -\alpha(i^* + \mu) . \tag{1.4}$$

Subtracting (1.4) from (1.3) shows that

$$e^s - \bar{e} = \alpha\mu > 0 .$$

Consequently, the shadow exchange rate is always higher than the fixed parity, no matter how high $\bar{e}$ or how large the amount of foreign reserves held by the central bank. Thus, if the monetary authority plans to sterilize an attack and announces these plans credibly, a fixed rate regime can never prevail, since there will always be positive arbitrage profits available from successfully attacking the fixed parity.

The result of this model strongly underlines the so-called "open economy trilemma": with free capital mobility a fixed exchange rate peg is never sustainable, if the monetary authority is unwilling to let monetary policy play a secondary role to exchange-rate policy. This statement holds for any amount of foreign reserves backing the fixed parity. As such, there is no sufficient amount of foreign reserves to defend a fixed currency peg, and fixed exchange rates are incompatible with complete sterilization.

1.2.2 Sterilization and Risk Premia

Although the model above clearly shows that fixed exchange rates are incompatible with complete sterilization, this policy has been common practice in the past, even though central banks had their parities fixed. Flood, Garber and Kramer (1996) recognized this incompatibility and found that, in essence, sterilization policies simply shift the effects of a speculative attack from the money market to the bond market. In their model, they assume that domestic credit increases at a rate of μ, but that the effects of the speculative attack are completely sterilized. Instead of the simple uncovered interest parity, they introduce a risk premium based on bonds

$$i = i^* + E(\hat{e}) + \beta(b - b^* - e) , \tag{1.5}$$

where b and b^* are the logs of domestic government bonds and foreign-currency bonds in private hands. Increasing domestic credit creates an incentive for private portfolio reallocations, so that private market participants try to increase the proportion of international bonds in their portfolios. Consequently, as foreign reserves decline, b^* increases.

Since in this model the money supply does not change, the domestic interest rate cannot jump to keep the money market in equilibrium. Hence, in order to prevent a movement of the fixed exchange rate, the risk premium must jump downwards, which can be seen from (1.5). Introducing a risk premium into the interest-rate parity thus makes sterilization compatible with a fixed exchange rate parity. While money supply is constant due to complete sterilization, the risk-premium keeps money demand constant, so that the money market is balanced throughout. However, assuming the existence of a risk premium in a model with perfect foresight is rather problematic, evidently. Subsequent approaches therefore concentrate on a stochastic modelling of crises with rational expectations on the part of the speculators.

1.2.3 Assuming Uncertainties

The typical first-generation models of currency crises examine the timing of an attack when agents with perfect foresight optimize intertemporally. The important contribution of these types of first-generation models is to show that large events, like the collapse of an exchange rate system, need not be associated with a large shock. Instead, they demonstrate how a sequence of small, predictable events, i.e. the buying of foreign reserves by speculators, may cumulate into the predictable collapse of the whole system. However, recent years showed that speculative attacks are massively characterized by uncertainties on the part of the speculators. Moreover, the perfect-foresight models are clearly not able to explain the observed forward discount on collapsing currencies. Finally, these models assume that attacking the fixed parity does not lead to a transfer of wealth from the government to the speculators. In reality, however, some agents indeed become rich through a speculative attack.

These unsatisfactory aspects of perfect-foresight models have been tackled in several papers (Flood and Garber, 1984; Flood and Marion, 1996; Daniel, 2000) by introducing uncertainties into the currency crisis models. In a discrete-time model by Flood and Garber (1984) for instance, it is presumed that domestic credit, instead of increasing at a rate of μ as before, depends on last period's level of domestic credit and on a random disturbance with zero mean. Thus, domestic credit growth fluctuates randomly around a trend growth rate. An attack on the fixed parity still takes place whenever the unconditional expected exchange rate of the next period is higher than the fixed rate. The expected value of e_{t+1}, however, is given as the average of the fixed rate and the expected exchange rate, conditional on an attack having succeeded. Each part is weighted with the probability of the respective event. The model is then not only able to explain the forward-rate discount in anticipation of a crisis, but also implies that foreign reserves are lower under fixed rates than the reserve level implied by the nonstochastic model. This, of course, is a result of the positive forward discount, since it raises the domestic-currency interest rate and hence reduces money demand relative to the certainty case. This reduction is absorbed by the stock of reserves. A major drawback of the model by Flood and Garber is, however, that the timing of an attack can no longer be perfectly foreseen. Instead, T becomes a random variable.

The model by Daniel (2000) deviates from the perfect-foresight assumption only in the initial period. She analyzes uncertainty about the fiscal use of additional seigniorage revenues following from increasing domestic credit creation. Her model results in showing that, first, uncertainty about the growth rate of domestic credit eliminates the viability of the fixed exchange rate, and secondly, that the timing of the collapse is contingent on the fiscal use of seigniorage.

A different approach of incorporating uncertainty into a model with full sterilization has been chosen by Flood and Marion (1996). They introduce a risk-premium, which is derived from expected utility maximization. Whenever expected utility is rising in expected wealth and decreasing in the variance of wealth, this model contains nonlinear private behavior that even allows for multiple equilibria outcomes. Hence, with a stochastic risk-premium, currency crises can still be the consequence of inconsistent policies, as has been the emphasis of the typical first-generation models. However, crises can also arise from self-fulfilling expectations on the part of speculators. This is also a crucial issue of second-generation currency crisis models, which will be delineated in the next chapter.

2

Second-Generation Model – Obstfeld (1994)

Despite the large number of extensions and modifications, the models classified as first-generation research on currency crises were hardly able to explain the observed speculative attacks on several fixed exchange rate parities in the 1990s (for instance in Europe 1992–1993, Mexico 1994–1995).[1] The foreign exchange turmoil in the first half of the 1990s was so great, that even currency pegs generally believed to be sustainable, were observed to be threatened and subsequently abandoned. Moreover, it was argued that for industrial European countries and most of the Latin American countries with free access to world capital markets, reserve adequacy, one of the major explanatory variables in first-generation models, should not have been as severe a concern as it had been for the crisis countries in the 1970s and 1980s. Hence, following these recent crises a new type of model had to be generated in order to keep track of the events. What differentiates these newer, "second-generation" approaches from the first-generation ones are both macroeconomic issues but also formal aspects of the structure of these models. Whereas first-generation research was centered on seigniorage aspects, the newer models rather focus on the importance of the governmental target function, which is influenced by several different issues, such as the effects of high interest rates, growing unemployment or real overvaluation. Therefore, the newer models are able to take account of the numerous policy options available to the authorities and of the ways how to balance the costs of exercising these options.

Concerning the formal structure of crisis models, we find that first-generation currency crisis theories are typically characterized by linearities. The Krugman (1979) model, for instance, combines a linear behavior rule for the private sector (the money demand function) with a linear rule for the government (domestic credit growth). In the classical first-generation models, these linearities interact with the assumption of certainty and perfect fore-

[1] Krugman (1997) opposes this view and shows that a slight modification of his 1979-model might account for the features of currency crises as observed in the 1990s.

sight, so that equilibrium is characterized by the nonexistence of foreseeable profit opportunities. Consequently, there is a unique point in time, at which a speculative attack on the fixed exchange rate takes place.

Second-generation models, in contrast, introduce one or more nonlinearities. Typically, they focus on nonlinear behavior on the part of the government. There are different ways to generate this. For instance, the government respectively central bank might react to changes in private behavior. Generally, it is assumed that the government faces a trade-off between the fixed exchange rate policy and other policy objectives (Obstfeld and Rogoff, 1995). Whereas in first-generation models, crises are generated by inconsistent policies prior to the attack, second-generation models point out that due to the nonlinearities, attack-conditional policy changes may trigger the crisis (Obstfeld, 1986; Calvo, 1988). Other types of second-generation models demonstrate that a shift in speculators' expectations can alter the governmental trade-offs and spark self-fulfilling crises (Obstfeld, 1994, 1996). Hence, even fundamentally sustainable currency pegs may be attacked and subsequently abandoned. Quite generally, however, all models of second-generation research emphasize the role of multiple equilibria, that arise from nonlinearities in behavior.

In the following, we will present the typical second-generation model by Obstfeld (1994). In this model, he derived a closed-form solution for a monetary rule with an escape clause that represents the crisis. Concerning the formal structure of the model, it can be seen as a direct adaption of the Kydland and Prescott (1977) and Barro and Gordon (1983) models of time inconsistent policymaking. Note that we deal with time inconsistency here and not with inconsistencies concerning the underlying economic fundamentals as in the first-generation models. The chapter closes with a brief overview of empirical tests trying to verify the results from both first- and second-generation research on currency crises.

2.1 The Classical Second-Generation Model by Obstfeld (1994)

In the typical Obstfeld-model, nonlinearities are generated by taking into account that the government faces a trade-off between different policy targets. On the one hand she wants to maintain the fixed exchange rate parity, on the other hand she realizes that abandoning the peg might foster the realization of other targets like economic growth or full employment. In deciding whether or not to defend an exogenously specified exchange rate parity, the government therefore has to take several aspects into account. There are some reasons why the government would like to depreciate the fixed exchange rate. By acceding to a devaluation, she might hope to reduce unemployment by increasing international economic competition, or to lower the real value of the governmental debt burden. Thus, a discrete depreciation of the fixed parity might lead to a positive payoff for the government in general. Moreover, the costs of maintaining the fixed exchange rate are influenced by speculators' expectations: the higher the expected rate of depreciation, the higher the costs of staying with the peg. This might be attributed to the fact that an expected depreciation of a currency leads to higher domestic interest rates. This in turn might have negative effects on the governmental budget or on the private economy. However, it is also costly for the government to abandon the fixed parity. The reasons underlying this fact are reputational aspects, since a government in a fixed-rate regime typically stakes a large part of its credibility on the maintenance of the parity. The costs of abandoning the peg may therefore be referred to as political costs.

In the following, we will present a reduced form of the general Obstfeld (1994) model to highlight the important issues, instead of portraying the complete history of the model.[2] Thus, instead of deriving the government's objective function we will rather use the following loss function, which represents the government's optimizing behavior and captures all the necessary characteristics

$$L = [a(e^*(\theta) - e) + bE(\hat{e})]^2 + C, \quad a, b > 0 . \tag{2.1}$$

In this equation, e denotes the log of the (actual) exchange rate, e^* is the log of the exchange rate preferred by the government, θ represents an index of fundamentals with a high value of θ signalling a good fundamental state, and vice versa for θ being low. Since the exchange rate is given in terms of domestic currency units per foreign currency unit, e is decreasing in θ. $E(\hat{e})$ gives the expected depreciation and C comprises the political costs of a potential depreciation. Let the fixed exchange rate moreover be given by $\bar{e}$. As such, the term in parenthesis on the right-hand-side of (2.1) represents the government's loss from keeping the fixed peg. This loss depends on two factors. First of all, it increases with deteriorating fundamentals, i.e. with a growing difference between the actual exchange rate (which in the fixed-rate case is equal to the fixed parity) e and the exchange rate $e^*(\theta)$ that would be optimal for the underlying state of fundamentals. Additionally, the loss from maintaining the fixed exchange rate increases in the expected level of depreciation. The stronger the speculators' belief in a devaluation, the

[2] The basic framework of the original Obstfeld-model (1994) is taken from Barro and Gordon (1983), but assumes an open economy instead of a closed one. The government minimizes the loss function

$$L = (y - y^*)^2 + \beta\hat{e}^2 + C(\hat{e}) ,$$

with y being output, y^* the government's target output and $\hat{e}$ the exchange rate change. Output is determined by the expectations-augmented Phillips curve

$$y = \bar{y} + \alpha(\hat{e} - E(\hat{e})) - u ,$$

where $\bar{y}$ gives the natural output level, $E(\hat{e})$ is the expected exchange rate change based on lagged information, and u is an iid shock with mean zero. The inconsistency problem is introduced by assuming that $y^* > \bar{y}$.

higher the costs of withstanding this expectation will be for the government. The second term on the right-hand side of (2.1) denotes the loss incurred by abandoning the peg. The more strongly the government has pegged its own credibility to the goal of maintaining the fixed exchange-rate system, the higher the "political" loss from a devaluation will be.

Following Kydland and Prescott (1977) and Barro and Gordon (1983), policymaking can be conducted either according to a rule or according to discretion. In the context of currency crises, the rule requires the government to keep the exchange rate fixed regardless of the current state of the economy and the expected depreciation. Discretion, in contrast, allows the government to set its policy after observing the state, so that it is possible to decide on a depreciation of the fixed parity whenever necessary. The Kydland and Prescott (1977) result concerning the optimal choice between rule or discretion holds for the Obstfeld-model as well: absent any shocks, the economy is better off with a rule, with shocks, however, discretion should be more suitable. What is crucial here is that shocks in the Obstfeld-model refer to changes in the expectation of a possible depreciation of the fixed parity. This, in turn, depends on the respective policy chosen by the government: rule or discretion. What is optimal for the government, therefore, depends on what is expected by the private sector to be optimally chosen on the part of the government.

Analyzing loss function (2.1), we find that in deciding on whether to abandon (discretion) or keep (rule) the peg, the government simply has to compare the loss from staying in the peg with the credibility cost of leaving it. Thus, the government will choose to maintain the peg, whenever the loss incurred by this action is lower than the loss from abandoning the peg

$$L(\text{maintain}) < L(\text{devalue})$$

$$[a(e^*(\theta) - \bar{e}) + bE(\hat{e})]^2 < C.$$

What is optimal in this game crucially depends on whether or not speculators expect a depreciation to happen. If no depreciation is expected, it might be optimal for the government to fulfill this expectation. She will keep the peg whenever

$$[a(e^*(\theta) - \bar{e})]^2 < C.$$

Assuming quite generally that $\bar{e} \leq e^*(\theta)$, so that the currency is vulnerable to a devaluation rather than a revaluation, it is easy to see that this inequality is satisfied as long as fundamentals are strong enough, so that $e^*(\theta)$ is not too high when compared to $\bar{e}$. Thus, for strong fundamentals it is reasonable for the speculators to expect a stable currency. In turn, the government will then maintain the peg, which vindicates the initial beliefs. Absent any expectation of depreciation, the government would abandon the peg only for sufficiently bad fundamentals that lead to a high enough e^*, so that

$$[a(e^*(\theta) - \bar{e})]^2 > C\,.$$

However, even if a depreciation is expected, the government will be willing to maintain the peg as long as

$$[a(e^*(\theta) - \bar{e}) + bE(\hat{e})]^2 < C \, .$$

This requires fundamentals to be much stronger than in the former case with no expectation of depreciation, so that a devaluation will be optimal for a larger range of fundamentals, and the government will abandon the peg whenever

$$[(a+b)(e^*(\theta) - \bar{e})]^2 > C \, .$$

Note that the slight change in the above formula stems from the fact that speculators know that a devaluation will bring the exchange rate to its optimal level, so that $E(\hat{e}) = e^*(\theta) - \bar{e}$.

Consequently, if fundamentals are sufficiently bad, speculators will believe the fixed exchange rate to be doomed to become devalued. This expectation will raise the government's loss from further maintaining the peg, so that the government indeed will abandon the peg, again validating the traders' initial expectations by this action. Note that it is assumed in this model that speculators actually know the exact fundamental state of the economy in order to determine their optimal actions.

It is easy to see that, whenever a depreciation is expected by the speculators, the fixed parity is much more vulnerable as compared to a situation with no expected devaluation. This is due to the fact that whenever speculators expect an abandonment of the peg, the government's loss from maintaining the peg increases, so that speculators will be willing to attack the fixed parity even for intermediate fundamentals. Instead, if speculators do not believe in a devaluation, the loss from keeping the peg is much lower, so that speculators will only want to attack the currency peg if fundamentals are sufficiently bad.

Hence, if economic fundamentals take on intermediate values and put the economy into a range so that

$$[a(e^*(\theta) - \bar{e})]^2 < C \; < [(a+b)(e^*(\theta) - \bar{e})]^2,$$

there might be a devaluation of the fixed parity as well as financial stability. This is the typical case of multiple equilibria arising from second-generation models. Both types of expectations are consistent with equilibrium for this range of fundamentals: if speculators anticipate a devaluation, it will be optimal for the government to abandon the peg. If, however, there is no devaluation expected by the market, there is no reason for the government to abandon the fixed parity and the peg will be stable. As such, expectations are self-fulfilling, since they force a certain action on the part of the government.

Note that multiple equilibria due to self-fulfilling beliefs on the part of the speculators do not reflect irrational behavior. Rather, they represent an indeterminacy of equilibrium, which arises when speculators expect an attack to sharply change the optimality condition for the government's policy. Since traders' anticipations depend on the conjectured government responses, which in turn are contingent on the speculators' expectations, this circularity brings about the potential for crises that need not have occurred, had not speculators expected them to. Currency crises occurring in the "multiple equilibria" range of fundamentals may therefore be characterized as inefficient, since they are not purely caused by weak fundamentals, but rather by speculators' expectations.

However, underlying macroeconomic fundamentals are far from irrelevant for the outcome of the model, since they determine the range of possible equilibria. Whenever fundamentals are sufficiently weak, the "attack"-outcome will be the only equilibrium. Vice versa, for sufficiently strong fundamentals only the tranquillity-equilibrium without an attack prevails. Multiple equilibria are possible only for intermediate fundamentals. If fundamentals are not so strong as to make a successful attack impossible, nor so weak as to make it inevitable, speculators may or may not coordinate on an attack. Hence, underlying macroeconomic factors still play a certain role in determining the outcome of a currency crisis model, even with self-fulfilling expectations. However, the derivation of equilibrium cannot be based on fundamentals exclusively.

One of the major drawbacks of the typical Obstfeld-model therefore is that for a large range of fundamentals it does not allow predictions of whether a currency crisis will occur or not. As a consequence, it is not possible to characterize the influence of economic parameters on the market outcome and, hence, no policy advice can be given. A second disadvantage of second-generation currency crisis models is the lacking foundation of speculators' expectation formation. In the original Obstfeld-model, traders' beliefs are assumed to be exogenous to the model. Therefore, switches from one equilibrium to the next are not explained by the model. As a result, the timing of an attack on the fixed parity becomes indeterminate (Obstfeld, 1995). In order to explain the switches between stability situations and financial turmoil without a major change of the underlying fundamentals as observed in recent currency crises, so-called "sunspots" were used as an auxiliary instrument to explain the change in speculators' beliefs and subsequent actions.[3] Note, however, that sunspots as artificial constructs, which do not necessarily have to be linked to economic fundamentals nor to financial markets in general, do not help to predict the onset of a crisis and therefore do not solve the overall problem of multiple equilibria models.

Hence, although second-generation models correctly perceive and reflect the important role that expectations play for the interaction between government, respectively central bank, and foreign exchange traders, the severe drawbacks of this type of model diminish its explanatory power. Models extending second-generation research on currency crises largely elaborated on the trade-offs in the governmental objective function, trying to further mo-

[3] For information on sunspots and their role in multiple equilibria models see also Blanchard and Fischer (1996).

tivate the switch in policies due to the speculative attack and the preceding shift in traders' anticipation of the governmental policy (Flood and Marion, 1997; Jeanne, 1999). Another strand of literature introduces shocks, for instance concerning the political costs of abandoning the fixed rate system, and thereby attempts to differentiate between the multiple equilibria (Isard, 1995).

The models we want to concentrate on in the following parts of this book, however, depart from a different point of criticism on the Obstfeld-model. They emphasize the fact that the multiple equilibria result does not provide an explanation of the coordination mechanism on the part of the speculators (Morris and Shin, 1999b). In the Obstfeld-model either all speculators attack the fixed parity, or they all refrain from participating in an attack. As we will see, the underlying reason for this behavior is that the model requires traders to have common knowledge of the fundamental state of the economy. Deviating from this very strong assumption on traders' knowledge helps to solve the above mentioned problems of models relying on self-fulfilling expectations.

2.2 Empirical Tests

Generally speaking, results from empirical work on currency crises are rather mixed. Whereas some models find the predictions from first-generation theory to hold for some of the observed currency crises of the past, others contradict this view or only find evidence for the results of second-generation research.

Concerning the testable implications of both first- and second-generation crisis models, we can state that the former ones rely on the importance of a fundamental deterioration preceding the collapse of the exchange rate regime, whereas second-generation models predict a policy-switch into a more expansionary direction in response to the attack with unchanged fundamentals.

For identifying characteristics of first-generation models, a fiscal deficit financed by domestic credit creating was considered as the root cause of speculative attacks. Empirical studies trying to verify the content of first-generation models were mainly conducted using structural models on data of Latin American crises during the 1980s. Blanco and Garber (1986) found for the Mexican Peso crisis that fundamental variables (in particular domestic credit growth and an interest rate rise) were important determinants of the probability of a devaluation, measured as the probability of the estimated shadow exchange rate exceeding the fixed parity. Similar analyses were conducted by Goldberg (1994) and by Cumby and van Wijnbergen (1989), who demonstrated that domestic credit growth was the major factor triggering the crisis in Argentina in the early 1980s. Edwards (1989) in a nonstructural approach finds for a set of developing countries between 1962–1983 that with the devaluation coming nearer, the countries increasingly displayed expansive macroeconomic policies with a declining current account, appreciating real exchange rate and a rundown of international reserves.

Whereas empirical tests for the crises in the 1980s rather strongly supported the main predictions from first-generation models, this finding no longer holds for the later years. Eichengreen, Rose and Wyplosz (1994) distinguish between an ERM- and non-ERM subsample for the period leading up to the ERM crisis during the first half of the 1990s. They find that fundamentals still play a major role for explaining foreign exchange market turmoil in the non-ERM subsample. However, this does not hold for the ERM countries. Yet, their test does not find evidence for the predictions from second-generation models either. Tests by Kaminsky, Lizando and Reinhart (1997) on the Mexican and Argentine crises in the 1980s, the Mexican crisis in 1994 and the 1992 crises in Finland and Sweden demonstrate that fundamental variables at least partly helped to predict these crises. A similar result has been derived by Sachs, Tornell and Velasco (1996a) for a sample of twenty developing countries over the period 1994–95.

Tests of second-generation currency crisis models give even more mixed results. This, however, is largely due to the difficulty of finding a testing procedure and appropriate empirical proxies for the relevant parameters of second-generation models. In this respect, Rose and Svensson (1994) concentrate on credibility effects in crisis situations. They show for the ERM crisis that prior to August 1992 the credibility of the system did not deteriorate markedly. According to them, prior to the actual attacks most of the ERM currency pegs were therefore not believed to succumb to a crisis . Hence, their model characterizes the ERM crisis as rather unexpected, which supports the predictions from second-generation research. Similarly, Jeanne (1997) demonstrates in a structural estimation that the attacks on the French Franc exhibited major signs of self-fulfillingness, which he takes as a sign for the validity of second-generation models.

A quite different approach of testing the theoretical properties of second-generation models has been chosen by Jeanne and Masson (2000). Departing from the argument that the nonlinearities displayed by second-generation models complicate empirical testing, they apply a Markov-switching model to a linearized version of a second-generation-type model. The switches across regimes correspond to the jumps between the "not-attack" and "attack"-equilibria. They find that their model performs very well for predicting the movement in the French Franc over the period 1987–1993.

Even though some tests find evidence for the results of self-fulfilling currency crises, most of the models advocating the view of second-generation research have to admit that the observed crises of the recent past were not purely self-fulfilling. Rather, they state that the effect of deteriorating economic fundamentals was augmented by self-fulfilling elements.

Part II

Self-Fulfilling Currency Crisis Model with Unique Equilibrium – Morris and Shin (1998)

3

Introduction

Financial markets are typically characterized by a large amount of risk and uncertainty on the part of the market participants, not only concerning the underlying fundamental values but also about the behavior of the other market participants. The basic currency crisis models of the first and second generation, however, completely neglected these issues. Rather, first-generation models assumed agents to have perfect foresight about the future development of fundamentals, and second-generation models additionally presumed speculators to have common knowledge of their opponents' behavior in equilibrium. Whereas modifications and extensions of these "classical" currency crisis models at least took account of uncertainties about fundamentals, as has been delineated in Sect. 1.2, the aspect of uncertainty about behavior did not play a role in the earlier models. However, behavioral issues gained importance in explaining the onset of financial market crises in the recent past. In the context of currency crises, it was argued that traders' decisions typically display characteristics of strategic complementarities in the sense that similar actions reinforce each other: attacking the fixed parity is the more advantageous for a speculator, the larger the number of other market participants who attack as well. However, earlier models of currency crises generally stuck to the assumption of certainty, both about fundamentals and about behavior. Since each speculator's optimal action depends on both the economic fundamentals and on the actions taken by his opponents, these models typically give rise to multiple equilibria for an intermediate range of fundamentals, i.e. for fundamentals not so bad that it would always be optimal to attack, nor so good that it would never reward to attack. Multiple equilibria in these models are a result of self-fulfilling expectations. One set of beliefs motivates actions that bring about the outcome envisaged in those beliefs, while another set of beliefs leads to a completely different result that has again been foreseen in these expectations. Therefore, whenever speculators expect the currency peg to be sufficiently weak, they will all attack and as such force the central bank to abandon the peg. Yet, the parity could have been maintained if only the proportion of attacking speculators had been smaller.

Although having been seen as a major contribution to a more realistic modelling of financial markets due to the emphasis of behavioral aspects at first, the second-generation approach to explaining currency crises has achieved large critique lately. The critique is based on two aspects: first, due to the numerous potential outcomes it is not possible to predict from the observed state of economic fundamentals whether a crisis will occur or not. Related to this fact is the problem that, of course, it is not possible either to analyze comparative statics in order to give advice to government and central bank on how to conduct optimal policy (Milgrom and Roberts, 1994). Secondly, the assumption of complete foresight of both the fundamental state of the economy and the behavior of market participants has clearly been dismissed as unrealistic (Jeanne and Masson, 2000). Due to the growing size and complexity of financial markets, uncertainty about behavior and fundamentals rather increases. For a realistic modelling of the processes taking place on foreign exchange markets, economists clearly are forced to take account of this cumulating uncertainty.

In addition to these theoretical aspects, empirical findings are calling for a new attempt at explaining the onset of currency crises as well. Second-generation models typically did not give reasons for the shift in beliefs which leads to the switch from an attack-equilibrium to the stability outcome or vice versa. Instead, it has been presumed that pure sunspots, i.e. factors not necessarily related to financial markets, incite speculators to change their beliefs and to attack a formerly stable currency. As such, the derived equilibria are no longer contingent on the fundamental state, at least not for intermediate ranges, where multiple equilibria are possible. However, as stated in Sect. 2.2, several empirical studies on the currency crises of the 1990s showed that the turmoil on foreign exchange markets in Europe, Latin America, Asia and Russia has not been completely independent of economic fundamentals after all. Consequently, a new theory was needed to take account of the role of fundamental and behavioral uncertainties for triggering a crisis and to emphasize the importance of economic fundamentals for the market equilibrium.

Surprisingly, a rather simple assumption introduced to the typical second-generation framework of modelling currency crises satisfies both claims. By presuming that speculators are uncertain about the fundamental state of the economy, Morris and Shin (1998) succeeded in showing that multiplicity of equilibria can be avoided even in a second-generation setting with self-fulfilling expectations on the part of the speculators. What is important in this respect is that the introduction of uncertainty into this framework not only necessitates the analysis of speculators' beliefs about fundamentals and their opponents' behavior, but also of the beliefs about beliefs etc. As such, this new approach of explaining currency crises takes account of numerous layers of uncertainty. Due to the uniqueness of equilibrium derived in the Morris/Shin-model, it is possible to predict whether there will be an attack on the fixed parity or whether the peg can be maintained. Moreover, the outcome of the game between speculators and the central bank can be shown to unequivocally depend on the underlying fundamentals, while expectations about the opponents' behavior are still self-fulfilling.

In order to eliminate all but one equilibrium in the setting of a second-generation currency crisis model, Morris and Shin used a method derived earlier by Carlsson and van Damme (1993). Carlsson and van Damme strongly criticized the facilitating assumption in game theory that agents have common knowledge about the underlying state of the game. As they pointed out: "There seems to be almost general agreement that game theory's agents are excessively rational and well-informed in comparison with their real-life counterparts" (Carlsson and van Damme, 1993). They argued that this is a much too strong premise and showed in a simple game-theoretic context that if common knowledge is replaced by uncertainty about the state of the game, a unique equilibrium prevails. The introduction of uncertainties forces players to broaden their scope from an individual game to a whole class of possible games, so that their method is also referred to as "global games" approach. Provided that uncertainties are not too large, multiple equilibria can be iteratively eliminated until only one equilibrium remains.

By embedding a typical second-generation currency crisis model into a global game, Morris and Shin (1998) were able to derive a unique equilibrium that depends on both fundamentals and on speculators' beliefs. Before analyzing the currency crisis model by Morris and Shin, however, we will present the method by Carlsson and van Damme in more detail. In order to go over the global games approach smoothly, it is necessary to introduce some game-theoretic definitions and concepts beforehand. Chapter 4 therefore presents some general game-theoretic preliminaries in Sect. 4.1. Section 4.2 focusses on the specific class of coordination games, which is most appropriate for modelling currency crises. Section 4.3 presents the method by Carlsson and van Damme (1993) on how to eliminate multiple equilibria in coordination games. A generalization of this method, which will be required for the currency crisis context, is given in Sect. 4.4. Based on the necessary game-theoretic underpinnings, the Morris/Shin-model is delineated in Chap. 5. Chapter 6 presents several extensions of this currency crisis model concerning aspects of transparency and expectation formation.

4

Game-Theoretic Preliminaries

4.1 Games, Strategies and Information

Game theory can quite generally be described as the study of multiperson decision problems. It is "concerned with the actions of decision makers who are conscious that their actions affect each other" (Rasmusen, 1995). Game theory is therefore suitable as a modelling tool for a large number of economic problems, among them decision problems on financial markets. In the following, let us characterize and explain the most basic game-theoretic terms, starting with the definition of games, players and strategies, continuing with a description of equilibrium concepts and closing with a differentiation between the most important types of information.

A game is identified by players, actions and outcomes (or payoffs). Often these terms are collectively referred to as the rules of the game. The players are the individuals who make decisions. Their aim is to maximize their utility by optimal choice of action. In some games, as in the games we are going to use in order to model currency crises, there is an additional (pseudo-) player, namely nature. Nature takes random (payoff-relevant) actions at specified points in the game, usually at the beginning, with specified (prior-) probabilities. An action, denoted by a_i, is a choice that player i can make out of his action set A_i, which represents the entire set of actions available to player i.

A strategy s_i for player i is a rule (or function) that tells him what action he should choose at any point in the game, conditional on his information. A strategy set S_i contains the set of all strategies available to player i. A strategy profile is an ordered set $s = (s_1, s_2, ..., s_n)$, consisting of one strategy for each of the n players in the game. A player's payoff is either defined as the player's utility after the game has been played out, or his expected utility as a function of his own strategy and his opponents' strategies.

An equilibrium is defined as a strategy profile $s^* = (s_1^*, s_2^*, ..., s_n^*)$ consisting of a best strategy for each of the n players in the game. The equilibrium strategies for the players are therefore characterized as the strategies that maximize their respective payoffs, i.e. the strategies which they pick in order to maximize their utility. It is important to note that an equilibrium is not equal to the outcome of a game, but instead is defined as the strategy profile that generates the outcome.

In order to derive an equilibrium, it is necessary to define a concept of a best strategy or best response strategy for the players in the game. An equilibrium concept can be characterized as a rule that determines the equilibrium based on the possible strategy profiles and the respective payoff functions. The most common equilibrium concepts are the dominant strategy equilibrium, the iteratively dominant strategy equilibrium and the Nash equilibrium. These equilibrium concepts will be delineated in the following.

In order to define an equilibrium consisting of dominant strategies, let us first consider the so-called best response strategy. A best response of player i to his opponents' strategies, denoted by s_{-i}, is the strategy s_i^* that gives him the highest payoff u_i

$$u_i(s_i^*, s_{-i}) \geq u_i(s_i, s_{-i}) \quad \text{for all } i .$$

The strategy is a strictly best response, if no other strategy yields the same payoff, i.e. if the "$>$"-sign holds, and weakly best otherwise, i.e. for "$\geq$".

Based on this definition of best responses, a strategy is defined as dominant, if it is a strictly best response to any other strategy that the player's opponents might take, i.e.

$$u_i(s_i^*, s_{-i}) > u_i(s_i', s_{-i}) \quad \text{for all} \quad s_{-i} \quad \text{and} \quad s_i' \neq s_i^* .$$

A dominant strategy is a strictly best response even to completely irrational actions chosen by the other players. The inferior strategies s_i' are called (strictly) dominated strategies. An equilibrium in dominant strategies is then given as a strategy profile that consists of each player's dominant strategy. The distinctive feature of this concept of equilibrium selection is that it does not constrain the opponents' actions, neither to only rational strategies nor to any other kind of restriction. A dominant strategy is simply the best response to any kind of action on the part of the other players in the game.

The concept of dominant strategies can be broadened to include an even larger set of equilibria, namely the equilibria in iterated dominant strategies. In order to define the iteration process, let a weakly dominated strategy s_i' be defined as a strategy such that there exists some other strategy s_i'' for player i that yields at least the same payoff, but never a lower payoff, i.e.

$$u_i(s_i', s_{-i}) \leq u_i(s_i'', s_{-i}) \quad \text{for all } s_{-i} ,$$
$$u_i(s_i', s_{-i}) < u_i(s_i'', s_{-i}) \quad \text{for some } s_{-i} .$$

An iterated dominance equilibrium then is a strategy profile that is characterized by an iterative deletion process of weakly dominated strategies. The equilibrium is found by eliminating a weakly dominated strategy of one player, rescheduling the remaining payoffs and searching for another weakly dominated strategy, which is then deleted and so on, until there is only one strategy left for each of the players. If the underlying game is one of incomplete information,[1] the iterated dominance equilibrium is also denoted as a rationalizable expectations equilibrium. This notion refers to the fact that with incomplete information (to be defined below) some expectations about other players' optimal actions are not rationalizable, in the sense that players' probability distributions on the strategy choices of other players are not stochastically independent (Brandenburger, 1992). The remaining equilibrium strategy profile, however, is characterized by expectations that are rationalizable and as such are realized.[2]

A quite different approach of selecting equilibria as compared to the concept of dominant strategies, is given by the Nash equilibrium. It is one of the most important and most frequently used equilibrium concepts. A strategy profile s^* is a Nash equilibrium, if no player has an incentive to deviate from this strategy given that all of his opponents stick to their equilibrium strategies. Thus, the Nash equilibrium is characterized by the fact that each player chooses his best response strategy, given that all other agents play their best response strategies as well. Formally, this condition is given as

$$u_i(s_i^*, s_{-i}^*) \geq u_i(s_i', s_{-i}^*) \quad \text{for all } i \text{ and all } s_i' \, .$$

However, a Nash equilibrium[3] is only a best response to other players' Nash strategies (and as such to their equilibrium strategies) but not to all strategies. The concept of Nash equilibrium therefore is less strict than equilibrium selection by iterated dominance. Hence, the Nash method is most often used in games, where it is not possible to find an iteratively dominant equilibrium (Myerson, 1999).

The description of different solution concepts up to now relied on the players' ability to choose optimal strategies. However, in order to make an optimal choice, players have to have certain information and knowledge of the game and its structure, of their opponents and their possible strategies and so on. In this respect, game theory distinguishes between several forms of knowledge[4], which are vital for deriving a certain type of equilibrium. Note that the following description of types of knowledge does not comply with a certain structure or ranking. Rather, the various forms of knowledge concern

[1] This is the case for the currency crisis models delineated in the chapters to follow.

[2] For more information on rationalizability of equilibria, see also Heinemann (1995) or Milgrom and Roberts (1990).

[3] The Nash equilibrium can be either weak or strong, depending on whether "$\geq$" or "$>$" holds.

[4] Often, the notions of knowledge and information are used interchangeably in game theory. However, since the currency crisis models very strongly emphasize certain types of information, we will try not to confuse these two subjects and refer to only knowledge in the following.

different aspects in games. Since the modelling of currency crises relies on only a few of the different types of knowledge, we will go over the rest rather briefly. Generally, the most important types of knowledge in game theory are perfect and complete knowledge. As they refer to different aspects of the players' information sets, however, they are hardly comparable. Other important forms of knowledge are certain, symmetric and common knowledge.

A game of perfect knowledge meets the strongest requirements on the players' information sets. In such games, players move sequentially, they can observe their predecessors' actions and the choices made by nature. Thus, players always know the history of the game as well as the current stage. Concerning the modelling of currency crises, it is quite easy to see that this type of knowledge is not appropriate for capturing the processes taking place on financial markets. Even if speculators know the historical development of the market, they are usually not able to directly observe their opponents' actions. Rather, they have to decide simultaneously on their optimal actions. More important, however, speculators mostly do not know the current state of fundamentals underlying the market, i.e. they do not know the exact "state of the game". Hence, currency crisis models typically are models of imperfect knowledge. Whereas Chaps. 5-12 analyze currency crisis models with simultaneous actions on the part of the speculators, Chap. 13 depicts a model where speculators decide on their optimal actions successively, after observing their predecessors' actions. Both types of models, however, display imperfect knowledge, since speculators in either game do not know the fundamental state underlying the economy.

A game with incomplete knowledge is characterized by the fact that nature moves first and is unobservable for the players. Referring to an older definition (Gibbons, 1992), incomplete knowledge is also described as lack of full knowledge of the rules of the game. Thus, in a game with incomplete knowledge, players do not know the history of the game and they cannot observe their predecessors' moves. They only know the other players, their potential actions and respective payoffs. It should be noted that a game with incomplete knowledge is always a game with also imperfect knowledge. In order to distinguish between games of perfect and complete information, note that in the former the history is common knowledge (to be defined below), whereas in the latter only the general rules of the game are common knowledge. The currency crisis models we will work with throughout the next chapters, belong to the class of games with incomplete knowledge.

In a game with certain knowledge, nature does not move after all the players have made their choices. However, nature is allowed to move initially, with its choice made public to all the players. If the game is one with uncertainty, such that nature's choice of the payoff-relevant fundamental variables is not observable, assumptions have to be made concerning the utility functions, since in this case players have to decide on their optimal strategies on the basis of expectations over payoffs. Usually, it is assumed for the players to have utility of the von Neumann-Morgenstern type (von Neumann and Morgenstern, 1974).

Symmetric knowledge is defined as equivalent information sets for all players. Asymmetric knowledge, in contrast, is assumed to influence a player's behavior in a payoff-relevant way. An essential source of asymmetric knowledge is so-called private information, i.e. information that is only contained in the information set of a single player. This is again a feature which prominently characterizes the modelling of currency crises with game theoretic tools. There, speculators have private information (and as such asymmetric knowledge) about the fundamental state of the economy underlying the market outcome.

A very important dimension of knowledge, completely different from the types delineated above, is the notion of common knowledge. Whereas the former types of knowledge referred to the pieces of information included in a player's information set, common knowledge refers to the overlapping of players' information sets (Brandenburger and Dekel, 1993). Generally, a piece of information is common knowledge, if everybody knows it, if everybody knows that everybody else knows it and so on to infinity.[5] Usually, it is presumed that all the players, their strategies and payoffs are common knowledge to all the participants in a game, so that the rules of the game are common knowledge. The assumption of the rules of the game being common knowledge is of vital importance for the above presented concepts of equilibrium selection (Geanakoplos, 1992; Rubinstein, 1989). In the case of the Nash equilibrium concept, this feature also enables the existence of more than one equilibrium at the same time (Brandenburger, 1992).

One last aspect to be discussed is the distinction between pure and mixed strategies. In addition to what has been said before, a strategy can be defined as a function that maps each of the players' information sets to a probability distribution over the possible actions. With the information set for player i denoted as I_i, we get

$$s_i : I_i \to a_i \ .$$

A (completely) mixed strategy then assigns a positive probability to every possible action, whereas a pure strategy attributes a probability of 1 to only one action and 0 to all other actions. However, the requirements for the strategies in the different equilibrium concepts are the same for pure as well as for mixed strategies. Thus, a Nash equilibrium in mixed strategies consists of mixed strategies that are mutual best responses. It is interesting to note that in a general coordination game (to be explained below) there is not always a Nash equilibrium in pure strategies, but there definitely exists a Nash equilibrium in mixed strategies (Van Damme, 1991). This is due to the fact that mixed strategies can be seen as a convexification of pure strategies, where con-

[5] For a more formal definition see Aumann (1976).

vexity of the pure strategies is a necessary condition for the Nash equilibrium to exist (Selten, 1975; Holler and Illing, 1996).

The interpretation of a mixed strategy usually is to assume that the players throw a dice in order to choose an action. In the Nash equilibrium, the probabilities for each of the players' possible actions to be chosen depend on the opponents' payoffs solely. The Nash equilibrium concept is therefore very sensitive to changes in the payoff structure of the game.

A different approach of interpreting mixed strategies takes into account the strategic uncertainties of the opponents' behavior. Mixed strategies are used to formalize the uncertainty over the opponents' choices. This is a very important characteristic of mixed strategies, which will be heavily drawn upon in the following sections. In this respect, Harsanyi (1973) came to the following conclusion: if we observe one game with complete knowledge and a second game that is conjured of the first game with very small but unobservable changes in payoffs, then the pure strategy equilibrium of this second perturbed game is equal to the equilibrium in mixed strategies of the first unperturbed game. Due to the uncertainty about the opponents' payoffs in the second game, each player has to randomize his best response strategy over the potential best responses of his opponents. The result is equal to the mixed strategy of the first game. Thus, a Nash equilibrium in mixed strategies is the limit of games in which the uncertainty over the players' payoffs becomes arbitrarily small.

The Nash equilibrium in such incomplete information games may also be referred to as Bayesian equilibrium (Binmore, 1992). The only difference between the two equilibrium notions is the fact that in the Bayesian game players have to form probabilities over their opponents' payoffs, since payoffs are perturbed. Each player therefore can only decide on an individually optimal action, if he assigns certain probabilities to his opponents' payoffs and thus to their actions. As in the complete information game with a Nash equilibrium, in the Bayesian equilibrium the probabilities of all the players' payoffs necessarily have to be common knowledge. These common probabilities are also denoted as common priors. The concept of common priors in a Bayesian game thus assumes a joint objective probability distribution over the moves of nature at the beginning of the game (Morris, 1995). Later on, players may receive additional private information, which incites them to update their beliefs over the opponents' payoffs, according to the Bayesian updating formula. The Bayesian updating-rule formalizes the process of learning in an incomplete information game and is defined as follows: let e_h be an event out of a set of possible events E and let I_i denote the private information set of player i. The posterior probability of event e_h occurring after player i has received his private information is given as

$$\mathrm{prob}(e_h|I_i) = \frac{\mathrm{prob}(e_h)\mathrm{prob}(I_i|e_h)}{\mathrm{prob}(I_i)} \, ,$$

with $\mathrm{prob}(e_h)$ denoting the common prior of event e_h.

After laying out the basic game-theoretic concepts, we still have to pinpoint which class of games to use in order to capture the characteristics of currency crises appropriately. Quite generally, one can distinguish between static games, where players have to decide on their optimal actions at the same point in time, and dynamic games, in which players have to make their choice successively. As mentioned above, there are currency crisis models which choose the second type of game. However, since most often currency crises are triggered by a large mass of speculators attacking a fixed parity at the same point in time, Chaps. 5-12 will concentrate on static games only, before briefly reviewing the case of dynamic games in Chap. 13. Since, moreover, speculators' payoffs in currency crisis situations typically depend on their coordinated behavior, one specific class of games, which seems to be appropriate for modelling currency crises, is the class of coordination games (Marshall, 2002).

Following Cooper (1999), coordination games in economics include aspects both of conflict but also of confidence and expectations. Quite generally they can be described by the following characteristics: first, they very often exhibit multiple (Pareto-ranked) Nash equilibria. And secondly, actions of players in coordination games typically are strategic complements. This implies that an increase in the level of activity of one agent creates an incentive for a higher level of activity of the remaining agents (Bulow, Geanakoplos and Klemperer, 1985).

In order to appropriately present currency crises as coordination games, the following section is dedicated to delineating the basic method but also the problems of solving coordination games. The process of equilibrium derivation will be described in detail. In order not to confuse the reader but clarify the basic features of coordination games, we will start with a simple 2×2-game, i.e. a coordination game with 2 players and 2 actions.

4.2 Solving Coordination Games

This section concentrates on 2×2-games only, in order to emphasize the basic characteristics of coordination games, i.e. we are dealing with 2 players who simultaneously have to choose between 2 different strategies. However, as will be seen later, extending this structure to many player, 2 strategy games, as would be appropriate for a currency crisis model, does not present any problems either.

To get the general idea of typical 2×2-games, consider the matrix of payoffs as given in table 4.1. U_1 and V_1 are the possible actions for player 1, yielding a payoff of either 0,1 or 2, depending on whether player 2 chooses U_2 or V_2. Payoffs in this game are von Neumann-Morgenstern utilities. The structure of the game as well as the payoffs are assumed to be common knowledge to both players. Moreover, players are supposed to be individually rational.

A pure strategy in this example is characterized by a probability of either zero or one for each of the two possible actions U and V for each player. A

Table 4.1.

	U_2	V_2
U_1	1, 1	1, 0
V_1	0, 1	2, 2

mixed strategy assigns a probability $0 < p < 1$ to the respective actions, with the two probabilities for each player summing up to one.

It can easily be seen that there are two pure Nash equilibria in this game as well as one equilibrium in mixed strategies. Whenever player 2 chooses action U_2, the best response of player 1 is to choose U_1 as well, since this will leave him with a payoff of one, whereas he would have obtained a payoff of zero if he had chosen action V_1. In contrast, if player 2 chooses action V_2, the best response of player 1 is to play V_1, which leaves him with a payoff of two instead of one by playing U_1. Additionally to these two pure Nash equilibrium strategies, there is another Nash equilibrium in mixed strategies where both players assign probability $\frac{1}{2}$ to action U (and, respectively, $\frac{1}{2}$ to action V).

Multiplicity of equilibria follows from agents' inability to coordinate on a unique equilibrium strategy. There is no way for them to tell which of the two strategies the opponent will choose in the first place. However, comparing only the two equilibria in pure strategies, we find that (V_1, V_2) clearly Pareto-dominates (U_1, U_2), in the sense that both players receive a higher payoff by choosing action V. Hence, (V_1, V_2) payoff-dominates (U_1, U_2). Pareto-suboptimal equilibria are also referred to as "coordination failures". Yet, even though (U_1, U_2) presents a coordination failure, it might still be the equilibrium which turns out to be chosen in this game. In economics, this is no news: think of a bank's impending default. In such an instance, depositors often choose to coordinate on the "bad" equilibrium, i.e. to run on the bank. This clearly presents a coordination failure, in contrast to a situation with the bank being saved by depositors keeping their faith in their bank's ability to manage the problem.

Following from this analysis, we find the obvious drawback of coordination games, and as such of currency crisis models which use coordination games to present the structure of crises, to be the large number of possible equilibria and the inability to predict which one of these will prevail. As a first step in order to solve this problem, it is advisable to explore the characteristics of the equilibria in more detail, as well as to investigate into the possible ways of coordination. In doing so, we follow the analysis by Harsanyi and Selten (1988).

In order to generalize it is useful to introduce some more notations. Let u_i and v_i denote the losses faced by player i, if he deviates from the equilibrium points $U = U_1U_2$ and $V = V_1V_2$, respectively, while the other player sticks to her chosen equilibrium strategy.[6] In this respect, consider the following matrix of payoffs as given in table 4.2. a_{ij} represents player 1's payoff, with

Table 4.2.

	U_2	V_2
U_1	a_{11}, b_{11}	a_{12}, b_{12}
V_1	a_{21}, b_{21}	a_{22}, b_{22}

i denoting the action that player 1 chooses and j depicting player 2's action. Here, $i, j = 1$ indicates action U, $i, j = 2$ indicates action V. b_{ij} in the same sense represents player 2's payoff, while i denotes the chosen action by player 1 and j shows the action chosen by player 2. Deviation losses are then given as

$$\begin{aligned} u_1 &= a_{11} - a_{21} \ , \\ u_2 &= b_{11} - b_{12} \ , \\ v_1 &= a_{22} - a_{12} \ , \\ v_2 &= b_{22} - b_{21} \ . \end{aligned}$$

By denoting the probability with which player i chooses strategy V_i as p_i, we can easily define best response strategies for each player to each of his opponents' actions. For player 1 we find the following: strategy U_1 is a best response to any action his opponent may take (i.e. player 2 may either choose the pure strategies U_2 or V_2, or a mixed strategy out of the two former ones), if

$$a_{11}(1 - p_2) + a_{12}p_2 \geq a_{21}(1 - p_2) + a_{22}p_2 \ ,$$

which simplifies to

$$\begin{aligned} (a_{11} - a_{21})(1 - p_2) &\geq (a_{22} - a_{12})p_2 \\ u_1(1 - p_2) &\geq v_1 p_2 \ . \end{aligned}$$

Player 1 will therefore optimally choose strategy U_1, if his loss from deviating from strategy U_1, which is given by $a_{11} - a_{21}$, while 2 plays U_2 with probability $(1 - p_2)$, is higher than the loss incurred by deviating from strategy V_1, which is $a_{22} - a_{12}$, with player 2 choosing V_2 with probability p_2. Likewise, V_1 is a best response for player 1 if,

$$a_{21}(1 - p_2) + a_{22}p_2 \geq a_{11}(1 - p_2) + a_{12}p_2 \ ,$$

[6] The loss is defined in dependence of one's own choice between the actions, while keeping the opponent's choice constant. This procedure is reasonable, since the Nash-equilibrium strategy is also defined by keeping the opponent's equilibrium strategy constant.

which again simplifies to

$$v_1 p_2 \geq u_1(1 - p_2) \ .$$

Thus, using the definition of u_i and v_i, we find that U_1 is the optimal response for player 1, if $0 \leq p_2 \leq \frac{u_1}{u_1+v_1}$, whereas V_1 is a best response for $\frac{u_1}{u_1+v_1} \leq p_2 \leq 1$. Similarly, for the second player it holds that U_2 is his best response as long as $0 \leq p_1 \leq \frac{u_2}{u_2+v_2}$, and V_2 is the best response for $\frac{u_2}{u_2+v_2} \leq p_1 \leq 1$. Thus, choosing action U is optimal for both players whenever their opponent selects action V only with a small probability. Otherwise, making a choice on V is optimal.

In order to analyze the importance of the best-response result in this game, we can use the following diagram, taken from Harsanyi and Selten (1988), which represents all strategy combinations as points in a rectangular system of coordinates. The horizontal axis measures the probability of player 1 choosing action V, while the vertical axis gives the probability of player 2 choosing V.

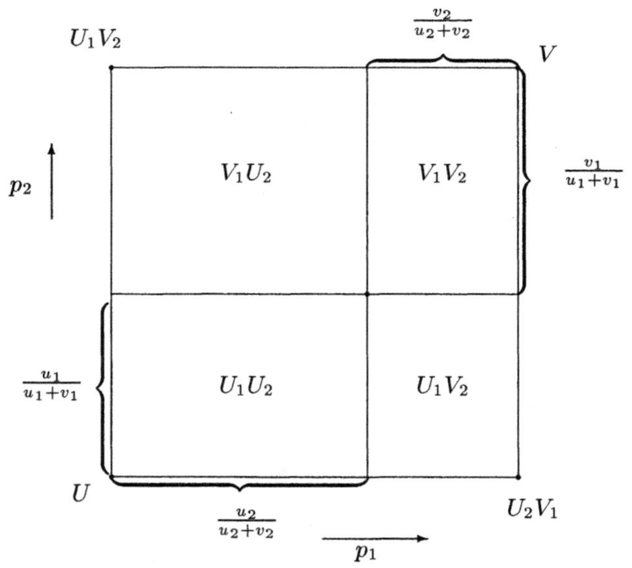

Fig. 4.1. Stability diagram

This so-called stability diagram shows for which combinations of p_1 and p_2 the two pure strategy combinations are best responses to each other. This is the case for two closed rectangles, one in the upper right of p_1 and p_2, and one in the lower left. If both players choose action V with a high probability (upper right rectangle), then (V_1, V_2) turns out to be a stable equilibrium.

In contrast, (U_1, U_2) is the stable equilibrium if both players attach only a very small probability to choosing action V (lower left rectangle). These two areas are called the stability regions of the game, since the actions of the players reinforce each other in these rectangulars. The upper left and lower right area, however, are characterized by the fact that one player attaches a high, the other a low probability to choosing action V. These rectangles therefore are not stable. The equilibrium in mixed strategies is given by the corner that both stability rectangles share, i.e. the point where $p_1 = \frac{u_2}{u_2+v_2}$ and $p_2 = \frac{u_1}{u_1+v_1}$.

Note that the best-reply of each player only depends on the ratios $\frac{u_1}{v_1}$ and $\frac{u_2}{v_2}$ of the agents' deviation losses, i.e. the payoff difference ratios, whereas absolute payoff levels do not matter. Player 1's risk situation is characterized by the ratio $\frac{u_1}{v_1}$, whereas player 2's risk situation is connected to $\frac{v_2}{u_2}$. Hence, player 1 is more strongly attracted to action U than player 2 to V, whenever $\frac{u_1}{v_1}$ is higher than $\frac{v_2}{u_2}$, which is the case for $u_1 u_2 > v_1 v_2$. Risk-dominance in the sense of Harsanyi and Selten (1988) can therefore be characterized as follows: action U risk-dominates V, if $u_1 u_2 > v_1 v_2$, and V risk-dominates U if $v_1 v_2 > u_1 u_2$. This is completely in line with the above analysis of best-reply structures, where the probabilities to be compared were given by $\frac{u_i}{u_i+v_i}$ and $\frac{v_i}{v_i+u_i}$. Hence, the definition of risk-dominance is fully complied with the notion of best reply functions. Moreover, leaning on the bargaining theory of Nash, the deviation-loss products $u_1 u_2$ and $v_1 v_2$ can also be referred to as the Nash-products of actions U and V, respectively. This is an additional argument for using risk dominance as a means of selecting equilibria, since this method can easily be compared to the argumentation with Nash products (Binmore, Rubinstein and Wolinsky, 1986).

The following game gives an example of the above reasoning. Consider the payoff matrix in table 4.3. The equilibrium (U_1, U_2) clearly yields higher pay-

Table 4.3.

	U_2	V_2
U_1	9, 7	0, 1
V_1	7, 2	8, 6

offs for both players than the second equilibrium in pure strategies, (V_1, V_2). Hence, U payoff-dominates V. However, analyzing aspects of risk, we find that V risk-dominates U, since

$$v_1 \cdot v_2 = (8-0) \cdot (6-2) = 32 \;>\; u_1 \cdot u_2 = (9-7) \cdot (7-1) = 12 \,.$$

In this game, payoff-dominance and risk-dominance point into different directions. Whereas both players are better off by choosing action U, player 1 has most to lose by deviating from V. Since players are assumed to be rational, they have to take into account the opponent's decision problem. Hence, they might as well coordinate on the risk-dominant equilibrium instead of the payoff-dominant one, if they both recognize that player 1 has a lot to lose by deviating from V_1.

Thus, in a game where risk- and payoff-dominant equilibria do not coincide, we cannot predict which of the possible outcomes will prevail. As long as the whole structure of the game is common knowledge to both players, we might expect the payoff-dominant equilibrium to hold, but we can never be sure. The next section will account for this problem and show how a solution method can be derived, which eliminates all equilibria but one. Surprisingly, the outcome is equal to the risk-dominant equilibrium. Moreover, this result not only holds for the simple 2×2-games considered so far, but quite generally for all n-player, 2 action games and also for some games with n players choosing among n actions.

4.3 Equilibrium Selection in Global Games – Carlsson and van Damme (1993)

In their paper of 1993, Carlsson and van Damme strongly criticize the common practice of game-theoretic models to assume the state of the game, in particular the payoff structure as well as rationality of the players, to be common knowledge. In their model, they deviate from this assumption by analyzing an incomplete information game. This incomplete information model, which is also referred to as a global game, is based on perturbations of the players' information about payoffs. The notion of a global game relates to the fact that incompleteness of information is introduced to the model by assuming that the game to be played is determined by a random draw from the whole class of (in this case) $2 \times 2-$games. Each player observes the selected game with some noise and, based on this observation, decides on his optimal action. In making their choice, players therefore have to take into account the whole class of games. Carlsson and van Damme are able to show that if the initial class contains games with different equilibrium structures, a unique equilibrium can be iteratively derived in the incomplete information game. Provided that the game which is actually selected is a game with two strict Nash-equilibria, the prevailing equilibrium coincides with the risk-dominant equilibrium. However, noise in player's observations has to be small.[7]

The uniqueness result of the Carlsson/van Damme (1993) method is driven by the fact that in a global game uncertainty forces the players to take into account the whole class of a priori possible games. This class may be large, even if noise is small. Whenever this class contains games with different equilibrium structures, players have to switch their optimal actions at some point of their

[7] A similar result is derived in a model by Burdzy, Frankel and Pauzner (2001), where players in a symmetric 2×2-game with randomly changing payoffs and small frictions in changing actions always coordinate on the risk-dominant equilibrium.

observation spaces. Equilibrium selection then stems from the conditions that optimal switching points have to satisfy in the limit with vanishing noise.[8] Equilibrium selection can be seen to be in accordance with risk-dominance, so that the equilibrium for the global game is equal to the limit of the equilibrium for the nearby game with incomplete information as the amount of noise goes to zero.

Carlsson and van Damme's analysis, although in line with several other attempts of perturbing information assumptions, delivers an intriguing result: whereas in earlier models strict equilibria have proved to be immune against most perturbations and refinements,[9] they succeed in showing that equilibria can iteratively be eliminated whenever they are dominated by arguments of risk. This apparent contradiction between the Carlsson/van Damme-method and earlier refinement approaches can be explained by the fact that in their model, players' observations of the game are correlated and all the players' higher order beliefs depend on their observations. In earlier models, for instance by Harsanyi (1973) or Selten (1975), it has been assumed, instead, that players' payoffs are independent.

To get the basic intuition for the Carlsson/van Damme-method of deriving a unique equilibrium in a coordination game with incomplete information, consider the following example of a 2 × 2-game, denoted by $g(\theta)$, as taken from Carlsson and van Damme (1993). The players can choose between two actions, either α or β. Payoffs are given by the following matrix and depend on θ, which is also referred to as the "state of the game".

Table 4.4.

	α_2	β_2
α_1	θ, θ	$\theta, 0$
β_1	$0, \theta$	$4, 4$

Depending on the value of the underlying state θ, this game has two strictly dominant equilibria: for $\theta < 0$ both players will rationally choose action β, so that $\beta = (\beta_1, \beta_2)$ is the strict Nash equilibrium that will be coordinated on. For $\theta > 4$, the prevailing Nash equilibrium is given by $\alpha = (\alpha_1, \alpha_2)$, i.e. both players will want to play strategy α. This follows from a simple best-response analysis. However, if θ takes on values between 0 and 4, both α and β are strict Nash equilibria. If, for $\theta \in (0, 4)$, the first player chooses action α_1, the best response for the second player is to play α_2, whereas it would be optimal to take action β_2, if the first player had decided on β_1. Since both players have to decide simultaneously which strategy to choose, the actions played in the game cannot be foreseen ex ante. Hence, if θ is commonly known to

[8] On this point, see also Carlsson and Ganslandt (1998).

[9] Actually, strictness of equilibrium has been defined as the fact that equilibrium does not change even with small perturbations of payoff. See also Cooper (1999).

lie between 0 and 4, we get the typical result of multiple equilibria with two equilibria in pure strategies and one equilibrium in mixed strategies.

However, for a certain range of values for θ within the interval $(0, 4)$, strategy α risk-dominates strategy β, whereas β is risk-dominant for the complementary region. Let us elaborate on this point in more detail. For player 1, the payoff associated with choosing strategy α is given by θ, whereas the payoff from deviating from α and deciding on β instead is given by zero whenever her opponent sticks to strategy α. Thus the product of deviation losses for strategy α is given by $(\theta - 0)^2 = \theta^2$. For strategy β the product of deviation losses is given by $(4 - \theta)^2$, since player 1 will receive a payoff of four from choosing β_1 and θ from deviating and choosing α_1, when player 2 sticks to his choice of β. Consequently, if θ takes on values in the interval $(0, 2)$, β is the risk-dominant strategy of the game. Here, most can be lost by deviating from strategy β, since $(4 - \theta)^2 > \theta^2$ for $\theta \in (0, 2)$. For $\theta \in (2, 4)$ instead, strategy α risk-dominates β, so that playing α in that subclass of games is less risky than playing strategy β. Note that for $\theta \in (2, 4)$, there is a conflict between risk-dominance and payoff-dominance, as α is the risk-dominant action whereas β is payoff dominant. For $\theta \in (0, 2)$, however, strategy β is both risk- and payoff-dominant.

Hence, for $\theta \in (0, 4)$, as long as there is common knowledge about the payoff structure (and as such about the exact game to be played), it cannot be predicted which of the possible equilibria will prevail. The best one can do is to find out motivations for the different equilibria that might be payoff-related or risk-related arguments.

Starting from this multiplicity result for general coordination games with common knowledge about the rules of the game, Carlsson and van Damme (1993) were able to show that introducing uncertainties about the payoff structure of the game eliminates all but the risk-dominant equilibrium, provided that the amount of noise is small. In order to make their argument more comprehensible, consider the following incomplete information game: let θ be the realization of a random variable Θ that is uniformly distributed over the interval $[\underline{\theta}, \bar{\theta}]$, with $\underline{\theta} < 0$ and $\bar{\theta} > 4$. Due to these assumptions, the two regions with strictly dominating strategies are included as subclasses of the game. Conditional on θ, each player observes a random variable x_i (signal), which is uniformly distributed on $[\theta - \varepsilon, \theta + \varepsilon]$, $\varepsilon > 0$. Hence, incomplete and asymmetric information arises, because players do not directly observe θ, but a noisy random variable x in form of a private signal. The magnitude of ε determines the informativeness of the signal. The two observation errors, $x_1 - \theta$ and $x_2 - \theta$, are assumed to be independent. Additionally, it is presumed that the structure of the class of games and the joint distributions of θ and x are common knowledge. After receiving their signals, players simultaneously have to choose their actions. Afterwards, they receive their payoffs according to the above delineated game $g(\theta)$.

It is straightforward to see that each player's posterior of θ is uniform on $[x_i - \varepsilon, x_i + \varepsilon]$, if he observes a signal $x_i \in [\underline{\theta} + \varepsilon, \bar{\theta} - \varepsilon]$. Thus, his expected payoff from choosing action α_i conditional on his signal will simply be equal to his signal x_i. Additionally, given signal x_i he believes his opponent's signal x_j to be symmetric around x_i with support on the interval $[x_i - 2\varepsilon, x_i + 2\varepsilon]$. Consequently, the probability he ascribes to his opponent receiving a higher or lower signal than himself is equal to $\frac{1}{2}$, respectively. Note, that the signal x_i is informative not only about the state θ, but also about the opponent's signal x_j, since signals are correlated.

If now the noise parameter ε is sufficiently small ($\varepsilon < -\frac{1}{2}\underline{\theta}$, so that $\underline{\theta}+2\varepsilon < 0$)[10], player 1 will optimally choose strategy β_1, whenever she observes a signal $x_1 < 0$. This is quite obvious, since her conditionally expected payoff from choosing α_1 is equal to x_1 and as such negative, whereas action β_1 would give her a payoff of at least 0. Thus, β_i is conditionally dominant for $x_i < 0$. However, iterated dominance arguments allow to go further. Since player 2 knows that whenever agent 1 observes a signal $x_1 < 0$ she will choose β_1, he will continue to choose strategy β, not only for negative signals, but also if he observes a signal of $x_2 = 0$. This follows from the fact that for a signal of $x_2 = 0$, he will assign at least probability $\frac{1}{2}$ to agent 1 receiving a signal smaller than 0. Consequently, player 2 will assume a probability of $\frac{1}{2}$ for player 1 to choose action β_1, so that his expected payoff from choosing β_2 equals $\frac{1}{2} \cdot 0 + \frac{1}{2} \cdot 4 = 2$. Since the expected payoff from deciding on α_2 is equal to his signal, he will rationally play β after receiving a signal of $x_2 = 0$. Thus, α_i can be rationally excluded not only for $x_i < 0$, but also for $x_i = 0$. If, however, player 1 follows this line of reasoning, it is rational for her to choose β_1 even for signals slightly higher than zero. Since this chain of thoughts holds for player 2 as well, he will be willing to choose strategy β for even higher values of the private signal, etc. With increasing values of the private signals, however, the difference between the expected payoffs from α and β will decrease. This is due to the fact that the expected payoff from selecting strategy α increases in the private signals, whereas the expected payoff from choosing strategy β is given by $0 \cdot \text{Prob}(\alpha_j|x_i) + 4 \cdot \text{Prob}(\beta_j|x_i)$.

Since in the depicted game player i's belief about her opponent's signal distribution is symmetric around her own signal x_i, the probability of one's opponent receiving a signal higher or lower than oneself is always equal to $\frac{1}{2}$, independent of one's signal. Starting from the lower dominance region as in the above argument, each player will therefore assign a probability of $\frac{1}{2}$ to his opponent receiving a lower signal than himself and hence to her still sticking to the decision rule of the lower dominance region and choosing β. Thus, α is iteratively eliminated until a point is reached where the inequality

$$0 \cdot \text{Prob}(\alpha_j|x_i) + 4 \cdot \text{Prob}(\beta_j|x_i) > x_i$$

no longer holds.

[10] It has to be assured, that a player receiving a signal on the borderline from the lower dominant strategy region to the multiple equilibria region assigns probability of at least $\frac{1}{2}$ to the event, that the posterior of θ lies in the dominant strategy area.

Denote the smallest value of the private signal for player i, for which α can no longer be eliminated and β no longer be established by iterated dominance arguments, as x_i^*. Due to the symmetry of the game it holds that $x_1^* = x_2^* = x^*$, i.e. the upper bound on the iteration process starting from the lower dominance region has to be the same for both players. Since for any signal $x_i < x^*$ player i will choose strategy β_i, player j will assign probability $\frac{1}{2}$ to player i's choosing β_i, if he observes signal $x_j = x^*$. Consequently, j's expected payoff from choosing strategy β_j when observing signal $x_j = x^*$ will be at most equal to 2. However, as has been said before, the expected conditional payoff for j from playing α_j is equal to the signal $x_j = x^*$. Since x^* is defined to be the smallest value of the signal for which strategy β is no longer chosen, the conditionally expected payoff from action α_j has to be at least equal to 2 (otherwise action β_j yielding a payoff of two would have been chosen). Thus, it is necessary that $x^* \geq 2$.

Proceeding from above, we can show that for noise values ε smaller than $\frac{\bar{x}-4}{2}$ (so that $\bar{\theta} - 2\varepsilon > 4$), strategy α is strictly dominant for $x > 4$ and iterated dominance leads to a value x^{**}, which is a lower bound in the sense that for $x \leq x^{**}$ strategy α is no longer iteratively dominant. This means that if player i conforms to that iterative dominance argument and if player j observes a signal of $x_j = x^{**}$, his expected payoff from choosing β_j is at least 2 (as he will have to assign probability at least $\frac{1}{2}$ to i's still choosing α_i), whereas his conditionally expected payoff from playing α_j is again given by $x_j = x^{**}$. Hence, as j chooses strategy β_j after receiving signal x^{**}, this value x^{**} cannot be higher than 2, for otherwise strategy α_j would have been chosen. Putting all the reasoning together we find that

$$x^* = x^{**} = 2 \,.$$

Thus, iterated dominance arguments force the players in this global game to choose an equilibrium strategy that coincides with the risk-dominant strategy. For $x < 2$, each agent will play strategy β, whereas α will be chosen for $x > 2$. As can be seen, this result critically depends on the existence of a subclass of dominance solvable games, which serve as take-offs for the iterated dominance argument and thus exert an influence on the complementary class of games with multiple equilibria.

Informally, the main idea of equilibrium selection in global games can be summed up as follows: shen θ lies between zero and four, and signals are very informative, the dominant strategy aspects of the two dominance regions ($\theta < 0$ and $\theta > 4$) will spill over to generate a unique equilibrium for the whole game. The crucial point is that in such a setting, players conceive of the possibility that their opponent has received an extreme signal that justifies the choice of only one unique action on the part of this player, and which then pins down the whole play.

The key to understanding the equilibrium structure is the fact that in a global game there is a sharp difference between knowledge and common knowledge. Take the example of $\theta = 3$. For $\theta = 3$, strategy β would be payoff-dominant. If noise variable ε is small, players receive signals close to 3 and as such know that choosing strategy β would yield a higher potential payoff than strategy α. The problem, however, is that this fact is not common knowledge. For ε being small, each player might know that his opponent must have received a signal which tells him that strategy β is Pareto-dominant, but he might not know whether his opponent knows that he knows, etc. Hence, due to the lack of common knowledge, remote areas have an influence on the players' behavior which would not prevail, if θ were common knowledge. In fact, in the game depicted above, the only information which is common knowledge is that some game $g(\theta)$ with $\theta \in [\underline{\theta}, \bar{\theta}]$ has to be played.

4.4 Generalizing the Method to n-Player, 2-Action Games

The appropriate form of modelling currency crisis situations as global games is given by n-player, 2-action games, since typically a large number (n) of speculators in the foreign exchange market has to decide whether or not to attack the fixed parity. Unfortunately, the Carlsson/van Damme (1993) method of deriving a unique equilibrium from a game with multiple equilibria generically has been derived for 2-player, 2-action games only. However, Frankel, Morris and Pauzner (2000) succeeded in generalizing the original result by Carlsson and van Damme to n-player, 2-action games as well.

Their generalization is based on reconstructing the result by Carlsson and van Damme (1993) in two logically separate parts. From the overall result that whenever players observe slightly noisy signals of the game's payoffs and if the ex ante feasible payoffs include those which make each action strictly dominant, iterative strict dominance eliminates all but one equilibrium, there follow two important separate aspects. First, there is a limit uniqueness result: as the noise of the incomplete information game becomes small, there is a unique action that survives iterative elimination of dominated strategies for almost all payoffs. Secondly, there is a noise independent selection result: as noise vanishes, the equilibrium played is independent of the distribution of noise.

Whereas Frankel, Morris and Pauzner (2000) found the first result to generalize quite easily to many player, many action games with strategic complementarities, the second result was much harder to prove for larger classes of games. However, it will be seen that the class of many player, 2-action games belongs to those games for which noise independent selection still holds. Since we do not want to go into the formal proof into detail here, we will simply give the outline of the argument by Frankel, Morris and Pauzner (2000), and state the main assumptions and conditions necessary to derive the results.

As Frankel, Morris and Pauzner (2000) were able to show, given that the following assumptions on the payoff structure of the game are satisfied, there is a unique equilibrium in the limit as noise vanishes: first, players' actions have to be strategic complements, i.e. for any state θ a player's best response has to increase in the actions of his opponents. This property can also be referred to as action monotonicity. Secondly, the global game has to include limit dominant actions. This means that at sufficiently low (high) states θ, each player's strictly dominant action is given by the lowest (highest) action. In case that each player's action space is finite, this assumption can be replaced by the weaker supposition that for $\theta \notin [\underline{\theta}, \bar{\theta}]$, the complete information game has a unique Nash equilibrium. The third requirement is single crossing, i.e. for any possible action profile of the other players, each player's best response is increasing in the state θ. This characteristic is also denoted as state monotonicity as opposed to action monotonicity. Lastly, it is required that the payoff structure is continuous with respect to both state θ and actions.

Under these assumptions, it can be shown that for any n-player, n-action game, iterative elimination of strictly dominated strategies selects an essentially unique Bayesian equilibrium as the signal errors go to zero.[11] The proof is in two steps: first, Frankel, Morris and Pauzner (2000) show that uniqueness holds in a simplified game, afterwards it is demonstrated that the original game converges to the simplified one as the signal errors shrink.

In the simplified game, payoffs depend directly on the signals x, instead of the state θ. Signals are given as $x_i = \theta + \nu\eta_i$ with $\nu > 0$ and each η_i smoothly distributed according to density f_i with support on the interval $[-\frac{1}{2}, \frac{1}{2}]$. θ is supposed to be uniformly drawn from a large interval including $[\underline{\theta}, \bar{\theta}]$. Note that with a uniform prior on states, player i's posterior of the normalized differences between her own and other players' signals, $\frac{x_j - x_i}{\nu}$, is independent of her own signal x_i and of the noise scale factor ν. The proof of a unique equilibrium requires showing that for $\nu \to 0$, players' posteriors over the differences in signal errors converge to the posterior that would result from a uniform prior distribution over θ. This, quite intuitively, follows from the fact that for small signal errors, the posterior of the signal error for a player with signal x is approximately the same as the posterior for a player with signal x'. Hence, $(x - \theta) - (x' - \theta) = x - x'$, so that a player's posterior over the difference between his signal and his opponent's signal is the same, no matter whether his signal is x or x'. This follows from the above stated uniform prior distribution of θ. Thus, a player receiving signal x, who believes that his opponent has observed a signal of x', must expect the same action distribution as a player who observes x' and thinks his opponent to have received a signal of x. Following from the structure of the game, they then must want to play the same strategy. Due to the assumed state monotonicity, however, x and x' cannot be equilibrium points at the same state, since a player's optimal action is strictly increasing in his estimate of θ. Consequently, x and x' must coincide, so that for shrinking noise, $\nu \to 0$, agents' behavior converges to the

[11] The "essential" qualification stems from the fact that either action may be played, if exactly the point of equilibrium is realized. See also Morris and Shin (2000).

weakly increasing strategy profile in x_i, which is the only one that survives iterative strict dominance arguments.

Additionally, Frankel, Morris and Pauzner (2000) find that with vanishing noise, it does not matter whether the players' payoffs depend on their signal or on the state θ. Hence, for $\nu \to 0$, the simplified game converges to the original game, so that the strategy profiles surviving iterative dominance in the original and simplified game converge to each other.

Consequently, given that the above assumptions are satisfied, the limit uniqueness result for vanishing noise holds for all n-player, n-action games and, as such, also for the n-player, 2-action game that we are going to use in the currency crisis context. However, the question remains whether this uniqueness result is independent of the assumed distribution of noise, f_i.

Concerning this latter question, Frankel, Morris and Pauzner (2000) demonstrate that the noise independent selection result holds for every local potential game with own-action concave payoffs. Thus, noise independent selection requires more stringent assumptions on the payoff structure of the game than the simple limit uniqueness result. However, since uniqueness is much more important for the currency crisis context to be analyzed later on, it should suffice here to note that many player, 2 action games with symmetric payoffs are included in the required class of local potential games,[12] so that noise independent selection holds for the typical currency crisis model as well. Potential games as defined by Monderer and Shapley (1996) are characterized by the property that there exists a common payoff function on action profiles, such that the change in a player's payoff from switching from one to the other action is always the same as the change in the common payoff function. For the complete information game with the same payoffs, the respective strategy is denoted as the local potential maximizer. This strategy must be played in the limit, since iteratively eliminating dominated actions will lead to the unique action that maximizes players' payoffs.

Summing up the arguments, we find that the appropriate form to model currency crises as global games is given by n-player, 2-action games, where a multitude of speculators can decide whether to attack the fixed parity or not. Since it is reasonable to assume that on the foreign exchange market speculators do not have perfect knowledge, neither about the underlying fundamental state of the economy nor about their opponents' behavior, the introduction of noise into the game can be seen as justified. This, however, enables the derivation of a unique equilibrium in the model, as compared to earlier second-generation currency crisis models with multiple equilibria, as long as the uncertainty on the market is not too large. Hence, it will become possible to predict whether or not a speculative attack on the fixed exchange rate is going to take place, and which influence the different parameters of the model will have on the probability of a crisis. Furthermore, the model enables us to analyze in more detail the role of information and subsequently to derive the

[12] Games with only two actions always satisfy the condition of own-action concavity.

optimal policy for a central bank that tries to prevent speculative attacks on the exchange rate.

Chapter 5 presents the global games model of a currency crisis by Morris and Shin (1998), and shows how a unique equilibrium can be derived in contrast to the multiplicity result and the ensuing controversies of the typical second-generation models. Chapter 6 delineates some further aspects of the Morris/Shin-model: questions of transparency and the influence of speculators' expectations will be analyzed. The reader will find that all the results to be derived throughout the following chapters have their game-theoretic counterpart in Chap. 4. However, the results coming up in the next sections are meant to also be self-explaining in their respective contexts.

5

Solving Currency Crisis Models in Global Games – The Morris/Shin-Model (1998)

The current chapter describes the type of models introduced by Morris and Shin (1998), who used a global games setting to derive a unique equilibrium from a currency crisis model with self-fulfilling beliefs. Their paper provides the framework that we are going to use in order to derive further results concerning the role of information dissemination in the chapters to follow. In a first step, however, we will present the procedure of eliminating equilibria in a basic currency crisis model, where speculators do not know the fundamental state of the economy but receive noisy information about it. The emphasis in this chapter therefore is on the method of iteratively eliminating dominated strategies in a currency crisis setting and on showing that the prevailing equilibrium indeed is the risk-dominant one, as has been stated in Chap. 4.

The main insight of the Morris/Shin-model is the fact that although the central bank's reaction function still displays nonlinearities due to a multitude of different policy targets and even though speculators' expectations are still self-fulfilling, the equilibrium derived is unique. This is very much in contrast to the typical second-generation models of currency crises à la Obstfeld as presented in Chap. 2, where a multiplicity of equilibria holds for the game between speculators and central bank. Hence, nonlinear government behavior and self-fulfilling prophecies obviously are not enough to enforce multiple equilibria. Rather, as we will see, it is the amount of overlapping information on the part of the speculators which accounts for either multiplicity or uniqueness of optimal actions.

The method by Morris and Shin of applying the results from global games theory as derived by Carlsson and van Damme (1993) to economic problems, has met with unanimous approval. Starting with the Morris/Shin-paper in 1998, a large number of economists have applied this method to all kinds of coordination problems in economics, for instance to bank runs (Goldstein, 2000; Goldstein and Pauzner, 2000), multiple source lending (Hubert and Schäfer, 2001), pricing debt (Morris and Shin, 1999a; Brunner and Krahnen, 2001) or competing order systems (Dönges and Heinemann, 2000). In the context of this book, however, we will concentrate on the application of the Morris/Shin-method to currency crises only.

5.1 The Basic Model by Morris and Shin (1998)

The seminal paper by Morris and Shin (1998) is concerned with finding the unique equilibrium of a game between the central bank and a group of speculators on the foreign exchange market, where the exchange rate is pegged to a certain level. The model assumes a continuum of speculators indexed in $[0, 1]$, each disposing of one unit of domestic currency. Hence, each individual speculator is negligibly small in "financial power". Due to this assumption, a single speculator can neither force a devaluation from the central bank nor prevent an impending attack by his opponents. The economy is characterized by the state of fundamentals, indexed by θ, with θ being uniformly distributed over the unit interval $[0, 1]$. A high value of θ represents strong fundamentals, a low value of θ corresponds to a weak fundamental state of the economy. The natural or shadow exchange rate, i.e. the rate which prevails in the absence of central bank intervention, is given by $f(\theta)$, where f is a continuous and strictly increasing function in θ.

Initially, the exchange rate is pegged at a level of $\bar{e}$, with $\bar{e} \geq f(\theta)$ for all θ.[1] Each speculator can decide whether to attack the fixed parity, for instance by short-selling his unit of domestic currency over the foreign exchange market, or to refrain from doing so. Attacking the exchange rate peg is associated with costs of t, which comprise both the interest rate differential between domestic and foreign currency as well as simple transaction costs from short-selling. If the attack is successful and the central bank abandons the peg, the net payoff from this action to the individual speculator is given by $\bar{e} - f(\theta) - t = D(\theta) - t$, which corresponds to the fall in the exchange rate free of transaction costs. If, however, the central bank succeeds in defending the peg, each attacking speculator ends up with a negative payoff of $-t$. Choosing not to attack does not lead to any costs.[2] It is assumed that $\bar{e} - f(1) = D(1) < t$. Thus, in the best state of fundamentals ($\theta = 1$), the pegged exchange rate is so close to the natural exchange rate, that the gain from a successful attack is outweighed by transaction costs, so that any rational speculator will refrain from attacking. The complete payoff structure of the game can be seen from the matrix in table 5.1.

The central bank derives a value v from keeping the exchange rate fixed, but also faces costs c from defending the parity, which decrease in the state of fundamentals, θ, and increase in the number of speculators attacking the

[1] The exchange rate is given in terms of units of foreign currency per unit of domestic currency.

[2] Opportunity costs from not participating in a successful attack on the fixed parity are not taken into account, since speculators might reasonably be expected to simply maximize their payoffs.

Table 5.1.

	success	no success
attack	$D(\theta) - t$	$-t$
not-attack	0	0

currency, l. It is assumed that $c(\theta, l)$ is a continuous and differentiable function. The central bank's net payoff from defending the peg is then given as $v - c(\theta, l)$, whereas the payoff from abandoning the peg is equal to zero.

In this set-up, the following presumptions are made: first, it is assumed that $c(0,0) > v$, i.e. in the worst state of fundamentals ($\theta = 0$), the costs from defending the peg always exceed the benefit from maintaining it, even if none of the speculators attacks. Additionally, the authors suppose that $c(1,1) > v$, i.e. even in the best state of fundamentals ($\theta = 1$), if all speculators decide to attack, the costs from defending the peg exceed the benefit from doing so.

Under these assumptions it is possible to define the following two specific values for the fundamental index θ

$$\underline{\theta}: \quad c(\underline{\theta}, 0) = v$$

and

$$\bar{\theta}: \quad D(\bar{\theta}) = t\,.$$

Thus, $\underline{\theta}$ is the value of the fundamental state for which the central bank is indifferent between abandoning the peg and defending it in the absence of any speculative selling. For $\theta = \bar{\theta}$, speculators are indifferent between attacking the peg and refraining from doing so.

Assuming that $\underline{\theta} \leq \bar{\theta}$, Morris and Shin classify three different groups of fundamentals, similar to the currency crisis model à la Obstfeld as depicted in Chap. 2: for $\theta \in [0, \underline{\theta})$ the currency peg is unstable, since fundamentals are so bad that the central bank will always devalue the peg even if none of the speculators attack. For $\theta \in [\underline{\theta}, \bar{\theta}]$ the currency peg is said to be ripe for attack. Here, if only few speculators attack, the costs from defending the peg are lower than the benefit for the central bank, so that the fixed exchange rate will be kept, which in turn justifies the decision not to attack. However, if a large enough proportion of speculators attacks, the central bank will no longer defend but abandon the peg. Since for all θ in this interval speculators would make a positive profit if the exchange rate were to be abandoned, attacking the peg is the rational action if speculators believe in the success of this action. For fundamentals in this interval, therefore, multiple equilibria arise. For $\theta \in (\bar{\theta}, 1]$, the currency peg is stable due to good fundamentals. Here, the dominant action for the speculators is not to attack the fixed parity and the peg will be kept.

From this tripartition of fundamentals it can be seen that there are two intervals in which a unique equilibrium prevails ("attack/devalue" in the first interval and "not-attack/defend" in the third one), whereas multiple equilibria exist in the "ripe for attack" region. Since speculators' actions influence the central bank's strategies, these multiple equilibria display the property of making speculators' expectations self-fulfilling. Note that the two pure equilibria are asymmetric, since speculators gain a positive payoff if the attack is successful, but receive zero in case the peg is not abandoned.

What differentiates the model by Morris and Shin from the original Obstfeld-model with self-fulfilling beliefs and multiple equilibria, is that in the former speculators do not exactly know the fundamental state θ. However, they individually receive noisy signals about θ. Due to this uncertainty, θ is no longer common knowledge, as has implicitly been assumed by Obstfeld.

Formally, it is presumed by Morris and Shin that nature chooses the state of fundamentals θ according to a uniform distribution over the unit interval. The realized value of θ cannot be verified by the traders. However, conditional on the chosen θ, each speculator observes a signal x_i, drawn uniformly from the interval $[\theta-\varepsilon, \theta+\varepsilon]$. Noise ε (> 0) is assumed to be small, in particular $2\varepsilon < \min[\underline{\theta}, 1-\bar{\theta}]$. Conditional on θ, the private signals are i.i.d. across individuals with independent signal errors. After having observed the signals, speculators simultaneously have to decide whether to attack the fixed parity or to refrain from doing so. The central bank observes θ and the proportion of attacking speculators, l, and devalues the peg whenever the costs of defending are higher than the value from maintaining the parity.

In order to exactly pinpoint the equilibrium, Morris and Shin additionally have to make a prediction of both the central bank's and speculators' behavior in case of indifference. In this respect, they presume that whenever a speculator is indifferent between attacking the peg and not-attacking, he will refrain from attacking, whereas the central bank in case of indifference between her two actions is supposed to abandon the peg.

An equilibrium in this game between speculators and central bank consists of strategies for both types of players, such that no one has an incentive to deviate from the chosen strategy. Hence, the equilibrium concept the Morris/Shin-model relies on is one of best response strategies. In order to derive the equilibrium, Morris and Shin solve out first the central bank's strategy at the last stage of the game and then analyze the reduced-form game between speculators.

The critical mass of speculators attacking the peg at state θ is denoted by $a(\theta)$. Due to the assumed cost-benefit structure, the central bank will abandon the peg for a given fundamental state θ, whenever the proportion of attacking speculators is higher than or equal to $a(\theta)$. Taking this optimal strategy for the central bank as given, the payoff structure for the speculators in the reduced-form game results in the following: denote by $s(x)$ the proportion of speculators who attack the currency peg after having observed a signal of x. Moreover, denote by $l(\theta, s)$ the proportion of speculators who end up attacking the peg when the state of the economy is given by θ, and aggregate selling is described by strategy s. From the assumed distribution of signals it follows that

$$l(\theta, s) = \frac{1}{2\varepsilon}\int_{\theta-\varepsilon}^{\theta+\varepsilon} s(x)dx \ .$$

Given the fundamental state θ, private signals are uniformly distributed in $[\theta-\varepsilon, \theta+\varepsilon]$, with each value of x being realized with a probability of $\frac{1}{2\varepsilon}$. In order to simplify on notation, Morris and Shin denote by $A(s)$ the event that the central bank abandons the peg, i.e.

$$A(s) = \{\theta | l(\theta, s) \geq a(\theta)\} \ .$$

The payoff for a speculator attacking the currency peg is then given as

$$h(\theta, s) = \begin{cases} D(\theta) - t & \text{if } \theta \in A(s) \ , \\ -t & \text{if } \theta \notin A(s) \ . \end{cases}$$

Since speculators cannot observe θ, they have to condition their decision on whether or not to attack the fixed parity on the posterior distribution of θ, given the observed private signal x. Let the expected payoff from attacking the fixed parity after having received a signal of x be given by

$$\begin{aligned} u(x, s) &= \frac{1}{2\varepsilon}\int_{x-\varepsilon}^{x+\varepsilon} h(\theta, s)d\theta \\ &= \frac{1}{2\varepsilon}\left[\int_{A(s)\cap(x-\varepsilon, x+\varepsilon)} (D(\theta))d\theta\right] - t \ . \end{aligned} \tag{5.1}$$

Speculators are exactly indifferent between attacking and not-attacking, if both actions lead to the same expected net payoff. This condition is what triggers the unique equilibrium, since it can be shown that there is exactly one value of the private signals, denoted by x^*, such that a speculator observing this signal is indifferent between attacking and refraining from doing so. Consequently, there is also exactly one value for the fundamental index, denoted by θ^*, such that the central bank after observing θ^* is indifferent between defending and keeping the peg. Hence, the following proposition holds:

Proposition 5.1. (Morris and Shin, 1998)
There exists a unique equilibrium (x^*, θ^*), such that each speculator observing a signal $x \leq x^*$ attacks the fixed parity, and the central bank abandons the currency peg if and only if $\theta \leq \theta^*$.

The proof consists of several steps. First it is shown that if a strategy profile s contains a larger proportion of attacking speculators than s' for a given signal x, then the payoff to attacking the parity is greater given s than s', i.e. $u(x, s) \geq u(x, s')$. This is due to the fact that $l(\theta, s) \geq l(\theta, s')$ for all θ, so that the range of fundamentals for which the central bank is forced to devalue the peg is larger under s than under s': $A(s) \supseteq A(s')$. Since A is the range of integration for the calculation of u, it follows directly from (5.1) that $u(x,s) \geq u(x,s')$.

The second step of the proof involves assuming that speculators follow a cut-off strategy around k, so that all speculators receiving a signal x smaller than k attack, and refrain from attacking if $x \geq k$. Let aggregate short-selling s in this case be denoted by $J_k(x)$, such that

$$J_k(x) = \begin{cases} 1 & \text{if } x < k \,, \\ 0 & \text{if } x \geq k \,. \end{cases}$$

It is then quite easy to see that the payoff from attacking, $u(k, J_k)$, is continuous and decreasing in k. This is to say that with improving fundamentals, the payoff from attacking the parity of a speculator on the margin from attacking to not attacking decreases. However, proving this property is quite difficult, since increasing k has two effects. On the one hand, if the cut-off value for the private signal increases, the proportion of attacking speculators increases for every θ. As such, the payoff from attacking rises. However, for k to be the equilibrium cut-off signal, the above indifference conditions have to be satisfied. Thus, a higher cut-off k can only be an equilibrium point, if the fundamental state θ is higher as well, since only for better fundamentals a larger proportion of attacking speculators is required to make the central bank indifferent between abandoning and keeping the peg. Increasing θ, on the other hand, reduces the payoff from a successful attack on the peg, since gross payoff $D(\theta)$ decreases in θ. It can be shown that this second effect weakly outweighs the first, so that $u(k, J_k)$ strictly decreases in k (Morris and Shin, 1998, 2000).

The last step of the proof consists in showing that there can be only one value of the private signal, denoted by x^*, such that in any equilibrium of the game with imperfect information on fundamentals, each speculator will attack the currency if the observed signal x is lower than x^*. This unique value of the private signal must then be the k for which

$$u(k, J_k) = 0 \,,$$

so that indeed attacking the peg leads to the same expected payoff as not attacking. As $u(k, J_k)$ is decreasing in k, we know that there will be a k, which satisfies the above condition, provided that $u(k, J_k)$ is positive for low values of k and negative for high values of k. Since for $\theta \in [0, \underline{\theta}]$ the fixed parity will be abandoned with certainty, the payoff to attacking must be positive whenever the private signal x is lower than $\underline{\theta} - \varepsilon$. If, however, the private signal x is higher than $\bar{\theta} + \varepsilon$, the payoff from an attack will certainly be negative. Due to the continuity of $u(x, I_x)$ there must be a unique value x^*, such that $u(x^*, I_{x^*}) = 0$. Morris and Shin then define two specific values of the private signals as follows

$$\underline{x} = \inf\{x | s(x) < 1\} \qquad (5.2)$$

and

$$\bar{x} = \sup\{x | s(x) > 0\} . \tag{5.3}$$

Thus, $\underline{x}$ is the lowest value of the private signal, which is still so good that not all of the speculators decide to attack. Likewise $\bar{x}$ is the highest value of the private signal, which is still so bad that not all speculators refrain from attacking, though. Since $\inf\{x|0 < s(x) < 1\} \leq \sup\{x|0 < s(x) < 1\}$, it follows that $\underline{x} \leq \bar{x}$. At $\underline{x}$, some speculators are not attacking the peg. This is only consistent with equilibrium, if the payoff from not-attacking is at least as high as the payoff from attacking $u(\underline{x}, s) \leq 0$.

From the definition of $\underline{x}$ it follows that $J_{\underline{x}} \leq s$, so that from the above derived results we find that $u(\underline{x}, J_{\underline{x}}) \leq u(\underline{x}, s) \leq 0$. Since $u(k, J_k)$ is decreasing in k, and x^* is the only value of k for which $u(x^*, J_{x^*}) = 0$, we know that

$$\underline{x} \geq x^* . \tag{5.4}$$

A similar line of reasoning leads to

$$\bar{x} \leq x^* . \tag{5.5}$$

From (5.2) and (5.3), however, we know that $\underline{x} \leq \bar{x}$, so that together with (5.4) and (5.5) it follows that

$$\underline{x} = \bar{x} = x^* .$$

Hence, x^* gives the unique cut-off value for the private signal: speculators attack the fixed parity whenever they observe signals smaller than x^*, but refrain from attacking if their signals are higher than x^*.

In equilibrium, therefore, strategy profile s is given by the step function J_{x^*}, and aggregate short sales at state θ are given as

$$l(\theta, J_{x^*}) = \begin{cases} 1 & \text{if } \theta < x^* - \varepsilon, \\ \frac{1}{2} - \frac{1}{2\varepsilon}(\theta - x^*) & \text{if } x^* - \varepsilon \leq \theta < x^* + \varepsilon , \\ 0 & \text{if } \theta \geq x^* + \varepsilon . \end{cases}$$

For $\theta \in (0, 1)$ we find that aggregate short sales $l(\theta, J_{x^*})$ are decreasing in θ, whereas $a(\theta)$, the proportion of attacking speculators necessary for a successful attack, is increasing in θ. Thus, both functions intersect exactly once, with θ^* being the value of the fundamental state at the intersection. For $\theta \leq \theta^*$,we know that $l(\theta, J_{x^*}) \geq a(\theta)$. Hence, the central bank will devalue the peg if and only if $\theta \leq \theta^*$. Fig. 5.1 presents the unique equilibrium. □

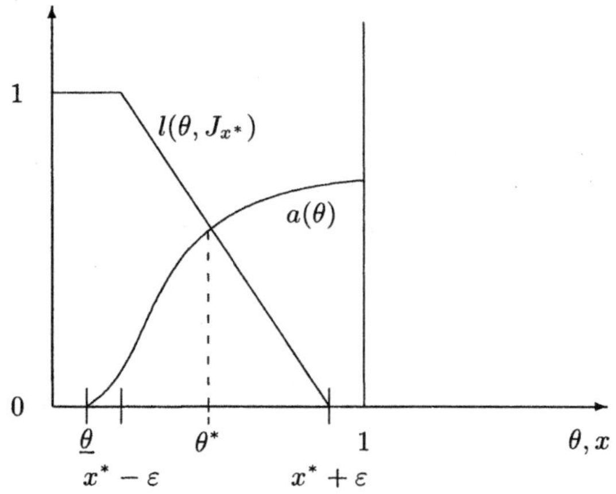

Fig. 5.1. Derivation of the unique equilibrium in the Morris/Shin-model (1998)

5.2 Interpretation of the Results

As has been shown by Morris and Shin, introducing noisy private information about the fundamental state of the economy into a second-generation crisis model is sufficient to eliminate all indeterminacy that resulted from complete information. At first sight this is a paradoxical result, since one might expect noisy information and the associated fundamental uncertainty to worsen the multiplicity problem. The basic intuition for the uniqueness result lies in the fact that even if speculators can infer from their signals that the reward from a speculative attack will pay off transaction costs, they cannot be sure how many other agents get these signals. Furthermore, they do not know how many of these other agents in turn are optimistic that their opponents have received those signals. In order to determine their optimal action, agents therefore have to compare potential gains with the losses from an attack. This leads to an additional equilibrium condition, which does not exist in the case of complete information. Under the assumed distribution of private information, this auxiliary condition eliminates all equilibria but one. Note, however, that it is not the lack of knowledge about the fundamental state of the economy which renders the unique equilibrium, but rather the uncertainty about other agents' information.

Thus, in contrast to the typical second-generation currency crisis models with complete information, introducing incomplete information derives a unique equilibrium, so that a successful currency attack will take place with certainty for all fundamental states lower than θ^*. In a model with complete information, however, a devaluation is going to happen with certainty only for values of θ below $\underline{\theta}$, with $\underline{\theta} \leq \theta^*$. Hence, the range of fundamentals for which a currency crisis will happen with certainty is smaller under complete information than with uncertainties about fundamentals. However, incomplete information about the fundamental state of the economy eliminates currency crises for fundamentals better than θ^*, while a devaluation is still possible to occur up to a level of $\bar{\theta} \geq \theta^*$ in models with complete information. It should therefore be noted, that, the uniqueness result notwithstanding, the occurrence of a crisis in the Morris/Shin-model can still be inefficient, so that the model may still deliver coordination failures on the part of the speculators. This is due to the fact that up to a fundamental level of $\underline{\theta}$ a devaluation can be attributed to weak fundamentals solely, whereas for fundamentals in the interval $(\underline{\theta}, \theta^*)$ an abandoning of the peg is forced by speculative mass and is not justified by a deterioration of fundamentals only. As such, the event of a currency crisis for fundamentals between $\underline{\theta}$ and θ^* might reasonably be denoted as an inefficient crisis.

It is easy to see that the unique equilibrium derived by Morris and Shin corresponds to the risk-dominant equilibrium of the underlying complete information game. The payoff-dominant strategy instead would be to attack the fixed parity up to a fundamental value of $\bar{\theta}$, since an attack by all speculators would be successful exactly up to this point and would lead to a positive net-payoff of $D - t$.

Several more aspects are worth analyzing in the Morris/Shin currency crisis model. These issues mainly refer to the robustness of the uniqueness result. A first question in this respect is whether restoring transparency about the fundamental state, i.e. decreasing uncertainty in the incomplete information game, is going to change the derived equilibrium. This issue has been explored by Heinemann and Illing (1999), who demonstrated that increasing the precision of private information may reduce the probability of a crisis event. An important second aspect to be examined is the influence of expectation formation on the part of the speculators on the outcome of uniqueness versus multiplicity of equilibria. Sbracia and Zaghini (2001) have questioned this point and found that assuming more general forms of expectations (instead of those stemming from uniformly distributed private signals) might hinder the elimination of multiple equilibria.

6

Transparency and Expectation Formation in the Basic Morris/Shin-Model (1998)

6.1 Transparency

The main insight of the Morris/Shin-model is that information plays a very subtle role in triggering speculative attacks on a fixed exchange rate parity. What matters is not the amount of information about the economic fundamentals per se, but rather whether this information is common knowledge or not. This idea is not quite intuitive. Let us therefore consider the following argument: in the Morris/Shin-model with noisy information, it will never be common knowledge that fundamentals are consistent with a fixed peg, i.e. that $\theta \geq \bar{\theta}$. Why is that? A single speculator knows that the true value of the fundamental index must lie in the stability area, if she receives a private signal $x_i > \bar{\theta} + \varepsilon$. However, in order to be sure that all other speculators know that the currency peg is stable, she must observe a signal of at least $\bar{\theta} + 3\varepsilon$, since signals can differ from her own information by at most 2ε. Yet, in order to believe that others also know that her signal tells her of a stable parity, she has to receive a signal of at least $\bar{\theta} + 5\varepsilon$. Proceeding in this way, Morris and Shin explain that there is "n-th order knowledge" of the fact that $\theta \geq \bar{\theta}$ only if everyone has observed a signal greater than or equal to $\bar{\theta} + (2n - 1)\varepsilon$. By definition, however, common knowledge of $\theta \geq \bar{\theta}$ requires n-th order knowledge for every n. Clearly, for fixed ε, n-th order knowledge will eventually fail for some level of n. Hence, it will never be common knowledge that the fundamental index is in the stable region.[1]

Since observing noisy signals might be interpreted as learning differential information about the fundamental state of the economy with small error, any information disseminating source plays an important role for triggering or preventing the onset of a crisis. In this respect, it should be questioned whether the central bank as the primary source of fundamental information by announcing aims and measurements of monetary policy can diminish the

[1] For an extensive analysis of the logical structure of common knowledge, see also Shin (1993).

danger of a crisis by making her policy more transparent, i.e. by decreasing noise ε.

Concerning the role of transparency in the basic Morris/Shin-model, the following interesting proposition by Heinemann (2000) holds:

Proposition 6.1. (Heinemann, 2000)
In the limit as ε tends to 0, θ^* approaches $\theta_0 \in (\underline{\theta}, \bar{\theta})$ given by the unique solution to

$$(1 - a(\theta_0))D(\theta_0) = t \, .$$

With this proposition, Heinemann corrected a slightly flawed finding by Morris and Shin (1998) referring to the effect of the noise variable ε converging to zero. The proof of proposition 6.1 revises the two equations, which describe the unique equilibrium of the basic Morris/Shin-model: the indifference condition for the speculators

$$u(x^*, J_{x^*}) = \frac{1}{2\varepsilon} \int_{x^*-\varepsilon}^{\theta^*} D(\theta) d\theta - t = 0 \tag{6.1}$$

and the central bank's indifference condition

$$l(\theta^*, J_{x^*}) = \frac{x^* - \theta^* + \varepsilon}{2\varepsilon} = a(\theta^*) \, . \tag{6.2}$$

Equation (6.2) can be rewritten as

$$1 - a(\theta^*) = \frac{\theta^* - x^* + \varepsilon}{2\varepsilon} \, . \tag{6.3}$$

Recalling the fact that $\frac{\partial D(\theta)}{\partial \theta} < 0$, equation (6.1) implies that:

$$\begin{aligned} \frac{1}{2\varepsilon} \int_{x^*-\varepsilon}^{\theta^*} D(\theta) d\theta &= t \\ &> \frac{1}{2\varepsilon} \int_{x^*-\varepsilon}^{\theta^*} D(\theta^*) d\theta = (1 - a(\theta^*))D(\theta^*) \end{aligned} \tag{6.4}$$

and

$$\begin{aligned} \frac{1}{2\varepsilon} \int_{x^*-\varepsilon}^{\theta^*} D(\theta) d\theta &= t \\ &< \frac{1}{2\varepsilon} \int_{x^*}^{\theta^*} D(x^* - \varepsilon) d\theta = (1 - a(\theta^*))D(x^* - \varepsilon) \, . \end{aligned} \tag{6.5}$$

It can be seen from (6.2) that the switching values for signals and fundamentals, x^* and θ^*, converge to each other for $\varepsilon \to 0$. From the continuity of D and a, together with the above inequalities (6.4) and (6.5), it then follows that

$$\lim_{\varepsilon \to 0}(1 - a(\theta^*(\varepsilon)))D(\theta^*(\varepsilon)) = t . \qquad (6.6)$$

Due to the assumed properties of the a- and D-functions, Heinemann (2000) concludes that (6.6) must have a unique solution given as θ_0, so that

$$\lim_{\varepsilon \to 0} \theta^*(\varepsilon) = \theta_0 ,$$

which completes the proof. □

Note that the limit point θ_0 for vanishing variance of private signals is independent of the assumed probability distribution of noise (Frankel, Morris and Pauzner, 2000). Moreover, the limit point is characterized by so-called Laplacian beliefs over the opponents' behavior. Hence, θ_0 is the optimal threshold for a trader who holds a uniform belief over the proportion of other traders attacking the parity (Morris and Shin, 2000).

As a response to several financial crises of the past, international policy makers often called for more transparency about economic fundamentals in order to avoid speculative attacks. They assumed that a more transparent governmental policy would enable private agents to better infer the true economic fundamentals from their information. It was hoped that this might incite speculators to refrain from attacking, at least in the cases where crises would be "inefficient". However, it remains to be seen whether or not increasing transparency, in the sense of decreasing noise in private information, will actually raise or lower θ^*, and hence broadens or reduces the region of fundamentals for which the central bank will always devalue the peg.

The effects of restoring transparency in the basic Morris/Shin-model have been analyzed by Heinemann and Illing (1999). They succeed in answering the question whether higher transparency reduces the likelihood of an attack in the affirmative. Starting point of their analysis are equations (6.1) and (6.2), which give the indifference conditions for speculators and central bank. Total differentiation and rearranging terms delivers

$$\frac{d\theta^*}{d\varepsilon} = 2\frac{(1 - a(\theta^*))D(x^* - \varepsilon) - t}{D(x^* - \varepsilon) - D(\theta^*) + 2\varepsilon a'(\theta^*)D(x^* - \varepsilon)} .$$

Due to D being positive and decreasing in θ, the denominator of this derivative is always positive. The numerator, however, is positive only if transaction costs are small enough, i.e.

$$t < (1 - a(\theta^*))D(x^* - \varepsilon) .$$

From (6.1) and (6.5) Heinemann and Illing (1999) infer that

$$t < \frac{\theta^* - x^* + \varepsilon}{2\varepsilon} D(x^* - \varepsilon) .$$

Recalling that $\frac{\theta^* - x^* + \varepsilon}{2\varepsilon} = 1 - a(\theta^*)$, they find that indeed $t < (1 - a(\theta^*))D(x^* - \varepsilon)$ and thus θ^* increases in noise ε: $\frac{d\theta^*}{d\varepsilon} > 0$. Consequently, increasing noise

ε raises the probability of speculative attacks, whereas higher transparency decreases the danger of a crisis. Note, however, that this result only holds for $\frac{dD(\theta)}{d\theta} < 0$, i.e. for cases where the reward of a successful speculative attack decreases in the fundamental state of the economy. Moreover, the effects of increasing transparency as derived by Heinemann and Illing (1999) rely on the assumption of noisy information on the foreign exchange market necessarily being of private type. Hence, their model neglects the existence of other forms of information. As we will see in part III of this book, the result concerning transparency changes completely, if we take account of several types of information in the model.

6.2 Expectation Formation

As has already been stated above, what delivers the unique equilibrium result in the basic Morris/Shin-model is not only the assumption that speculators do not exactly know the true fundamental state of the economy, but additionally that they do not know what the other market participants know. Hence, there are two types of uncertainty included in the model: uncertainty about fundamentals and uncertainty about the behavior of other speculators. The latter type is also referred to as Knightian uncertainty and is typically assumed away in Nash equilibria (Hirshleifer and Riley, 1992). There, all agents are supposed to know the strategies of all other agents in order to determine mutually optimal equilibrium strategies. In the complete information game, represented by the typical second-generation currency crisis model à la Obstfeld, this feature is captured by the presumption that an attack on the fixed exchange rate is always successful, if conducted by all speculators. Since for a single trader it is optimal to attack only if all other agents do so as well, they either all attack or all refrain from attacking. If they do attack the parity, it is assumed that they can indeed force the central bank to abandon the peg. In the incomplete information game as described by Morris and Shin (1998), however, this Knightian uncertainty plays a major role. As players' actions are strategic complements, each speculator has to make a best guess about his opponents' behavior in order to decide on his optimal action.

After having analyzed the basic Morris/Shin-model with both uncertainty about fundamentals and opponents' behavior in Chap. 5 and the effects of a subsiding fundamental uncertainty in Sect. 6.1, the question remains whether multiple equilibria will reemerge once we assume away Knightian uncertainty again. This aspect has been analyzed by Sbracia and Zaghini (2001) in a framework of the basic Morris/Shin-model.[2] They assume that speculators cannot observe the true fundamentals, but have common expectations about θ, in the form of a probability distribution, which is common knowledge.

[2] In the following, we constantly refer to Sbracia and Zaghini (2001), unless otherwise stated.

Hence, there is uncertainty about the fundamental state, but not about the opponents' behavior, since speculators' information sets are the same and common knowledge. Before we start presenting the model by Sbracia and Zaghini, let us briefly classify the different models that will be or already have been depicted, by referring to the respective type of uncertainty they allow for. In this respect, consider the following matrix of table 6.1.

Table 6.1.

	Fundamental Certainty	Fundamental Uncertainty
Knightian Certainty	Obstfeld (Chap. 2)	Sbracia/Zaghini (Chap. 6.2)
Knightian Uncertainty	Heinemann/Illing (Chap. 6.1)	Morris/Shin (Chap. 5)

The set-up of the model by Sbracia and Zaghini is very similar to the basic Morris/Shin model, except for the fact that speculators' expectations about the fundamental state are not given individually with different private signals, but as a common probability density function, referred to as η. By denoting the "attack"-action of agent i as a_i, and the action of "not-attacking" by n_i, Sbracia and Zaghini state the following facts concerning the expected payoff for a single speculator: a speculator refraining from an attack always receives a payoff of 0, irrespective of what the other agents do. If a speculator attacks, while all other market participants do so as well, she receives a payoff of $u(a_i, a_{-i}) = \int_0^1 (\bar{e} - f(\theta) - t)\eta(\theta)d\theta = \bar{e} - E[f(\tilde{\Theta})] - t$. If a speculator attacks, while all other agents refrain from attacking, her expected payoff is $u(a_i, n_{-i}) = \int_0^{\underline{\theta}} (\bar{e} - f(\theta) - t)\eta\theta d\theta - \int_{\underline{\theta}}^1 t\eta(\theta)d\theta$. This is due to the fact that in the interval $[0, \underline{\theta}]$ the central bank abandons the peg, while the peg is sustained for $\theta \in [\underline{\theta}, 1]$ if only a single speculator attacks.

Clearly, having all speculators attack is an equilibrium if $u(a_i, a_{-i}) \geq 0$, whereas the strategy profile in which all agents abstain from attacking is an equilibrium if $u(a_i, n_{-i}) \leq 0$. In order to facilitate on notation, Sbracia and Zaghini refer by p to the probability of an "unforced" devaluation, i.e. to the probability that the parity is abandoned for sufficiently bad fundamentals $\theta \leq \underline{\theta}$. They then find that

$$u(a_i, a_{-i}) = \bar{e} - E[f(\tilde{\Theta})] - t \quad \text{and} \quad u(a_i, n_{-i}) = \bar{e}p - E[f(\tilde{\Theta})|\tilde{\Theta} \leq \underline{\theta}]p - t\,. \tag{6.7}$$

It can easily be seen that, since $u(a_i, a_{-i}) \geq u(a_i, n_{-i})$, speculators' actions are strategic complements. Three situations can therefore be distinguished: if $u(a_i, a_{-i}) > 0$ and $u(a_i, n_{-i}) > 0$, there is a unique equilibrium with all speculators attacking the exchange rate parity. If $u(a_i, a_{-i}) < 0$ and $u(a_i, n_{-i}) < 0$, there is a unique equilibrium with all speculators refraining from an attack on the currency peg. For $\theta \leq \underline{\theta}$, however, the central bank nevertheless devalues the exchange rate. If $u(a_i, a_{-i}) \geq 0$ and $u(a_i, n_{-i}) \leq 0$ at the same time, the model displays multiple equilibria, since it is rewarding to attack if all others attack, while a speculator will refrain from short-selling, if her opponents do not attack either.

From (6.7), it follows that the condition of multiple equilibria may also be written in the form of the fixed exchange rate $\bar{e}$ lying in the following interval

$$\bar{e} \in \left[E[f(\tilde{\Theta}] + t, \quad E[f(\tilde{\Theta}|\tilde{\Theta} \leq \underline{\theta}] + \frac{t}{p}\right] .$$

Sbracia and Zaghini denote this interval as H. Whenever $\bar{e}$ is higher than the upper boundary of this interval, speculators expect a large profit from a successful attack. Hence, they will all attack. If, however, $\bar{e}$ is fixed at a level which is lower than the lower boundary of interval H, speculators reckon an attack to yield a negative payoff, so that they will all refrain from attacking. For intermediate values of $\bar{e}$, i.e. for $\bar{e} \in H$, both outcomes are possible, so that multiple equilibria result.

A necessary condition for multiple equilibria to exist in this model, therefore, is that H is not empty: $H \neq \varnothing$. This is the case for

$$E[f(\tilde{\Theta}|\tilde{\Theta} \leq \underline{\theta}] + \frac{t}{p} \geq E[f(\tilde{\Theta}] + t ,$$

which is equivalent to

$$p \leq \frac{t}{t + E[f(\tilde{\Theta})] - E[f(\tilde{\Theta})|\tilde{\Theta} \leq \underline{\theta}]} \equiv w . \qquad (6.8)$$

Given condition (6.8) for multiple equilibria, Sbracia and Zaghini analyze what influence small changes in speculators' common expectations have on the onset of a crisis. In this respect, they assume that the initial common probability function η is such that $p \leq w$ and $\bar{e} \in H$. Additionally, it is considered that speculators in the multiple equilibria case initially coordinate on the "not-attack" equilibrium, so that the central bank can maintain the fixed parity. Compared to this situation, they presume that expectations change from η to η', with $p' > w$, while t, $E[f(\tilde{\Theta})]$ and $E[f(\tilde{\Theta})|\tilde{\Theta}] \leq \underline{\theta}]$ stay constant. With the new probability distribution there are no longer multiple equilibria, but it can be shown that now speculators all attack the currency peg with a devaluation being the unique equilibrium. As Sbracia and Zaghini point out, this result stems from the fact that $\bar{e}$ now is higher than the upper bound of the multiplicity interval. Hence, speculators believe that there is more to gain than to lose from attacking the parity. Since this belief is common knowledge, they will all attack. Note that the examined change in beliefs does not necessarily have to coincide with a commonly believed worsening of the fundamental state, since the new probability distribution η' might be mean-preserving when compared with η. As Sbracia and Zaghini show, there is an infinite number of probability distributions, which contain the same mean as η but have a bigger believed probability p of an "unforced" devaluation of the peg. All of them naturally must be characterized by a higher variance of speculators' expectations over fundamentals, which renders the mentioned result. Thus, the speculative attack on the fixed parity is triggered by higher uncertainty about fundamentals. From this, Sbracia and Zaghini conclude that changes in speculators' expectations can have breaking consequences for the maintenance of a fixed exchange rate.

Interestingly, the authors are also able to show that when payoff function f is linear, having a fundamental state of $\theta \leq \bar{\theta}$ is sufficient for an equilibrium with a speculative attack on the parity to prevail. Hence, whenever θ is in the ripe-for-attack zone and p is sufficiently high, the strategy not to attack can be iteratively eliminated, so that a currency crisis occurs as unique equilibrium. Thus, in the incomplete information game by Sbracia and Zaghini there might be an attack on the peg, depending on speculators' beliefs about an "unforced" devaluation. As long as agents presume the event of an "unforced" abandoning of the peg to be likely enough, an attack will take place with certainty, due to the fact that the beliefs of all agents are common knowledge. In contrast, in the complete information game as represented by the Obstfeld-model, a devaluation might be prevented for the same range of fundamentals if only agents refrain from attacking.

Summing up the results, Sbracia and Zaghini point out the following interesting fact: if the fundamental state of the economy is common knowledge, as long as fundamentals are neither too bad nor too good, i.e. for θ in the ripe-for-attack region, the economy is vulnerable to an attack since speculators may trigger a devaluation, but a crisis does not have to occur necessarily. However, if there is uncertainty about fundamentals so that the economic state is not common knowledge, but nevertheless speculators' beliefs about it are, the fixed parity is doomed to be abandoned for the same range of fundamentals. Hence, with speculators' expectations being common knowledge, the economy is as fragile for intermediate values of fundamentals as for completely unstable fundamentals. Moreover, the outcome of the game between speculators and central bank is very susceptible to even small changes of speculators' beliefs, so that the economy might very easily move from stability to a crisis, due to a slight increase in speculators' perception of the central bank's willingness to devalue.

Part III

The Influence of Private and Public Information in Self-Fulfilling Currency Crisis Models

7

Introduction

Analyzing currency crisis models in a global games setting allows to take into account the influence of different parameters on speculators' actions. As such, it is possible to give policy advice to the government or central bank on how to possibly prevent the occurrence of currency crises in the future. In this respect, one of the most urgent questions to be answered refers to the optimal use of information. The importance of informational aspects in currency crises arises from two facts: first, the currency crises of the past, most notably in Europe 1992–93 and Mexico 1994–95, quite strongly demonstrated the impact of information on triggering an attack. In particular for Mexico 1994, numerous economists argued that the obvious withholding of information on the part of the government increased fundamental uncertainty among the market participants and finally caused the major attack on the fixed Peso exchange rate in December 1994. Secondly, disseminating information about the fundamental state of the economy is a quite exclusive policy instrument for the central bank or government. Hence, by using this instrument sensibly, the political authorities should be able to stabilize the market in times of financial turmoil. However, analyzing optimal informational policy measurements has not yet received the appropriate attention among economists. Although the importance of information has often been commented on (Friedman, 1979; Hirshleifer and Riley, 1992; Lawrence, 1999), a surprisingly small number of papers has yet tried to analyze exactly why and in which way information influences speculators' behavior. The current part of the book therefore presents own research on the influence of information disclosure and of different types of information on the event of a currency crisis (Metz, 2002a).

During financial crisis situations throughout the last years, the large impact of informational aspects has often been pointed out as an important feature (Morris and Shin, 2000, 2001). Whether it was the lack of information available about economic fundamentals, such as about international reserves as in the case of the Mexican crisis in 1994, or rumors about a government's subsiding interest in sticking to a fixed exchange rate system as in the EMS crisis 1992–93, it was always some aspect of information that has been surmised to have triggered the collapse of the parity. Going into informational issues in more detail, we often come across the general claim that markets seem to "overreact" to informational announcements from authorities, for instance from central bankers. This is the more astonishing, since often only the obvious is stated or already known facts are reaffirmed. Numerous anecdotal evidence from a variety of contexts seem to confirm the exaggerated reaction to this form of information. Information common to all market participants has therefore been suspected to have a disproportionate effect on agents' decisions, relative to the impact of an individual's private information. However, it stands to reason whether such seemingly exaggerated behavior in reaction may not be completely rational. Since in the precedence of financial turmoil market participants clearly are concerned about other participants' reactions to news, information common to the whole market obviously contains much more than the simple face value of the announcement. It is one of the great advantages of the global games method to recognize these aspects, as we will see in the following.

In the subsequent chapters we investigate into the role of different types of information for triggering currency crises in more detail. Referring to the above mentioned concerns about the disproportionate influence of common information on the occurrence of a currency crisis, we distinguish two forms of information: private and public. Whereas private information presents individual information that will most certainly be different from one trader to the next, public information is common to all market participants. Public information can be interpreted as publicly observable events which influence economic fundamentals, or a statistic thereof. Chapter 8 is concerned with giving a detailed description and characterization of the two types of information. In Chap. 9, a currency crisis model is then laid out, where speculators receive both private and public information. The model is a modification of the basic Morris/Shin-model (1998) as analyzed in Chap. 5.[1] In accordance with Morris and Shin (1999a), we will demonstrate that a unique equilibrium in this model prevails whenever private information is sufficiently precise relative to public information. The major part of Chap. 9 is dedicated to analyzing the influence that the informational parameters exert on the probability of a currency crisis. In this respect, we find that increasing the precision of private and public information not necessarily has to reduce the danger of a crisis. Rather, the influence of the information's precision depends on the "market sentiment", i.e. on the economic performance generally expected by the market participants. Additionally, we can show that the influence of more precise private information most of the time is opposite to the effect of disseminating more precise public information. After providing an explanation of these intriguing findings, Chap. 10 uses the results in order to find the optimal in-

[1] Actually, the model with both private and public information is similar to a model by Morris and Shin (1999a), which, however, is applied to liquidity crises and the pricing of debt.

formation policy for a central bank trying to prevent a speculative attack on the fixed exchange rate. The analysis of Chap. 10 is conducted along the lines of Heinemann and Metz (2002). We find that the optimal policy design not only depends on the commonly expected state of the economy, but furthermore is also contingent on whether the fixed parity is vulnerable to an attack, due to a highly profitable devaluation for the speculators, or not. In the case of a vulnerable peg, it can be demonstrated that whenever prior expectations concerning fundamentals are weak, the central bank should maximize fundamental risk and disseminate private information of maximal precision. The opposite policy is found to minimize the probability of a crisis in case of a strong market sentiment concerning the fundamental state. A quite different combination of policy is seen to be useful if the exchange rate parity initially is rather viable. In this case, the central bank should always disseminate private information of minimal precision. Additionally, she should commit to the highest possible precision of public information for a good market sentiment, but lowest possible precision for the commonly expected fundamental state being weak.

8

Characterization of Private and Public Information

Although there are several ways to characterize different forms of information, one of the commonest classification systems is to differentiate between private and public information (respectively "signals"). In the context to be analyzed here, both types of signals inform about the unknown fundamental state, i.e. about the index that comprises the relevant economic fundamentals of the respective country.

Formally, the difference between private and public information lies in the degree to which they are "known". On a first stage we can state that private information is known only to an individual market participant, whereas public information is known to a larger group of persons. With respect to this "group-contingent" feature, it is therefore quite reasonable to refer to private and public information also as private and public signal. In this sense, a private signal contains informational aspects that are known only to a single person. As such, he or she receives this private signal individually, without anyone else knowing the content of the signal. A public signal in contrast is observed by all members of a group, so that they all know the informational content of this signal. However, this is not the only difference between the two types of information. On a second stage, we find that not only everyone observes the informational content of the public signal, but additionally everyone knows that everyone in that group has observed the public signal. For the private signal, however, it holds that everyone knows that no one else has observed the own private signal, which is also the case for all stages to follow. The public signal, yet, is also known to be known one further stage, so that, following this process up to an infinite round, the content of the public signal becomes common knowledge. Everyone knows that everyone has received the public signal, everyone knows that everyone knows this fact, everyone knows that everyone knows that everyone knows this fact, and so on to infinity.

As such, each speculator's information set contains two types of information that are completely different. First, there is information which is exclusive to the individual agent. This type of signal might also be interpreted as insider information. Second, there is information which has been commonly agreed upon. This part of information might be interpreted as the "market sentiment" about the fundamentally relevant economic variables.

Concerning the content of the two types of signals, we assume that they inform about the distribution of the unknown fundamental state of the economy. From the point of view of a currency crisis model, this is the most comprehensive modelling of information, since the signals then – each in its own way – comprise all that has to be known about the fundamental state of the economy, without θ becoming obvious. Whereas the public signal gives information about the unconditional distribution of θ, the private information is conditional on θ itself. Due to this state-contingency of the individual signals, private information is prevented from becoming completely "unrealistic", as there is always the true (although unknown) fundamental state underlying this type of information.

Since the information set of each speculator contains both private and public information, all information sets have one identical "ingredient", represented by the public signal. As such, the public signal not only gives information about the unknown fundamental state of the economy, but also about the information sets of the other market participants. Public information therefore conveys strategic information on the likely beliefs held by other speculators, which explains the importance that market participants ascribe to this type of information and which – as we will see – should not be taken as an "overreaction". It is on the contrary a completely rational decision to give more weight to public information whenever strategic complementarities influence the possible payoffs of players, and is as such determined by the inherent logic of equilibrium selection in global games.

In our model, public information about the fundamental state of the economy is assumed to be disseminated by the central bank. This might be the case through publishing economic data and other statistics, or by announcing monetary policy measurements that influence the development of economic fundamentals (Popper and Montgomery, 2001). Every market participant has costfree access to this information and everyone knows that everyone receives this information. Since this argument holds for an infinitely large number of iterations, this information indeed becomes common knowledge. However, publicly available information can still be quite noisy. This might be due to the fact that economic concepts, which are the basis of statistical measurements, are faulty, or due to preliminarily published statistics with some underlying data still missing (Morris and Shin, 1999b,c). Also, chosen monetary policy measurements may lead to unexpected results, which erratically change the fundamental development.

Private information about economic fundamentals, in contrast, is information that is known only to a single speculator. Apart from the interpretation as insider information, private signals may also be taken as speculators' different perceptions of the unknown fundamental state. Another possible way to motivate private information is to assume that speculators receive pieces of information at different points in time, or from different information disseminating agencies at a time. For instance, although newspapers give reports about the same facts, they all use a slightly different way of presenting news, so that speculators quite credibly may form different interpretations of these news. Note that the source of private information may also be the central bank.

In contrast to the basic Morris/Shin-model (1998), where only private signals about the fundamental state of the economy were allowed, the next chapters analyze, what influence the introduction of both private and public information and their interaction have on the outcome of the model. As we will see, the existence of public information additionally to private signals does not restore certainty about agents' behavior. Hence, the currency crisis model with both private and public information still contains both fundamental uncertainty as well as Knightian uncertainty, and therefore may display a unique equilibrium.

9

The Currency Crisis Model with Private and Public Information

In contrast to previous sections where a unique equilibrium has been derived in a currency crisis model with noisy private information, the model to be used in the following section includes a more complex information structure. Consequently, the influence of the two types of information on the event of a currency crisis turns out to be very complex as well. However, the derivation of the unique equilibrium at first sight seems to be surprisingly clear and simple. It is nonetheless quite interesting to go into more detail and analyze the influence of higher order uncertainty as well as of information in the limit, i.e. with infinitely high precision, to get a deeper understanding for the interaction of both types of information.

Concerning the model set-up, we use a very simple structure of normally distributed signals, similar to the model by Morris and Shin (1999 a,b). The general setting of the model is introduced in the first section of this chapter. It closely follows the work by Metz (2002a). Sections 9.2 and 9.3 analyze special or limiting cases for the assumed distribution of signals, where multiplicity might be reinvited into the model, contingent on the presumed structure of information. These sections are dedicated to drawing parallels to the models of Chaps. 5 and 6. Section 9.4 presents the general form of the currency crisis model to be elaborated on, by taking into account both noisy private and public information. It is demonstrated how a unique equilibrium can be derived, provided that information satisfies certain conditions. The main part of this chapter in section five is based on this general model and analyzes the influence of the different model parameters on the event of a currency crisis, with special emphasis on the impact of private and public information.

9.1 The Structure of the Model

We consider a small open economy where the central bank has pegged the exchange rate at a certain parity. There is a continuum of risk-neutral speculators in the foreign exchange market, indexed by the unit interval $[0, 1]$.[1] Each speculator disposes of one unit of the currency and can decide whether to short-sell this unit, i.e. attack the currency peg, or not to do so. If the attack is successful he gets a fixed payoff D, $D > 0$.[2] Taking a speculative position in the market, however, also leads to costs of t, $t > 0$, which comprise both transaction costs and the interest rate differential between the considered countries. We assume that costs t are small relative to the available payoff D, i.e. $t < D$, so that there is a potential incentive to attack the currency peg in the first place. If a speculator refrains from selling the currency he is not exposed to any costs, but he does not gain anything either.[3] The matrix of net payoffs is given in table 9.1.

Table 9.1.

	success	no success
attack	$D - t$	$-t$
not-attack	0	0

Since we abstract from welfare considerations, the central bank is supposed to be willing to defend the peg as long as the international reserves, that she is endowed with, are above a predetermined critical level. This critical level depends on the central bank's assessment of the fundamental state of the economy. If economic fundamentals are good, the critical level is low, so that the central bank is willing to use a large amount of international reserves to defend the exchange rate. However, if fundamentals are bad, the central bank will only want to lose few reserves before giving in to the attack and devalue the peg.[4] In our model, an index of the fundamental state of the economy is given by θ, with a high value of θ referring to strong fundamentals and a low value of θ representing a weak fundamental state. Let the proportion of attacking speculators be denoted by l. In compliance with usual second-generation currency crisis models, we assume that the costs of defending the peg against a speculative attack increase in the amount of speculative pressure, i.e. in the number of attacking speculators l, but decrease in economic fundamentals.

[1] Due to the assumption of a continuum of speculators, each of them is negligibly small, so that an individual speculator cannot force a specific outcome of the game.

[2] The assumption of a fixed payoff is made for simplicity reasons. It should, however, be kept in mind that generally the payoff from a successful attack on the fixed parity decreases in economic fundamentals, i.e. the stronger the fundamentals the closer will the shadow exchange rate be to the fixed rate.

[3] Again (see Chap. 5), the model does not account for the possibility of opportunity costs from not-attacking.

[4] An alternative argument is to concentrate on the political costs for the central bank arising from a devaluation of the fixed parity. These are high when the fundamental state of the economy is strong and vice versa.

To keep arguments simple, we assume that the central bank is able to defend the fixed parity whenever the proportion of attackers falls short of a specific threshold which depends on the fundamental state. More precisely, if $l < \theta$, the central bank keeps the peg and an attack is unsuccessful. If $l \geq \theta$, the central bank devalues the peg, so that an attack leads to success.

Given the central bank's strategy, we can solve the model backwards in order to derive the solution of the reduced-form game for the speculators. In doing so, we can distinguish between three different cases. First, we analyze the case of the fundamental index θ being common knowledge, which leads back to the original second-generation model à la Obstfeld. Secondly, we assume that there is only public information about the fundamental state of the economy, but that this public information is noisy.[5] Lastly, we analyze the case of both noisy public and private information about economic fundamentals.

9.2 The Complete Information Case - Multiple Equilibria

Whenever the fundamental state of the economy θ is not only known to each individual speculator but is moreover common knowledge, the model results in the original Obstfeld model with multiple equilibria for intermediate values of θ, i.e. for $0 < \theta \leq 1$. This can easily be seen by noting that each individual speculator is negligibly small, so that a single trader cannot force a certain outcome of the game from the central bank. Since speculators' actions are assumed to contain strategic complementarities, the rational strategy for each speculator is to decide on the same action that he expects his opponents to choose.

We consequently get the following tripartition of fundamentals à la Obstfeld: for $\theta > 1$, the currency peg is said to be stable. In this interval, fundamentals are so good that the central bank is always able to defend the peg, irrespective of the actions chosen by speculators. Thus, even if all of them attack, so that the proportion of attacking speculators is equal to one, the critical mass condition of a devaluation ($l > \theta$) is not satisfied. Since θ is common knowledge, speculators will therefore refrain from attacking if the fundamental index is known to lie in this region. For $\theta \leq 0$, however, the currency peg is unstable. In this range of fundamentals, the condition of a devaluation is always satisfied, even if none of the speculators attack. As such, the central bank can never keep the peg. Since speculators know this, they will all attack and each will receive a net payoff of $D - t$ with certainty. For $0 < \theta \leq 1$, the exchange rate parity is said to be ripe for attack. If a speculator expects his opponents to attack the fixed parity, it is rational for him to attack as well. However, if he reckons the other speculators to refrain from

[5] Recall that the case of noisy private information only is given by the basic Morris/Shin-model (1998).

attacking, he will do the same, as he himself is too small to force a devaluation on his own. Since all traders follow this chain of thought, they will either all attack or all refrain from attacking, so that $l \in \{0, 1\}$. If, now, all speculators attack in this region of fundamentals, the critical mass condition is satisfied, as $l = 1 \geq \theta$. In contrast, whenever they refrain from attacking, the central bank can always maintain the peg, since $l = 0 < \theta$. As such, for this intermediate range of fundamentals, speculators' expectations are self-fulfilling. If they believe in the success of an attack, they will (all) attack and thereby force a devaluation. In contrast, if they believe in the failure of an attack, they will (all) refrain from attacking, so that the central bank can always keep the peg.

For the case of economic fundamentals being common knowledge for all market participants, the typical criticism concerning second-generation currency crisis models applies. Thus, if θ is commonly known to lie in the range from zero to one, even incidences that seem to be absolutely unrelated to economic fundamentals (so-called sunspots) can induce speculators to sell the currency and consequently lead to a speculative attack. Although in this interval the state of fundamentals can coordinate speculators' actions as well, the shift in beliefs, which leads to a shift from an "attack"-equilibrium to a "no-attack"-equilibrium and vice versa, does not necessarily depend on the fundamental index. Obviously, this property of multiple equilibria models runs counter to the intuition that, above all, countries in economic distress should be vulnerable to speculative attacks.

9.3 Incomplete Public Information - Multiple Equilibria versus Unique Equilibrium

In order to analyze the influence of incomplete public information about economic fundamentals as the only form of information, consider the following structure of the game between speculators and central bank: Nature chooses the value of the fundamental index θ according to a normal distribution with mean y and variance $\frac{1}{\alpha}$, $\alpha > 0$. Whereas the central bank can observe the selected fundamental value θ, speculators cannot. However, they get to know the distribution of θ, $\theta \sim N(y, \frac{1}{\alpha})$, from a public disclosure by the central bank. Thus, the distribution of θ becomes common knowledge to all market participants. According to the literature, this commonly known fundamental distribution is also referred to as public signal (Morris and Shin, 1999a,b, 2000, 2001). It is important to note that the distribution of θ and as such the public signal has two different meanings. First of all, it describes the development of economic fundamentals. Additionally, it represents information disclosed to the public by the central bank. Thus, the lower the variance, the more precise this information will be in the sense that speculators know the unobserved θ to be close to the mean y. α is therefore also referred to as the precision of public information. This twofold nature of public information can be interpreted in the following way: let the market have a common belief about the unknown fundamental state of the economy. Since traders are assumed to have rational expectations, the common belief about fundamentals will be equal to the mean y. This common belief can also be denoted as the market sentiment. By choosing monetary policy measurements, the central bank can influence the development of the true fundamental state by determining its variance $\frac{1}{\alpha}$. A high variance represents a risky policy, whereas a low variance will lead to a realization of the fundamental state being quite close to the commonly expected level. Moreover, the central bank has to inform speculators about the chosen policy measurements and is supposed not to cheat. As such, speculators get to know the exact value of α and know whether the chosen policy is risky or not. After deciding on the value of α and communicating the associated policy to the speculators, the fundamental state is realized by nature as a stochastic variable from the distribution $N(y, \frac{1}{\alpha})$.[6] Note that in this model, the central bank is supposed to choose α before observing both θ and y. Hence, y and α can be taken to be exogenous and to stay constant throughout the course of the game. This assumption will partly be modified in Chap. 10, where the optimal policy for the central bank is derived by endogenizing the precision of information.

After receiving public information, speculators simultaneously have to decide whether or not to attack the fixed parity. The central bank observes the proportion of attacking speculators and abandons the peg whenever $l \geq \theta$. Note that the complete information case of the previous section is obtained whenever public information is completely precise, i.e. whenever $\alpha \to \infty$. For infinitely precise public information, the fundamental state θ takes on its mean value y, which is then common knowledge to all traders. In order to be able to examine the influence of public information on the event of a crisis, we therefore assume α to be finite, so that the public signal is not completely precise. The derivation of results in this case follows a reasoning by Prati and Sbracia (2001).

[6] A similar way of modelling this problem would be to assume that θ is chosen from a uniform distribution over the real line. Nature's choice of θ can be observed by the central bank, but not by the speculators. After having observed θ, the central bank disseminates the public signal as a noisy representation of the observed fundamental state: $y = \theta + \nu$. It is assumed in this respect, that the noise parameter is distributed according to a normal distribution with mean 0 and variance $\frac{1}{\alpha}$, $\nu \sim \mathrm{N}(0, \frac{1}{\alpha})$, with $E(\nu\theta) = 0$, so that the noise parameter is independent of the chosen fundamental state. The distribution of noise parameter ν is assumed to be common knowledge to all market participants. The improper prior distribution of θ with infinite mass presents no difficulties as long as we are concerned with conditional beliefs only (see also Hartigan, 1983). The assumption of a uniform prior distribution of θ can be interpreted as the limiting case, where speculators have very diffuse or almost no prior information about economic fundamentals and their development. It is then completely plausible that they take each possible value of θ as equally likely, which is equivalent to the assumed uniform distribution over the real line (Hellwig, 2000).

Given the central bank's strategy, the model can be solved as follows. Each speculator will attack (refrain from attacking) the fixed parity whenever the net payoff from attacking is higher (lower) than the net payoff from not-attacking, which is assumed to be equal to zero. Each trader's net payoff from attacking, however, depends on the actions chosen by his opponents. Denoting by $u(a_i, a_{-i})$ the expected net payoff of speculator i attacking (a_i) when all of his opponents attack as well (a_{-i}), we find

$$\begin{aligned} u(a_i, a_{-i}) &= \int_{-\infty}^{1} (D-t) \cdot \mathrm{No}(\theta) d\theta - \int_{1}^{+\infty} t \cdot \mathrm{No}(\theta) d\theta \\ &= D \cdot \Phi\big(\sqrt{\alpha}(1-y)\big) - t \,, \end{aligned}$$

where $\Phi(\cdot)$ represents the cumulated normal density. Similarly, the net payoff from attacking when all of the opponents refrain from attacking (n_{-i}) is given by

$$\begin{aligned} u(a_i, n_{-i}) &= \int_{-\infty}^{0} (D-t) \cdot \mathrm{No}(\theta) d\theta - \int_{0}^{+\infty} t \cdot \mathrm{No}(\theta) d\theta \\ &= D \cdot \Phi\big(-\sqrt{\alpha} y\big) - t \,. \end{aligned}$$

Proposition 9.1. (Prati and Sbracia, 2001)
The "attack"-strategy in which all speculators attack the currency is an equilibrium if $u(a_i, a_{-i}) \geq 0$. *The "don't attack"-strategy in which all speculators refrain from attacking the currency is an equilibrium if* $u(a_i, n_{-i}) \leq 0$.

As such, a necessary and sufficient condition for both "attack"- and "do not attack"-strategy profiles to be equilibria of the game is given by $u(a_i, a_{-i}) \geq 0$ and $u(a_i, n_{-i}) \leq 0$ at the same time. It can easily be shown that this condition is satisfied whenever

$$y \in \left[\frac{\Phi^{-1}(\frac{t}{D})}{\sqrt{\alpha}}, \quad 1 - \frac{\Phi^{-1}(\frac{t}{D})}{\sqrt{\alpha}} \right]. \tag{9.1}$$

Thus, the game with incomplete public information might display multiple equilibria contingent on whether condition (9.1) is satisfied.

We can now analyze the influence of the two parameters of public information, mean y and precision α, on both the "attack" and "do not attack"-strategy profile. The results by Prati and Sbracia are given in proposition 9.2.

Proposition 9.2. (Prati and Sbracia, 2001)
The value of the public signal y has a decreasing influence both on $u(a_i, a_{-i})$ and $u(a_i, n_{-i})$. However, $u(a_i, a_{-i})$ is increasing in α if $y < 1$, and decreasing in α if $y > 1$. $u(a_i, n_{-i})$ is increasing in α if $y < 0$, and decreasing in α if $y > 0$.

Thus, a "better" public signal in the sense of a higher value of y makes the range of values for the fundamental index broader where the "do not attack"-strategy is an equilibrium, and makes the interval smaller where the "attack"-strategy profile is an equilibrium. Since the multiple equilibria interval still prevails, however, it is not possible to tell from this specification of the model whether a stronger market sentiment, i.e. a higher y, is going to decrease the probability of a currency crisis.

Interestingly, the influence of the precision parameter α on the maintenance of the peg depends on the commonly expected fundamental, y. If expected fundamentals are extremely bad ($y < 0$), increasing the precision of public information will make the "attack"-equilibrium more likely and the "do not attack"-equilibrium less likely. The reverse holds, if α is raised while the public signal is extremely high ($y > 1$). In order to interpret this result, recall that a high value of α will make speculators more confident that the unknown value of θ lies in a close neighborhood to y. Thus, if y is low, a higher precision α will incite speculators to attack, since they expect the central bank to be easily forced to abandon the peg in this case. Conversely, if y is high, a higher precision α makes speculators more confident that the fixed parity will be kept due to good expected fundamentals.

Again, be reminded that due to the prevalence of multiple equilibria in these particular cases for private and public information as analyzed in Sects. 9.2 and 9.3, we cannot specify the influence that the informational parameters exert on the event of a currency crisis. Hence, no policy advice can be given yet. The following section, however, will show that this problem can be resolved for the general case of speculators possessing both private and public information.

9.4 Incomplete Public and Private Information - Unique Equilibrium

The game between speculators and central bank with both public and private information is structured similarly to the model of the previous section with public information only. The following presentation of the model as well as of the results is taken from Metz (2002a).

Nature selects the fundamental state θ from a normal distribution with mean y and variance $\frac{1}{\alpha}$. The choice of θ is known to the central bank, but unobserved by speculators. However, additionally to observing the common public signal, each speculator individually receives a private signal about economic fundamentals. The private signal of speculator i is denoted as x_i. It is defined as a noisy representation of the unknown fundamental state of the economy: $x_i = \theta + \varepsilon_i$, with $\varepsilon_i \sim \mathrm{N}(0, \frac{1}{\beta})$, $\beta > 0$. The noise value in the private signal is hence assumed to be normally distributed with a mean of 0 and a precision of β. Additionally, the noise parameters of the private signals are presumed to be independent of each other and of the fundamental state: $E(\varepsilon_i \varepsilon_j) = 0$ for $i \neq j$ and $E(\varepsilon_i \theta) = 0$. Again, the distributional properties of the noise parameters in the private signals are supposed to be common knowledge to all speculators. However, as long as precision β of the private signals is not infinitely high, private signals might differ from each other and speculators cannot accurately establish their opponents' signals contingent on their own information.

The information set I of speculator i in this model consists of two parts, the common public signal and the individual private signal: $I_i = (y, x_i)$. Based on their information, speculators simultaneously have to choose whether to attack the currency or to stay with the peg. The central bank observes the proportion l of attacking agents, and decides on maintaining the peg (for $l < \theta$) or abandoning it (for $l \geq \theta$).

In order to derive the equilibrium of this model, it is crucial to correctly define which elements of the game are common knowledge. These are payoff D, cost t, the commonly expected fundamental state y (market sentiment) and the precision parameters of public and private information α and β respectively. Whether the fundamental state θ is common knowledge as well, is endogenous to the model. θ does become common knowledge, if the public signal is infinitely precise, i.e. for $\alpha \to \infty$. Not only is then θ commonly known, but each speculator can infer his opponents' optimal equilibrium strategies, which invites multiple equilibria as formerly shown. Note, however, that the private signals being completely precise does not lead to multiple equilibria. This is due to the fact that even if the variance of the private signal's noise value is close to zero, i.e. $\beta \to \infty$, the fundamental state of the economy still does not become common knowledge.[7]

Thus, the distinction between the models with unique equilibrium and multiple equilibria depends on the structure and precision of information. In all types of models analyzed here, the structure of the game is common knowledge. Assuming that public information is completely precise, even with noisy private signals, leads back to the original Obstfeld-model as shown in a simplified version in Sect. 9.2. However, if public information is sufficiently noisy relative to private information, we find that our model results in a unique equilibrium. The degree of lack of common knowledge of the fundamental state θ thus decides on whether there are multiple equilibria or a unique equilibrium, when several forms of information are at work.

9.4.1 Derivation of the Unique Equilibrium

In the model of incomplete information we assume that α and β take on finite values, so that θ is prevented from becoming common knowledge. Hence, speculators do not know the true value of θ, but obtain signals that are more or less close to the realized value of θ. In accordance with Morris and Shin (1999a) we can then state the following condition for a unique equilibrium:

[7] For a more thorough treatment of this point see Hellwig (2000).

Proposition 9.3. (Morris and Shin, 1999a)
If private information is sufficiently precise relative to public information, i.e. for $\beta > \frac{\alpha^2}{2\pi}$, *there exists a unique equilibrium. It consists of a unique value of the fundamental index* θ^*, *up to which the central bank always abandons the peg, and a unique value of the signal* x^*, *such that every speculator who receives a signal lower than* x^* *attacks the currency peg.*

The general intuition behind this proposition is the following. In the depicted model there is a unique fundamental value, denoted by θ^*, which generates a distribution of private signals, such that there is exactly one signal x^* that makes a speculator receiving this signal indifferent between attacking and not-attacking. At the same time, if all speculators with signals smaller than x^* decide to attack, it generates a proportion of exactly $l = \theta^*$ of attackers that just suffices to make the central bank indifferent between abandoning or defending the fixed parity.

Deriving a unique equilibrium from a model, which renders multiplicity for intermediate values of θ whenever the state of the world is common knowledge, crucially requires the two regions characterized by a unique equilibrium in the complete information case to be at least "possible", given the noisy information.[8] This condition has been explained thoroughly when describing the game-theoretic underpinnings of global games in Chap. 4. Thus, in the model to be analyzed here, after observing private and public signals, speculators must attach a non-negative probability to the event that θ belongs to the interval of either $(-\infty, 0)$ or $(1, +\infty)$, so that "attacking" respectively "not-attacking" would be the uniquely optimal action. Since signals are assumed to be normally distributed in the current model, this condition is always satisfied in the game with incomplete information. Hence, one of the necessary conditions for deriving the unique equilibrium is met.

The equilibrium can easily be found by noting that the equilibrium concept relies on best responses. Hence, θ^* and x^* must represent a situation of indifference: for $\theta = \theta^*$, the central bank must be indifferent between defending the currency peg and abandoning it, whereas speculators receiving a signal of $x = x^*$ must be indifferent between attacking the peg and refraining from doing so.[9] Thus, the equilibrium values θ^* and x^* can be obtained as follows. Due to the assumption of normally distributed noise parameters, the distribution of θ conditional on private and public information is normal as well, so that the expected value of the unknown fundamental index, conditional on player i's information set, is given by

[8] Under particular circumstances it can be shown that it is also possible to derive a unique equilibrium even if there is only one region in the original game with a uniquely optimal strategy. See for this aspect also Goldstein and Pauzner (2000), or Chan and Chui (2002).

[9] For reasons of mathematical tractability we assume that after receiving a signal of $x = x^*$, a speculator decides to attack rather than not-attack.

$$E(\theta|I_i) = \frac{\alpha}{\alpha+\beta}y + \frac{\beta}{\alpha+\beta}x_i = \theta^e(x_i)$$

with variance

$$\mathrm{Var}(\theta|I_i) = \frac{1}{\alpha+\beta}.$$

As can be seen, the posterior expectation of θ is a weighted average of the information the speculator possesses. The higher the precision of the public information, α, the more important the public signal y gets, i.e. the larger the weight attached to the public part of information. Similarly, the private signal gains importance - and as such a higher weight - the higher its precision β is. The conditional variance of the fundamental index decreases in the precision of both public and private signal, with each type of information being equally valuable.

Since the public signal y is common knowledge for all speculators and as such does not help to distinguish player i's behavior from player j's, we will in the following skip the public signal y as conditional argument whenever possible and only use the private signal x_i (respectively x_j).

In order to understand the interference of the two types of information, consider each speculator's beliefs about his opponents' beliefs. Given the own private signal x_i, each speculator expects his opponents' private signals x_j to be equal to

$$E(x_j|x_i) = \frac{\alpha}{\alpha+\beta}y + \frac{\beta}{\alpha+\beta}x_i = \theta^e(x_i)$$

with variance

$$\mathrm{Var}(x_j|x_i) = \frac{\alpha+2\beta}{\beta(\alpha+\beta)} > \frac{1}{\alpha+\beta}.$$

Conditional on his signal, each speculator thus assumes his opponents' private signals to be equal to his posterior expectation of the fundamental index, $\theta^e(x_i)$. However, he assigns a higher variability to their signals than to his posterior of θ. Consequently, even if a speculator receives a signal, which rules out some states of the world, he cannot simply neglect these states in his decision-making process. This is due to the fact that the payoff from his action does not only depend on the true value of the fundamental index, but also on the actions of the other speculators, who might have got different signals that did not rule out the same states. Furthermore, even if all the other speculators neglected the same states of the world due to their signals, they might not know that he did the same, so that again he cannot rule out these fundamental states. This lack of common knowledge is the essential feature of the model which renders unambiguity of the equilibrium.

After receiving private and public signal, each speculator has to decide whether to attack the currency, which leads to costs of t and an uncertain payoff of D, or not to sell his unit of domestic currency, which is associated with a net profit of zero with certainty. As can be shown, there exists exactly one value of the private signal, namely x^* that makes each speculator indifferent between these two possibilities. Indifference in this sense is given, if both actions lead to the same expected net payoff.[10] For indifference it is thus required that

$$0 = D \cdot \text{Prob}(\text{attack successful}|x) - t\,.$$

Since the central bank will abandon the peg for all fundamental indices smaller than or equal to θ^*, the probability of a successful attack equals the probability that θ is smaller than or equal to θ^*, given x. Thus, with Φ denoting the cumulated normal density,

$$\begin{aligned} t &= D \cdot \text{Prob}(\theta \leq \theta^*|x) \\ &= D \cdot \Phi\left(\frac{\theta^* - E(\theta|x)}{\sqrt{\text{Var}(\theta|x)}}\right) \\ &= D \cdot \Phi\big(\sqrt{\alpha+\beta}(\theta^* - \frac{\alpha}{\alpha+\beta}y - \frac{\beta}{\alpha+\beta}x)\big)\,. \end{aligned} \tag{9.2}$$

The central bank, on the other hand, is indifferent between defending the currency peg and abandoning it, if the proportion of speculators attacking the peg, l, equals θ. The proportion of attacking speculators is given by the proportion of speculators who observe a private signal smaller than or equal to x^*. Since ε is assumed to be independent of the true value of θ, this proportion corresponds to the probability with which one single speculator observes a signal smaller than or equal to x^*, given θ. l can thus be calculated as

$$\begin{aligned} l &= \text{Prob}(x \leq x^*|\theta) \\ &= \Phi\left(\frac{x^* - E(x|\theta)}{\sqrt{\text{Var}(x|\theta)}}\right) \\ &= \Phi(\sqrt{\beta}(x^* - \theta))\,. \end{aligned} \tag{9.3}$$

Hence, the central bank is indifferent between defending the peg and abandoning it if

$$\theta = \Phi(\sqrt{\beta}(x^* - \theta))\,. \tag{9.4}$$

From (9.2) and (9.4) we can derive the indifference curve for the speculators, denoted by $x^{SP}(\theta)$, and for the central bank, denoted by $x^{CB}(\theta)$

$$x^{SP}(\theta) = \frac{\alpha+\beta}{\beta}\theta - \frac{\alpha}{\beta}y - \frac{\sqrt{\alpha+\beta}}{\beta}\;\Phi^{-1}\left(\frac{t}{D}\right), \tag{9.5}$$

and

$$x^{CB}(\theta) = \frac{1}{\sqrt{\beta}}\Phi^{-1}(\theta) + \theta\,. \tag{9.6}$$

The equilibrium is then given as the intersection point of the two indifference curves, which can be seen from Fig. 9.1. The equilibrium value of θ can be

[10] Recall that speculators have been assumed to be risk-neutral.

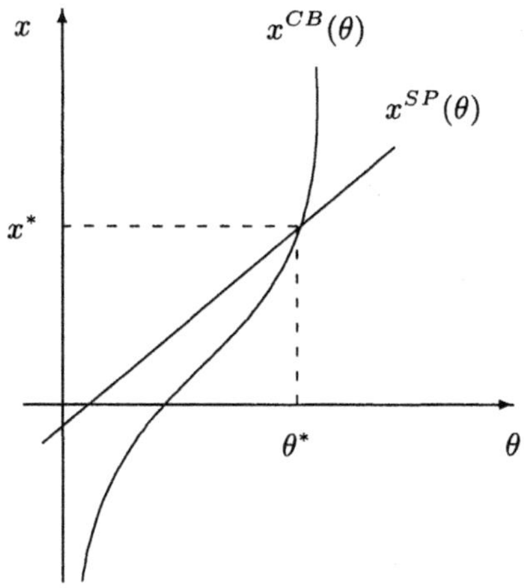

Fig. 9.1. Unique equilibrium

determined to be given by

$$\theta^* = \Phi\left(\frac{\alpha}{\sqrt{\beta}}\left(\theta^* - y - \frac{\sqrt{\alpha+\beta}}{\alpha} \quad \Phi^{-1}\left(\frac{t}{D}\right)\right)\right), \tag{9.7}$$

while x^* can be obtained from (9.5). θ^* can be seen to be a function of the payoff and cost parameters D and t, of the precision variables α and β, and of the public signal's value y, the commonly expected fundamental state. Moreover, θ^* is an implicit function, since it is contingent on itself.

Note that (θ^*, x^*) forms a trigger-point equilibrium in the following respect: a speculator observing a private signal x lower than the switching signal x^* chooses "attack" as his optimal action, whereas after observing a private signal higher than x^* "not attack" is the optimal action. In the same way, the central bank's optimal action is to "abandon the peg" whenever the observed fundamental value θ is lower than θ^*, but "keep the peg" is optimal if θ turns out to be higher than θ^*. Thus, the players in the game switch their actions exactly at the equilibrium points.

It is important to note that the equilibrium values θ^* and x^* are given by the exogenous parameters of the model, which are common knowledge to all players. Therefore, the equilibrium point can be determined before agents receive their individual private signals and before they take any actions. However, the choice of the true fundamental state θ by nature determines whether there will be a crisis, by giving the distribution of public and private signals that incite the speculators to run on the currency peg or not to do so, according to the above delineated decision process. Hence, the maintenance of the peg in the game with noisy public and private information hinges on the realized fundamental state of the economy. This is in contrast to second-generation crisis models, where the outcome of the game was triggered by speculators' beliefs. However, expectations still play a major role in this model with unique equilibrium, since they determine the trigger values θ^* and x^*.

9.4.2 The Uniqueness Condition

In order to show that the equilibrium is unique, we have to prove that there can be only one value of the fundamental index and one value of the private signal, which make both the central bank and the speculators indifferent at the same time, i.e. there is only one intersection point of the indifference curves $x^{SP}(\theta)$ and $x^{CB}(\theta)$. As can be seen from Fig. 9.1, this condition for a unique equilibrium is satisfied if one of the indifference curves runs steeper than the other throughout the whole range of possible values. As neither of the two indifference functions is limited to any range, the unique equilibrium then exists with certainty.

The slopes of the two indifference curves are equal to

$$\frac{\partial x^{SP}(\theta)}{\partial \theta} = \frac{\alpha + \beta}{\beta}$$

and

$$\frac{\partial x^{CB}(\theta)}{\partial \theta} = \frac{1}{\sqrt{\beta}} \frac{\partial \Phi^{-1}(\theta)}{\partial \theta} + 1 \,,$$

respectively. Thus, the sufficient (but not necessary[11]) condition for a unique equilibrium is satisfied, if

$$\frac{\alpha + \beta}{\beta} < \frac{1}{\sqrt{\beta}} \cdot \ _{min} \left(\frac{\partial \Phi^{-1}(\theta)}{\partial \theta} \right) \ + \ 1 \,.$$

For the following derivation of the uniqueness condition, note that the smallest value of $\frac{\partial \Phi^{-1}(\theta)}{\partial \theta}$ is equal to the reciprocal of the maximum value of the partial derivative of $\Phi(\theta)$ with respect to θ. This maximum value is given by the normal density $\phi(\theta)$ at its mean μ, with $\phi(\mu) = \frac{1}{\sqrt{2\pi}}$. The above sufficient condition of uniqueness is therefore fulfilled, if

$$\frac{\alpha + \beta}{\beta} < 1 + \frac{1}{\sqrt{\beta}} \frac{1}{\frac{1}{\sqrt{2\pi}}}$$

$$\beta > \frac{\alpha^2}{2\pi} \,.$$

Hence, for a given precision α of the public signal the depicted equilibrium is unique as long as the precision β of the private signal is high enough. If θ^* is unique, then x^* must be unique as well.

[11] The two necessary conditions for the unique equilibrium to exist are $D > t$, and $E(\varepsilon_i \varepsilon_j) = 0$.

As can be seen from Fig. 9.2, if the central bank's indifference function is not always steeper than $x^{SP}(\theta)$, we find that the game between central bank and speculators has three equilibria, two of them in pure strategies and one in mixed strategies.

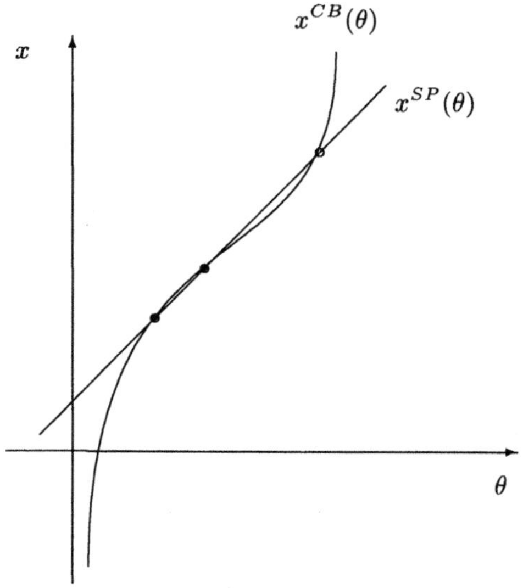

Fig. 9.2. Multiple equilibria

Note that additionally to proving that there is only one equilibrium trigger strategy around (θ^*, x^*), it can also be shown that the trigger strategy is the only strategy which survives the iterative elimination of dominated strategies. For a complete conduction of this proof, which follows Morris and Shin (1999a,c), see the appendix to this chapter.

9.5 Comparative Statics

After deriving the equilibrium and showing that is unique whenever private information is sufficiently precise relative to public, we are now able to examine the influence that the different parameters exert on the unique switching point (θ^*, x^*). It is important to analyze comparative statics in order to find answers to the question, which policy a central bank should conduct in order to prevent an attack on the fixed exchange rate parity. Due to the nature of the unique equilibrium, it is possible to define the probability of a currency crisis and investigate the effect that different parameters have on this probability. As we are mostly concerned with the impact of information on a currency crisis, most emphasis will be given to the influence of parameters y, α and β.

Since in the unique equilibrium model the central bank devalues the fixed exchange rate parity whenever the realized fundamental state θ falls into the interval bounded above by θ^*, it is reasonable to define the probability of a currency crisis as being proportional to the size of the interval $[-\infty, \theta^*]$. Thus, the higher the switching point θ^* turns out to be, the higher is the danger of a currency crisis and vice versa. All economic variables which increase θ^* therefore raise the probability of a currency crisis. Note that this definition of a currency crisis is an "ex-ante" definition, since the interval for the fundamental index, in which a crisis will occur, is determined before θ is realized.[12] From equation (9.7), which gives the equilibrium value of the fundamental index, we can infer the following propositions:

Proposition 9.4. (Metz, 2002a)
The probability of a currency crisis rises whenever t decreases and/or D increases.

Proof:
The partial derivatives of θ^* with respect to t and D are:

$$\frac{\partial \theta^*}{\partial t} = \phi(\cdot)\left(\frac{\alpha}{\sqrt{\beta}}\frac{\partial \theta^*}{\partial t} - \sqrt{\frac{\alpha+\beta}{\beta}}\frac{\partial \Phi^{-1}(\frac{t}{D})}{\partial t}\right) = \frac{-\sqrt{\frac{\alpha+\beta}{\beta}}\frac{\partial \Phi^{-1}(\frac{t}{D})}{\partial t}\phi(\cdot)}{1-\phi(\cdot)\frac{\alpha}{\sqrt{\beta}}} < 0$$

$$\frac{\partial \theta^*}{\partial D} = \phi(\cdot)\left(\frac{\alpha}{\sqrt{\beta}}\frac{\partial \theta^*}{\partial D} - (-1)\sqrt{\frac{\alpha+\beta}{\beta}}\frac{\partial \Phi^{-1}(\frac{t}{D})}{\partial D}\right) = \frac{\sqrt{\frac{\alpha+\beta}{\beta}}\frac{\partial \Phi^{-1}(\frac{t}{D})}{\partial D}\phi(\cdot)}{1-\phi(\cdot)\frac{\alpha}{\sqrt{\beta}}} > 0$$

The partial derivative of θ^* with respect to t (D) is always negative (positive), since due to the condition of uniqueness the denominator stays positive and nonzero. A rising t (D) thus decreases (increases) the switching value θ^* and thereby the probability of an exchange rate crisis. □

Increasing costs t reduce the expected net payoff of an attack for every probability of success. As such, the incentive to attack the fixed parity decreases. Consequently, controlling for the costs of international capital transactions might be a possibility to prevent speculative attacks on currency pegs.

[12] The ex-ante or prior probability of a currency crisis only refers to the switching value θ^*, without taking into account the realized fundamental value θ, since for all fundamental states worse than θ^* a devaluation will take place with certainty in the depicted model. The ex-post probability, in contrast, refers to the event of a currency crisis after the fundamental state has been realized. Since it takes on a value of either 0 or 1, depending on whether the realized state θ is higher or lower than θ^*, the ex-post probability is not helpful in finding an optimal policy rule for the central bank.

This result obviously favors the introduction of a tax on international capital transactions in order to avoid currency crises, for instance in the form of a Tobin tax.[13] In contrast, increasing the payoff D from a successful attack on the peg obviously rises the incentive to attack and as such increases the probability of a devaluation.

Proposition 9.5. (Metz, 2002a)
The public signal (i.e. the commonly expected value of the fundamental index), y, influences the probability of a currency crisis negatively.

Proof:

$$\frac{\partial \theta^*}{\partial y} = \phi(\cdot)\left(\frac{\alpha}{\sqrt{\beta}}\frac{\partial \theta^*}{\partial y} - \frac{\alpha}{\sqrt{\beta}}\right) = \frac{-\phi(\cdot)\frac{\alpha}{\sqrt{\beta}}}{1-\phi(\cdot)\frac{\alpha}{\sqrt{\beta}}} < 0$$

The higher the public signal, i.e. the higher the commonly expected economic state, the lower the switching point θ^* turns out to be, and thus the narrower gets the range of fundamentals for which an attack would be successful and vice versa. □

Hence, the higher the public signal about the fundamental state of the economy, the lower the switching point θ^* will be, and the narrower gets the range of fundamentals for which an attack would be successful. From this analysis it can be seen that expectations still play a major role in this model. The better the market sentiment, i.e. the higher the commonly expected fundamental state of the economy, the lower the probability of a currency crisis will be, since θ^* decreases in y. However, a bad market sentiment raises the danger of a crisis. From the partial derivative of θ^* with respect to y, it can also be found that the influence of the public signal is the stronger, the more precise this signal is, i.e. the higher α is.

Proposition 9.6. (Metz, 2002a)
If $\theta^* > y + \frac{1}{\sqrt{\alpha+\beta}}\Phi^{-1}\left(\frac{t}{D}\right)$, the precision of the private signal β exerts a negative influence on the probability of a currency crisis. If $\theta^* < y + \frac{1}{\sqrt{\alpha+\beta}}\Phi^{-1}\left(\frac{t}{D}\right)$, the precision of the private signal β exerts a positive influence on the probability of a currency crisis.

Proof:

$$\frac{\partial \theta^*}{\partial \beta} = \phi(\cdot)\left(-\frac{\alpha}{2\sqrt{\beta^3}}\theta^* + \frac{\alpha}{\sqrt{\beta}}\frac{\partial \theta^*}{\partial \beta} + \frac{\alpha}{2\sqrt{\beta^3}}y + \frac{\alpha}{2\beta^2}\sqrt{\frac{\beta}{\alpha+\beta}}\Phi^{-1}\left(\frac{t}{D}\right)\right)$$

$$= \frac{\phi(\cdot)\left(-\frac{\alpha}{2\sqrt{\beta^3}}\theta^* + \frac{\alpha}{2\sqrt{\beta^3}}y + \frac{\alpha}{2\beta^2}\sqrt{\frac{\beta}{\alpha+\beta}}\Phi^{-1}\left(\frac{t}{D}\right)\right)}{1-\phi(\cdot)\frac{\alpha}{\sqrt{\beta}}}$$

[13] For a thorough discussion of advantages and disadvantages of a Tobin tax see also Menkhoff and Michaelis (1995a,b) or Aizenman (1999). An application of the theory of a Tobin tax to the EMS is given by Jeanne (1996).

In the unique equilibrium, $\frac{\partial\theta^*}{\partial\beta}$ is negative, if θ^* is larger than $y+\frac{1}{\sqrt{\alpha+\beta}}\Phi^{-1}\left(\frac{t}{D}\right)$, so that the numerator becomes negative, whereas $\frac{\partial\theta^*}{\partial\beta}$ is positive if $\theta^* < y+\frac{1}{\sqrt{\alpha+\beta}}\Phi^{-1}\left(\frac{t}{D}\right)$. □

A changing value of β has three individual effects on the equilibrium value θ^*, with proposition 9.6 giving the net effect. The first is the direct influence on the distribution of private signals, since $\frac{1}{\beta}$ gives the variance of the distribution of private signals around the realized fundamental state θ. The second effect concerns the posterior variance of the fundamental index given the individual information: $\text{Var}(\theta|I_i) = \frac{1}{\alpha+\beta}$. The third effect refers to the posterior of the fundamental state given each speculator's information: $E(\theta|I_i) = \theta^e(x_i) = \frac{\alpha}{\alpha+\beta}y + \frac{\beta}{\alpha+\beta}x_i$.

The individual effects can be illustrated by means of Fig. 9.3 that describes the interaction between signals and fundamentals in the process of determining the unique equilibrium. The vertical axis depicts the value of the fundamental state, on the horizontal axis the values of the private signals can be found.

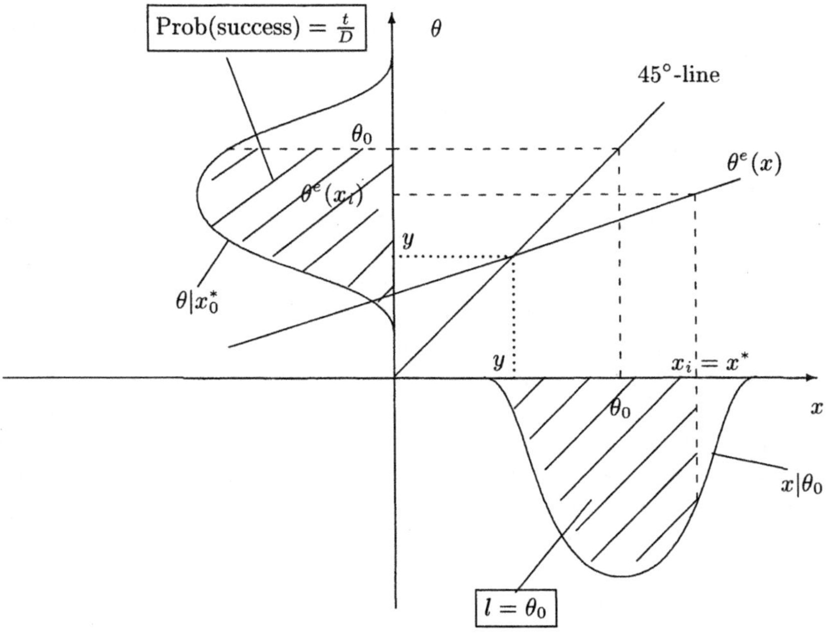

Fig. 9.3. Determination of the unique equilibrium

Let us first of all show how the equilibrium is derived in this type of figure, before analyzing the effects of a change in β. Suppose that nature chooses a fundamental index equal to θ_0, given on the vertical axis. This generates a distribution of private signals corresponding to a normal density with the following parameters: $x|\theta_0 \sim \mathrm{N}(\theta_0, \frac{1}{\beta})$. This distribution is depicted below the horizontal axis. After observing an individual private signal from the depicted distribution, the respective speculator with signal x_i expects the fundamental state to be normally distributed around a mean of $\theta^e(x_i) = \frac{\alpha}{\alpha+\beta}y + \frac{\beta}{\alpha+\beta}x_i$ with a variance of $\frac{1}{\alpha+\beta}$. The mean of this posterior distribution is given by the value of the $\theta^e(x)$-function corresponding to the observed value of the private signal x_i. The posterior distribution $\theta|x_i$ is depicted on the vertical axis with variance $\frac{1}{\alpha+\beta}$.

In Fig. 9.3, we find the equilibrium values of the private signal and the fundamental index as follows. Again, x^* and θ^* are determined by a situation of indifference. For the central bank to be indifferent between the two possible actions "defending" and "abandoning" the peg, the proportion of attacking speculators, l, has to be equal to the fundamental state. If the realized fundamental state θ_0 happened to be the equilibrium value, i.e. $\theta_0 = \theta^*$, then the proportion of attacking speculators required for indifference would have to be $l = \theta_0$. From the derived optimal trigger strategy for the speculators, we know that the trigger value for the private signals, x^*, has to be such that exactly a proportion of $l = \theta_0$ of speculators receive a signal lower than the searched-for trigger value $x^* = x^*(\theta_0)$.

It is important to keep in mind, that there is a multitude of combinations of fundamental values chosen by nature and affiliated trigger values of the private signal (one for each fundamental index) that render the central bank indifferent. From this multitude of (θ, x)-combinations there has to be chosen exactly one, which additionally makes each speculator receiving the respective private signal indifferent between his two actions. For a trader receiving a private signal of $x^*(\theta_0)$ in order to be indifferent between "attacking" and "not-attacking", the expected net payoff from an attack on the fixed parity has to be equal to the net payoff from not-attacking ($= 0$). As has been explained in the former section, this is equivalent to the requirement that the probability of a successful attack has to equal $\frac{t}{D}$. For x^* to be the optimal trigger value for the speculators while θ_0 is the optimal trigger for the central bank, the probability that the fundamental state is lower than θ_0, given that exactly a private signal of x^* has been observed, has to be equal to $\frac{t}{D}$. In the figure, this can be seen to be the case for the signal of x_i. As such, θ_0^* and x_i^* are the equilibrium values in the depicted situation of Fig. 9.3. They depend on the given payoff- and cost-parameters, the precision values α and β and the common prior y.

Let us now analyze a change in β. Since it is not possible to quantify each of the three different effects on the probability of a currency crisis, but only the direction of the net effect is assessable, we will at least briefly describe the potential consequences of changes in β. In doing so, we concentrate on the case of an increase in precision β, while a decrease in β would yield the opposite effects.

The first "direct" effect of an increase in β leads to a higher density of the private signals around their mean, given by the realized fundamental state θ. Since the critical mass of attacking speculators necessary to make the central bank indifferent stays constant, the switching value of the private signals x^* has to change. Whether x^* has to increase or decrease, depends on whether x^* has been higher of lower than θ before the change in β. If the trigger signal x^* has been higher than its mean θ, the higher precision of private signals leads to a higher proportion of speculators receiving signals below x^*, so that the mass of attacking traders increases. The opposite holds, if x^* has been lower than θ before the change in precision. In the former case, the trigger value has to be reduced, in the latter case it has to be raised, due to the more precise private signals.

The second effect of an increasing β refers to the posterior variance of fundamentals, contingent on the speculators' information. Due to an increase in β, the posterior distribution of θ, depicted on the vertical axis in Fig. 9.3, will become more dense around its mean. Similarly to the explanation of the "direct" effect above, the impact on θ^* depends on whether the trigger value of the fundamental state before the change in β lay above or below its mean, given by $\frac{\alpha}{\alpha+\beta}y + \frac{\beta}{\alpha+\beta}x$. In the case that θ^* has been higher than the mean, the probability that a fundamental state lower than θ^* is chosen will increase, following the higher precision of private signals. Since, however, the probability of a successful attack for a speculator observing the equilibrium signal x^* still has to equal $\frac{t}{D}$, the trigger value of the fundamental index therefore has to decrease. The opposite holds, if θ^* had been lower than the mean before the change in β.

The third "indirect" effect of a changing precision of private information concerns the posterior-mean function $\theta^e(x_i)$. A higher precision β will make this function steeper. Note, however, that the higher precision of private signals not necessarily makes speculators more optimistic concerning the fundamental state of the economy. Whether or not they believe fundamentals to be better than before, depends on whether the observed private signal is higher or lower than the public signal y, since the $\theta^e(x_i)$-function turns around the intersection point with the 45°-line, which is given at $x = y$. Hence, whenever the trigger value of the private signals x^* is higher than y, the posterior distribution of fundamental states, depicted on the vertical axis in Fig. 9.3, will be shifted upwards, since a speculator who observes the trigger value is more optimistic than before, due to the higher precision of his private signal. However, if x^* is lower than y, the posterior distribution of θ will shift downwards, following an increase in β. In the former case, the equilibrium value of the fundamental index θ^* has to increase in order to keep the probability of a successful attack equal to $\frac{t}{D}$, in the latter case it has to decrease.

The net effect of a change in the precision β of private information on the probability of a currency crisis depends on whether θ^* exceeds or falls short of a threshold function given by $y+\frac{1}{\sqrt{\alpha+\beta}}\Phi^{-1}(\frac{t}{D})$. Whenever the switching value θ^* exceeds this threshold, a rising precision of the private signals decreases the probability of a currency crisis. In contrast, if θ^* falls short of the threshold, a higher precision of the private signals increases the likelihood of a crisis. Since the threshold-function $y+\frac{1}{\sqrt{\alpha+\beta}}\Phi^{-1}\left(\frac{t}{D}\right)$ increases in y, whereas θ^* decreases in y according to proposition 9.5, there must be a value of y, denoted as y_β, such that θ^* is exactly equal to the threshold:[14] $\theta^*(y_\beta)=y_\beta+\frac{1}{\sqrt{\alpha+\beta}}\Phi^{-1}\left(\frac{t}{D}\right)$. It is easy to see that for all public signals lower than y_β, a higher precision of the private signals is associated with a lower probability of a crisis, whereas for all public signals higher than y_β, more precise private signals lead to a higher probability of a currency crisis.

For interpreting the influence of β on the probability of a currency crisis, note that a speculator deciding on his optimal action has to take two aspects into account. On the one hand, he wants to choose an action that is appropriate to the realized but unknown fundamental state. On the other hand, he knows that for the relevant intermediate range of fundamentals, i.e. for $0<\theta\leq 1$, it is possible to force a devaluation of the currency peg through sheer speculative pressure. As such, he wants to coordinate his own decision on his opponents' actions, so that even for good fundamentals in this interval a devaluation might be achieved.

Whereas both types of signals give information about the fundamental state of the economy, only the private signals have a direct effect on the coordination incentive described above. Speculators decide on their optimal action solely based on their specific information sets. Equivalent information sets therefore must lead to the same choice of actions. What makes speculator i's information set different from speculator j's is only the private part, since private signals might differ from each other. The more precise the private signals are, however, the more closely they will be distributed around the realized fundamental state θ, and the more similar the information sets will be. This amounts to saying that varying the precision of the private signals foremost affects the coordination incentive: the higher β, the easier it is to coordinate on a certain action. An individual speculator will be more confident in his private information, if he thinks that his private beliefs are shared by his opponents. This is the case whenever the precision of private signals is high, so that all signals are quite densely distributed around the unknown fundamental state θ. However, both private and public signal exert an indirect effect on the coordination incentive. The more precise one type of signal is, the higher is the respective weight that is attached to this part of information in calculating the expected value of the unknown fundamental index θ. Since the weighing scheme of the signals is common knowledge, this indirect coordination effect is not negligible but rather important.

[14] y_β exists with certainty, since the public signal y is not restricted to any range of values.

The interpretation of the effects of an increasing precision β is then quite intuitive. The more precise the private signals, the less weight will be given to the informational content of the public signal. Take the case of a good market sentiment, i.e. $y > y_\beta$. With an intermediate precision of private information, speculators tend to refrain from attacking, since they know that for good fundamentals a large proportion of agents has to coordinate on the attack-action in order to force a devaluation. If, in contrast, the precision of private information is extremely high, speculators will simply neglect the content of the public signal. Consequently, they will become more aggressive in attacking the peg as compared to a situation with less precise private signals, so that the probability of a currency crisis increases. In case of a bad market sentiment, the reverse holds. Here, the public signal is low, i.e. $y < y_\beta$, so that speculators should want to attack, since a devaluation can easily be achieved. If, however, private information is extremely precise, speculators will be incited to neglect the informational content of the public signal and refrain from attacking, which leads to a lower crisis probability.

Proposition 9.7. (Metz, 2002a)
The precision of the public signal α exerts a positive influence on the probability of a currency crisis, if $\theta^* > y + \frac{1}{2\sqrt{\alpha+\beta}}\Phi^{-1}\left(\frac{t}{D}\right)$. In contrast, if $\theta^* < y + \frac{1}{2\sqrt{\alpha+\beta}}\Phi^{-1}\left(\frac{t}{D}\right)$, the precision of the public signal α exerts a negative influence on the probability of a crisis.

Proof:

$$\frac{\partial\theta^*}{\partial\alpha} = \phi(\cdot)\left(\frac{1}{\sqrt{\beta}}\theta^* + \frac{\alpha}{\sqrt{\beta}}\frac{\partial\theta^*}{\partial\alpha} - \frac{1}{\sqrt{\beta}}y - \frac{1}{2\beta}\sqrt{\frac{\beta}{\alpha+\beta}}\Phi^{-1}\left(\frac{t}{D}\right)\right)$$

$$= \frac{\phi(\cdot)\left(\frac{1}{\sqrt{\beta}}\theta^* - \frac{1}{\sqrt{\beta}}y - \frac{1}{2\beta}\sqrt{\frac{\beta}{\alpha+\beta}}\Phi^{-1}\left(\frac{t}{D}\right)\right)}{1 - \phi(\cdot)\frac{\alpha}{\sqrt{\beta}}}$$

In the unique equilibrium, the partial derivative of θ^* with respect to the precision of the public signal α is positive if $\theta^* > y + \frac{1}{2\sqrt{\alpha+\beta}}\Phi^{-1}\left(\frac{t}{D}\right)$, whereas it is negative if θ^* is lower than $y + \frac{1}{2\sqrt{\alpha+\beta}}\Phi^{-1}\left(\frac{t}{D}\right)$. □

The effect of the public signal's precision is threefold as well. First of all, a changing α influences the range of possible values for the fundamental index, since the variance of the unconditional distribution of θ is given by $\frac{1}{\alpha}$. The higher α, the more closely the possibly chosen value of θ will be to its prior mean y, i.e. the market sentiment, whereas low values of α make extreme values of θ possible. The second effect is similar to the second effect of an increase in β. An increasing precision α of the public signal decreases the conditional variance of θ, so that the expected values of the fundamental index are more densely distributed around the conditional mean $\theta^e(x_i)$. Thirdly, there is also an "indirect" effect, since a rising α makes the $\theta^e(x_i)$-function steeper.

It is the first, "direct" effect, however, which makes the influence of α on θ almost opposite to the effect of β, since the second and third effect are completely the same for both types of information. Thus, if the equilibrium switching value of θ^* is high enough to exceed the threshold $y+\frac{1}{2\sqrt{\alpha+\beta}}\Phi^{-1}(\frac{t}{D})$, increasing the precision of public information raises the probability of a currency crisis. If, however, θ^* falls short of the threshold, increasing α decreases the likelihood of a crisis. Again, the threshold-function increases in the value of the public signal y, whereas θ^* decreases in y, so that there must be a value denoted by y_α, so that $\theta^*(y_\alpha) = y_\alpha + \frac{1}{2\sqrt{\alpha+\beta}}\Phi^{-1}(\frac{t}{D})$. Consequently, for public signals lower than y_α, i.e. for bad commonly expected fundamentals, a higher precision α of the public signal leads to a higher probability of a currency crisis. If, however, y is higher than y_α, so that the market sentiment is rather good, an increased precision of public information leads to a lower crisis probability.

These effects are again quite intuitive. In contrast to the private signal, the public signal only gives information about the fundamental state of the economy and is included in each speculator's information set. Since it cannot be used to differentiate between individual private signals, the public signal has no direct influence on possible coordination effects. Consequently, if the public signal is known to be very precise and if it indicates a bad fundamental state of the economy, this clearly tells speculators to attack the currency peg for two reasons: first, each speculator knows that in case of bad fundamentals the proportion of attacking agents necessary to force a devaluation is not very high, which increases the probability of a successful attack. Secondly, if the public signal is very precise, each agent knows that all other agents will put more weight on public information in calculating the expected value of θ, so that there is an indirect coordination effect. For good expected fundamentals, exactly the opposite effects occur. The results of propositions 9.6 and 9.7 are summed up in Fig. 9.4[15] For the market sentiment being sufficiently bad, so that $y < \min\{y_\alpha, y_\beta\}$, the probability of a currency crisis increases with higher precision of public information and lower precision of private information. For sufficiently strong expected fundamentals, however, i.e. $y > \max\{y_\alpha, y_\beta\}$, the danger of a crisis increases with lower precision of public and higher precision of private information.

For an overview of the influence of all parameters on the probability of a currency crisis, approximated by the value of θ^*, see Fig. 9.5. It represents equilibrium equation (9.7). On the vertical axis the trigger value θ^* is depicted.

[15] It has been assumed here that $0 < t < \frac{1}{2}D$, i.e. costs are small relative to the payoff from a successful attack. In this case, for all public signals between y_α and y_β, both α and β exert a positive influence on θ^*. If instead $\frac{1}{2}D < t < D$, increasing precision of private and public information will have a negative influence on θ^* for intermediate values of the prior mean y.

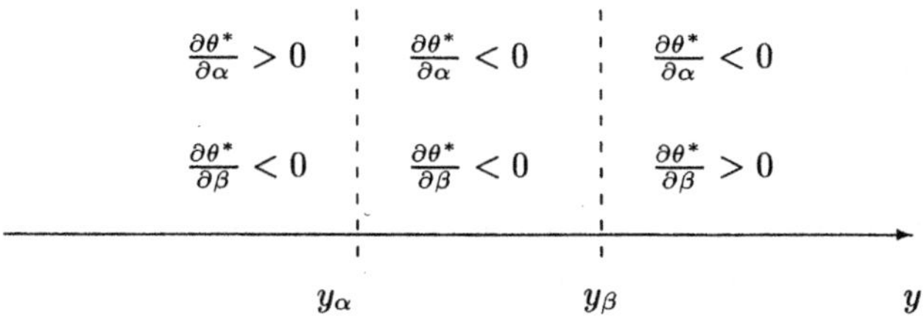

Fig. 9.4. Regions for influence of α and β

The equilibrium is defined by the intersection of the curve given by $\Phi(\frac{\alpha}{\sqrt{\beta}}[\theta^* - y - \frac{\sqrt{\alpha+\beta}}{\alpha}\Phi^{-1}(\frac{t}{D})])$, and the 45°-line, which represents the function θ^*. Uniqueness of equilibrium requires the slope of the equilibrium-curve to be less than one. In essence, Fig. 9.5 represents a normalization of the indifference curves for central bank and speculators. Instead of describing the effects of the different parameters on the indifference condition of speculators and central bank individually, Fig. 9.5 presents a concise overview of the overall effects of changes in the parameters on θ^*, and as such is more suited for illustrating our results.

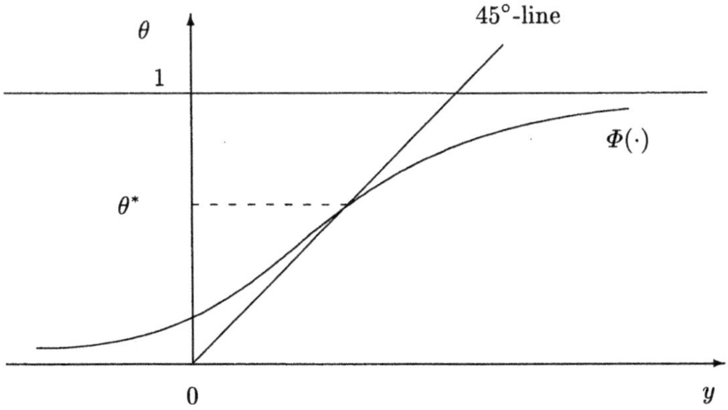

Fig. 9.5. Overall influence of the model parameters on θ^*

It is easy to see that parameter changes have different effects on θ^*, depending on whether they change the mean or the variance of the equilibrium-function $\Phi(\cdot)$. The mean of this function is given by $y + \frac{\sqrt{\alpha+\beta}}{\alpha}\Phi^{-1}(\frac{t}{D})$, the variance by $\frac{\beta}{\alpha^2}$. Increasing (decreasing) the mean shifts the function to the right (left), so that the intersection value θ^* decreases as long as the uniqueness condition is satisfied. Increasing (decreasing) the variance makes the curve more shallow (steep) and as such may both raise or diminish θ^*. Hence, increasing y or t decreases the danger of a crisis, whereas increasing D raises the probability of a currency crisis unambiguously, since these parameters only influence the mean of the distribution function. The impact of changing the precision parameters α and β, however, concerns both mean and variance of the function, and is as such more complex.

Consider the case of an increase in α first. A higher precision of public information will lower the variance $\frac{\beta}{\alpha^2}$ and makes the equilibrium-function steeper. Additionally, the mean will decrease since $\frac{\partial(y+\frac{\sqrt{\alpha+\beta}}{\alpha}\Phi^{-1}(\frac{t}{D}))}{\partial\alpha} < 0$, so that the function shifts to the left. The two effects can be seen from Fig. 9.6. Note that the "mean"-effect unequivocally leads to an increase in the

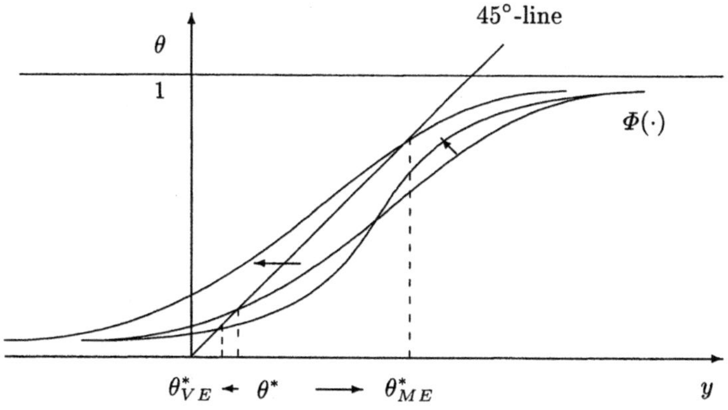

Fig. 9.6. Influence of α on θ^*

switching value from θ^* to θ^*_{ME}, due to the higher value of α. However, the decreasing effect on the variance makes the switching value of the fundamental index turn out to be lower in the depicted case: it decreases from θ^* to θ^*_{VE}. Yet, the effect of the changing variance is ambiguous and depends on whether the new intersection point with the 45°-line lies to the right or to the left of the mean. In the former case, θ^* will increase. In the latter case, the trigger value will decrease, as can be seen from the figure.

The effects of an increase in β are reverse. A higher β shifts the mean of the cumulated density function $\Phi(\cdot)$ to the right, while the variance increases, so that the function becomes less steep. The two effects can be seen from Fig. 9.7. Again, the "mean"-effect is unambiguous and leads to a decrease in

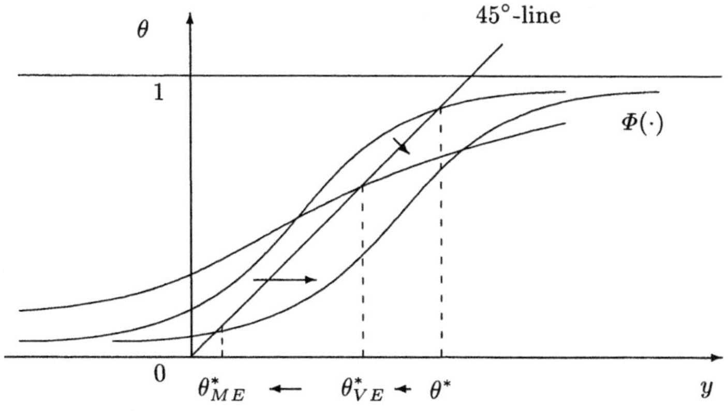

Fig. 9.7. Influence of β on θ^*

θ^* down to θ^*_{ME}, due to the increase in β. The "variance"-effect, however, is contingent on whether the new intersection point lies to the left of the mean, in which case θ^* decreases, or to the right, so that θ^* increases.

What can be seen from the discussion of comparative statics in this section is that "better" information, in the sense of more precise information, does not necessarily lead to a lower probability of a currency crisis, as has been suggested by former models (Heinemann and Illing, 1999). Moreover, the mechanisms of a changing informativeness are very complex. The most important result, however, is that with the given structure of private and public signals, the market sentiment, i.e. the commonly expected fundamental state of the economy, plays an important role in determining the influence of the information's precision on the probability of a currency crisis. If the market sentiment is good, a higher precision of public information leads to a lower probability of a crisis, whereas very precise private information tends to increase the likelihood of a crisis. For a bad market sentiment, the influence of information is exactly the reverse. As can be seen from Fig. 9.4, there is only a small range of common priors y, where both signals exert the same influence on the probability of a crisis. Moreover, this interval for y vanishes with increasing α and/or β.[16]

[16] The length of the interval of equal influence of α and β is given by $\frac{1}{2\sqrt{\alpha+\beta}}\Phi^{-1}(\frac{t}{D})$, which decreases in α, β and D, but increases in t.

9.6 Unique versus Multiple Equilibria and the Importance of Private and Public Information

Since we know that a unique equilibrium can only be sustained for rather precise private information relative to public information, a declining β, respectively a rising α, will eventually lead to multiple equilibria again. This can also be seen from Fig. 9.8, which depicts the sufficient condition for uniqueness of equilibrium.[17]

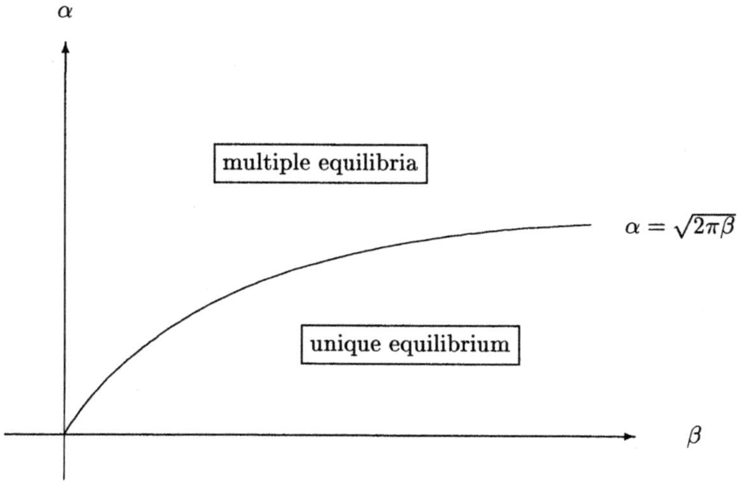

Fig. 9.8. Regions of unique versus multiple equilibria

If β declines while α stays constant, speculators are not able to precisely establish the private information received by the other agents, so that they are not able to coordinate on a specific action for a given θ. Since they cannot be sure that the necessary amount of coordination, i.e. the proportion of attacking agents, will be achieved, the optimal action for them at some point is to attack if everyone else attacks and to refrain from short-selling if that is what they expect everyone else to do. With β going to zero, the private part in the information sets will simply be neglected, so that information sets are the same for all speculators, which invites multiple equilibria. Similarly, if the precision of public information α increases for a given β, the informational

[17] Note, however, that due to the depicted condition only being sufficient but not necessary for uniqueness, there might be a unique equilibrium above the line $\alpha = \sqrt{2\pi\beta}$ as well. Yet, generally, we will refer to the upper area as the multiple equilibria region.

content of the private signal falls more and more behind, so that it is eventually neglected and, again, multiple equilibria arise.

Hence, in case that the fundamental state of the economy is commonly expected to be weak, both very precise and very imprecise public information, i.e. high as well as low α, may lead to an outcome of the game with "not-attack" being the chosen strategy: on the one hand, if α is sufficiently low relative to β, so that a unique equilibrium is guaranteed, a bad market sentiment leads to θ^* exceeding the threshold function $y + \frac{1}{2\sqrt{\alpha+\beta}}\Phi^{-1}(\frac{t}{D})$, so that a low α brings about a small probability of a currency crisis. On the other hand, if the public information's precision is extraordinarily high, so that the condition for uniqueness is violated, there is a certain, however not calculable, probability that in the revived multiplicity of equilibria speculators will coordinate on the no-attack equilibrium, since this coordination will no longer depend on the fundamental state of the economy. Yet, it obviously stands to reason if an increased uncertainty of the realized equilibrium will ever be preferred, even with very bad expected fundamentals.

9.7 Conclusion

From the delineated model we are able to see that the introduction of certain structures of noisy information eliminates multiplicity of equilibria. Since speculators are not sure about the underlying fundamental state of the economy and as such of their opponents' actions, they have to take into account a larger set of strategies to choose from. By starting from the uniquely optimal action for extremely good or extremely bad fundamental states, we can show that noisy information renders a unique equilibrium, provided that noisiness is limited to a certain ratio. This equilibrium can be found to be a trigger point, where speculators and central bank switch their optimal actions. If a speculator's information set indicates the fundamental state to be worse than the trigger value, he will choose to attack the fixed parity, as this action will perceivably deliver a positive payoff, whereas not-attacking will only give him a payoff of zero. However, if the information set makes the speculator believe that economic fundamentals are stronger than the trigger value, he will not attack, since in this case he reckons the expected payoff from short-selling the domestic currency to be negative. The introduction of noisy information therefore brings an additional crucial condition of a net expected payoff equal to zero into the model, which renders uniqueness of equilibrium whenever private information is sufficiently precise relative to public.

In contrast to the multiple equilibria outcome of second-generation models of currency crises à la Obstfeld, we are now able to give directions for policy advice. First, we find that the increase of transaction costs certainly reduces speculators' incentives to intervene on international financial markets and therefore reduces the probability of a speculative currency attack. Secondly, the stronger (i.e. the higher) the commonly expected value of the economic fundamental, the lower is the danger of a crisis. Thirdly, increasing the precision of information is obviously not enough to prevent currency crises. On the contrary, we find that increasing the precision of private and public information may have opposite influence on the danger of a crisis. Which sign of influence prevails crucially depends on the commonly expected fundamental state of the economy. Whenever the market sentiment concerning economic fundamentals is bad, disseminating very precise public information is dangerous, since it increases the probability of a currency crisis further, whereas a high precision of private signals will decrease it. In contrast, in case of a good market sentiment, higher precision of public information decreases the likelihood of a currency crisis, while more precise private information raises it. This finding is very much in contrast to the usual claim that a central bank should commit to a high degree of transparency about economic fundamentals in order to prevent speculative attacks on the fixed parity.[18]

However, this is only a first step to a thorough policy advice on how to prevent currency crises in a setting where strategic complementarities incite speculators to coordinate on an attack-strategy. A major weakness of the above analysis furthermore is that the results concerning informational influences are based on endogenous formulae. Whether increasing the precision of private or public information will raise or lower the danger of a crisis was found to depend on the ratio of the trigger value θ^* to certain threshold functions. Both θ^* and the threshold functions, however, are contingent on the parameters D, t, y, α and β. In order to give a thorough advice to the central bank on how to behave in situations of currency turmoil, therefore, the exogenous conditions for the influence of precision parameters α and β on the probability of a currency crisis remain to be found. This problem will be seen to in Chap. 10, where the optimal information policy for the central bank is derived in order to minimize the danger of a currency crisis.

[18] For a critical analysis of the optimal degree of transparency in monetary policy in general, see Jensen (2001).

Appendix

In accordance with Morris and Shin (1999a,c), we can show that the switching strategy around (θ^*, x^*) is not only the unique equilibrium strategy, but it is also the only strategy which survives the iterated elimination of dominated strategies. This is a much stronger argument than the simple Nash concept usually underlying equilibrium derivation, and as such deserves the appropriate attention.

In the setting of the model of Sect. 9.5, consider a single speculator who uses a switching signal of x, while all other speculators switch strategies at $\hat{x}$. Denote the payoff from attacking for the first speculator in this case as $u(x, \hat{x})$. This payoff satisfies the following three properties. Monotonicity: u is strictly decreasing in its first argument x, and strictly increasing in its second argument $\hat{x}$. Continuity: u is continuous with respect to x. Full Range: For $x \to -\infty$ it holds that $u(x, \hat{x}) \to D$ and for $x \to \infty$ it holds that $u(x, \hat{x}) \to -t$.

We can then define the following two sequences of real numbers. First:

$$\underline{x}^1, \underline{x}^2, ..., \underline{x}^k, ...$$

as the solutions to

$$\begin{aligned} u(\underline{x}^1, \infty) &= 0 \\ u(\underline{x}^2, \underline{x}^1) &= 0 \\ &\vdots \\ u(\underline{x}^{k+1}, \underline{x}^k) &= 0 \\ &\vdots \end{aligned}$$

Analogously, define the sequence:

$$\bar{x}^1, \bar{x}^2, ..., \bar{x}^k, ...$$

as the solutions to

$$\begin{aligned} u(\bar{x}^1, -\infty) &= 0 \\ u(\bar{x}^2, \bar{x}^1) &= 0 \\ &\vdots \\ u(\bar{x}^{k+1}, \bar{x}^k) &= 0 \\ &\vdots \end{aligned}$$

We can then show that the following lemmas hold:

Lemma 9.8. (Morris and Shin, 1999a)
Let x be the signal which solves the equilibrium conditions, so that $u(x,x) = 0$. Then

$$\underline{x}^1 > \underline{x}^2 > \ldots > x$$

and

$$\bar{x}^1 < \bar{x}^2 < \ldots < x\,.$$

Let $\underline{x}$ and $\bar{x}$ be the largest and the smallest solution to the equilibrium, then

$$\underline{x} = lim_{k\to\infty}\underline{x}^k \quad and \quad \bar{x} = lim_{k\to\infty}\bar{x}^k\,.$$

Proof:
Since $u(\underline{x}^1,\infty) = u(\underline{x}^2,\underline{x}^1) = 0$, and this regularity holds for the whole sequence, monotonicity implies that $\underline{x}^1 > \underline{x}^2$, and in general $\underline{x}^k > \underline{x}^{k+1} > \underline{x}$. The analogous argument holds for the second sequence. Monotonicity moreover implies that the decreasing bounded sequence $\{\underline{x}^k\}$ converges to its highest lower bound which is given by $\underline{x}$, and vice versa for $\bar{x}$. □

Lemma 9.9. (Morris and Shin, 1999a)
If σ is a strategy that survives k rounds of iterated elimination of dominated strategies, then

$$\sigma(x) = \begin{cases} refrain & if \quad x > \underline{x}^k\,, \\ attack & if \quad x < \bar{x}^k\,. \end{cases} \tag{9.8}$$

Proof:
Let now σ^{-i} be the strategy used by all other agents, and denote by $\tilde{u}^i(x,\sigma^{-i})$ the payoff to player i from attacking for signals lower than x, while all others use strategy profile σ^{-i}.

The incidence of a coordination failure is minimized if everyone attacks irrespective of the signal, whereas it is maximized if everyone refrains from attacking irrespective of the signal. Hence, for any signal x and any strategy profile σ^{-i} it holds that

$$u(x,\infty) \geq \tilde{u}^i(x,\sigma^{-i}) \geq u(x,-\infty)\,.$$

Recalling the definition of $\bar{x}^1$ and using monotonicity, we find that

$$x < \bar{x}^1 \Rightarrow \text{for any } \sigma^{-i}, \quad \tilde{u}^i(x,\sigma^{-i}) \geq u(x,-\infty) > u(\bar{x}^1,-\infty) = 0\,.$$

Thus, $x < \bar{x}^1$ implies that for signals lower than $\bar{x}^1$ not to attack the fixed peg is strictly dominated by attacking the peg. Similarly, we find that

$$x > \underline{x}^1 \Rightarrow \text{for any } \sigma^{-i}, \quad \tilde{u}^i(x,\sigma^{-i}) \leq u(x,\infty) < u(\underline{x}^1,\infty) = 0\,.$$

Hence, $x > \underline{x}^1$ implies that attacking the peg is strictly dominated by not attacking.

Consequently, (9.8) holds for $k = 1$ and strategy σ^i survives the first round of iterated deletion of dominated strategies. Assume that (9.8) holds for k and denote by S^k the set of strategies which satisfy (9.8). It has to be shown then, that if a player i faces a strategy profile from S^k, then any strategy that is not contained in S^k is dominated.

Since we know that for each round k the incidence of a coordination failure is minimized when the strategy profile σ^{-i} utilizes the strategy profile with the $\underline{x}^k$-trigger (which is the highest possible trigger in S^k), and the incidence of failure is maximized if σ^{-i} uses the $\bar{x}^k$-trigger (the lowest possible trigger in S^k), then for any x and σ^{-i} from S^k it holds that

$$x < \bar{x}^{k+1} \Rightarrow \tilde{u}^i(x, \sigma^{-i}) \geq u(x, \bar{x}^k) > u(\bar{x}^{k+1}, \bar{x}^k) = 0 .$$

In other words, when $x < \bar{x}^{k+1}$ and all others are using strategies from S^k, refraining from an attack is strictly dominated by attacking. Similarly,

$$x > \underline{x}^{k+1} \Rightarrow \tilde{u}^i(x, \sigma^{-i}) \leq u(x, \underline{x}^k) < u(\underline{x}^{k+1}, \underline{x}^k) = 0 .$$

Again, when $x > \underline{x}^{k+1}$ and all others are using strategies from S^k, attacking is strictly dominated by not-attacking. Thus, (9.8) holds for $k + 1$ rounds of iterated deletion of dominated strategies which proves lemma 2. □

With these preliminaries we can now prove that the trigger strategy around x is the only strategy, which survives iterated elimination of dominated strategies. If x solves the equilibrium condition, then $u(x, x) = 0$, so that if everyone else is using the trigger strategy around x, the payoff to attacking and refraining from an attack must be equal. Since u is strictly decreasing in the first argument and strictly increasing in the second, it holds that

$$x_* < x < x^* \quad \Leftrightarrow \quad u(x_*, x) > 0 > u(x^*, x) ,$$

so that the $x-$trigger strategy is the strict best reply to all other agents using the $x-$trigger strategy.

Finally, it has to be shown that if x is the unique solution to $u(x, x) = 0$, then there is no other equilibrium. From the first lemma in this appendix we know that

$$x = lim_{k\to\infty}\bar{x}^k = lim_{k\to\infty}\underline{x}^k ,$$

so that there is no other strategy, which survives iterated deletion of strictly dominated strategies. As such, the $x-$trigger strategy is the unique equilibrium strategy that survives iterated elimination of dominated strategies.

10

Optimal Information Policy - Endogenizing Information Precision

Although the previous chapter demonstrably showed that it is possible to identify conditions for which increasing the precision of private and public information reduces the probability of a speculative attack, we cannot yet give exact policy advice to the central bank on how to prevent a crisis. This is due to the fact that the identified conditions for the influence of α and β are given in terms of endogenous formulae: θ^* has to exceed or fall short of certain thresholds, with the parameters in the threshold-functions themselves influencing the value of θ^*. As such, it still remains an open question under which conditions on exogenous parameters disclosures of better information would enhance or harm the goals of the information providing principal.

In this chapter we reconsider the information problem. On the basis of the currency crisis model of Chap. 9, we derive the exogenous conditions for optimal information policy and optimal risk taking of a central bank, which intends to minimize the prior probability of a currency crisis. As can be seen, optimal policy is mostly used to shift fundamental risk from the central bank to the agents. This characteristic of the principal's optimal behavior has also been found in different models, both applied to currency crises and related topics such as multiple source lending, where firms face the risk of early liquidation of creditors (Allen and Gale, 1997, 2002; Brunner and Krahnen, 2001). Hence, our arguments can easily be extended to a broader range of contexts. The analysis of optimal risk taking and information policy as laid out in this chapter follows quite closely the work by Heinemann and Metz (2002).

In order to find the optimal policy that minimizes the probability of a speculative attack, a three-stage game is used. On the first stage, the central bank decides on the optimal policy measurements, i.e. the parameters concerning the distribution of economic fundamentals and the precision of posterior private information on fundamentals. In the second stage, traders receive private and public information about the realized fundamental state, whose exact specification is unknown to them, and decide whether to speculate against the fixed parity or not. In a third stage, the central bank makes the decision on whether to abandon the currency peg or maintain the parity. This decision is based on knowledge of the fundamental state and on the proportion of traders who attack the currency.

Note that in the setting of the model to be used here, risk policy concerns the development of economic fundamentals, which has also been denoted as public information in previous chapters. Risk taking behavior of the authorities hence refers to the accepted variability of the fundamental state around an exogenously given mean. The chosen distribution of parameters is again assumed to be common knowledge among market participants. According to our previous explanations on this subject, the prior mean of fundamentals is also interpreted as "market sentiment". Public information thus comprises the common belief concerning the central bank's reaction to market positions. Observable policy conducted in order to increase or decrease fundamental risk therefore also changes the precision of public information. The lower the risk chosen by the authorities, the closer is the realized fundamental state to its commonly expected value and, as such, the more precise public information will be.[1]

Information policy is conducted by disseminating individual signals on the realized fundamental state to the traders. Note that information is "private", in the sense that individual signals might and will almost certainly differ from each other. Precision of private information is measured by the conditional variance of signals for given fundamentals. The central bank's choice concerning information policy is described as a commitment to provide markets with private signals of a specific precision about fundamentals. The variance of private signals indicates how precisely the central bank disseminates her own information to agents. Thus, high precision of private information may be interpreted as transparency chosen by the principal.

The analysis of this chapter shows that optimal risk taking behavior and optimal information policy crucially depend on the a-priori expected mean of fundamentals and on the profitability of an attack for the speculators. There is a unique fundamental threshold θ_0^*, such that it is optimal to choose minimal risk if the prior expected mean of economic performance is above this threshold. For lower means, optimal risk policy is exactly reversed, avoiding any economic risks in order to minimize potential crises. Optimal information policy, however, also depends on the ratio of payoff and costs from a successful attack for the speculators. Whenever a devaluation is highly profitable for the traders, the central bank should disseminate completely precise information in case of weak prior means, while the reverse is optimal in case of strong expected fundamentals and also whenever the costs from attacking are high enough to significantly reduce the profitability of an attack.

[1] A similar approach to analyzing the influence of central bank interventions on the foreign exchange market has been chosen by Bhattacharya and Weller (1997). They show that it might be desirable for the central bank to keep its policy target secret instead of disclosing it publicly.

10.1 The Model

In the currency crisis model of the previous chapter, precision parameters α and β were assumed to be exogenous to the model, i.e. the values were chosen before the central bank observed the realized fundamental state of the economy. By assuming the precision parameters to be constant throughout the course of the game, it was then shown that under certain conditions for α and β there is a unique equilibrium in trigger strategies with thresholds x^* and θ^*. As such, a trader attacks the fixed parity whenever he receives a signal smaller than x^*, and the attack is successful if the realized fundamental state of the economy is lower than θ^*. The threshold for the fundamental index was given by

$$\theta^*(\alpha, \beta, y) = \Phi\left(\frac{\alpha}{\sqrt{\beta}}[\theta^* - y] - \sqrt{1 + \frac{\alpha}{\beta}}\Phi^{-1}\left(\frac{t}{D}\right)\right) . \tag{10.1}$$

The notation indicates that θ^* is a function which depends (among others) on the precision parameters α and β and the prior mean y. As has been shown by Heinemann (2000), for $\frac{\beta}{\alpha} \to \infty$ the equilibrium threshold θ^* converges to

$$\theta_0^* = 1 - \frac{t}{D} . \tag{10.2}$$

This limit point has the property that it is a best response to each agent believing that the proportion of attacking agents has a uniform distribution in $[0, 1]$ (Morris and Shin, 2000).

Propositions 9.6 and 9.7 of the last chapter showed that θ^* rises with increasing precision of private information β, if and only if

$$\theta^*(\alpha, \beta, y) < y + \frac{1}{\sqrt{\alpha + \beta}}\Phi^{-1}(\frac{t}{D}) . \tag{10.3}$$

Moreover, θ^* rises with increasing α, if and only if

$$\theta^*(\alpha, \beta, y) > y + \frac{1}{2\sqrt{\alpha + \beta}}\Phi^{-1}(\frac{t}{D}) . \tag{10.4}$$

Define y_β as the solution to (10.3) with equality and y_α as solution to (10.4) with equality. For $y < \min\{y_\alpha, y_\beta\}$, increasing the precision of private signals, β, and decreasing α reduce the probability of an attack. For $y > \max\{y_\alpha, y_\beta\}$ the effects are reverse. Yet, since θ^* itself depends on α and β, it cannot be concluded that a central bank should commit to accurate private and no public information under bad prior fundamentals and the reverse if prior fundamentals are good.

Even more problematic is an interpretation that the central bank should choose the precision of its released information posterior to the realization of state θ. The equilibrium, as derived, relies on constant precisions for all posterior realizations. If these would change across states, conditional probabilities would have to take account of that, which changes the whole equilibrium and basically makes it algebraically untractable.

In order to analyze the effects of α and β in more detail and find the exogenous conditions for optimal values of the precision parameters, Heinemann and Metz (2002) point out that one has to be careful in defining the timing and structure of events in the model. In the following we will depict their approach which extends the model of Chap. 9 by assuming that the central bank can influence the distribution of fundamentals and the precision of private information before observing the fundamental state. In particular, they analyze a game with the following stages. In the first stage, the central bank decides on parameters α and β in order to minimize the probability of a successful speculative attack, based on the market sentiment. While selecting optimal values of α and β, the central bank in any case tries to avoid instabilities arising from multiple equilibria. This restricts her choice to parameters, for which uniqueness condition

$$\beta \geq \frac{\alpha^2}{2\pi} \tag{10.5}$$

holds. In a second stage, nature selects the fundamental state from the distribution $\theta \sim N(y, \frac{1}{\alpha})$. Speculators receive private signals $x_i|\theta \sim N(\theta, \frac{1}{\beta})$ in the third stage. Additionally, they get to know the distribution of θ without learning θ itself, though, and decide on either attacking the fixed parity or not to do so. In the final stage, the central bank observes the proportion l of attacking speculators and abandons the peg whenever $l > \theta$, and keeps the peg otherwise.

Stages two to four are the same as analyzed in the previous chapter. The addendum by Heinemann and Metz (2002) as delineated in this chapter is the analysis of the optimal choice of fundamental variance $\frac{1}{\alpha}$ and the precision of private information β in the initial stage of the game.

10.2 Optimal Risk Taking and Information Policy

In order to analyze the optimal policy for the central bank, Heinemann and Metz (2002) take account of an even more comprehensive definition of crisis probability compared to the previous chapter. Whereas before, the probability of a currency crisis has simply been defined to be proportional to the trigger value θ^*, thereby taking into consideration that a currency crisis is going to occur whenever the realized fundamental state is worse than θ^*, the current definition goes one step further. Here, it is not only accounted for the length of the devaluation interval, but also for the distribution of θ, so that the probability of a crisis is given as

$$\mathrm{Prob}(\theta \leq \theta^*) = \Phi(\sqrt{\alpha}[\theta^*(\alpha, \beta, y) - y]) \ .$$

Hence, the central bank's optimization problem at stage 1 of the model is

$$\min_{\alpha,\beta} \Phi(\sqrt{\alpha}[\theta^*(\alpha,\beta,y) - y]) \quad \text{s.t. (10.1) and (10.5)} . \qquad (10.6)$$

The central bank's choice on β is a commitment to supply private agents with well specified kinds of information at stage 2. Following Cukierman and Meltzer (1986), Faust and Svensson (2000), and Illing (1998), economic transparency can be viewed as a high precision of private signals. The higher β, the more reliable are private signals and the better can private agents infer the information held by the central bank. The central bank's choice on α may be interpreted as monetary policy, influencing the real economy and leading to more or less risk for the economy.

The selected values of α and β are again supposed to be common knowledge. This is a natural assumption for β, since information policy must be determined and information must be reliable to allow Bayesian updating. Common knowledge of α can be justified by rational expectations: even if agents were not informed on the riskiness of economic policy, they would be able to deduce the government's choice of α from solving for the optimal strategy of the government, as the rules of the game are common knowledge. This is even more plausible, since a unique solution can be found for the government's optimization problem for every combination of exogenous parameters. Hence, complete transparency on the model and on the government's objective to minimize the probability of a crisis is assumed.

The prior mean of the fundamental state, y, is treated as an exogenous variable, since the only interest is in optimal risk taking behavior and optimal information policy. In any case, as long as we assume expectations to be rational, a policy that intends to change the mean of the fundamental's distribution would be foreseeable and thus lead to the true mean becoming common knowledge. The prior mean in the model should therefore be interpreted as the solution of such a political process with rational expectations. For a similar reason, cheating on the information policy by the central bank is excluded. Any possible way and incentive to provide one–sided information within the bands that commitments allow, is anticipated by private agents, who correct their posterior beliefs for any such information bias.

In the solution to (10.6), risk taking behavior and the commitment to provide information interact in different ways for different cases of the remaining exogenous parameters t, D and y. Keep in mind that the limit point of the equilibrium threshold for $\frac{\beta}{\alpha} \to \infty$ is given by $\theta_0^* = 1 - \frac{t}{D}$. The government therefore can always approach this default point by choosing a sufficiently large precision of private information β.

The analysis of optimal risk taking and information policy by Heinemann and Metz (2002) proceeds in two steps. First, it is solved for the optimal precision of private information β for any given α. Afterwards, the optimal risk parameter is searched for, given that information policy has already been chosen optimally.[2] The first step thus requires to find solutions to

$$\min_{\beta} \Phi\left(\sqrt{\alpha}\,[\theta^*(\alpha,\beta,y) - y]\right) \qquad \text{s.t. (10.1) and (10.5) hold .} \tag{10.7}$$

The derivative of the prior probability of a crisis with respect to precision β is given by

$$\frac{d\Phi(\sqrt{\alpha}[\theta^*(\alpha,\beta,y) - y])}{d\beta} = \phi(\sqrt{\alpha}[\theta^*(\alpha,\beta,y) - y]) \cdot \sqrt{\alpha}\frac{\partial\theta^*(\alpha,\beta,y)}{\partial\beta} . \tag{10.8}$$

Since $\phi(\cdot)$ takes on positive values always, it can be seen that the optimal choice of β only depends on the partial derivative of θ^* with respect to β. Note, that the range of optimal values for β is bounded below by the uniqueness condition. The following proposition states the results:

Proposition 10.1. (Heinemann and Metz, 2002)
The precision of information that minimizes the probability of a speculative attack for given variance of fundamentals $\frac{1}{\alpha}$ *is*

$$\beta^*(\alpha) = \begin{cases} = \frac{\alpha^2}{2\pi} & \text{if } y > 1 - \frac{t}{D} \text{ and } D < 2t \\ = \frac{\alpha^2}{2\pi} & \text{if } y > 1 - \frac{t}{D} \text{ and } D > 2t \text{ and } \alpha \geq \tilde{\alpha} \\ = \tilde{\beta}(\alpha) & \text{if } y > 1 - \frac{t}{D} \text{ and } D > 2t \text{ and } \alpha < \tilde{\alpha} \\ = \frac{\alpha^2}{2\pi} & \text{if } y < 1 - \frac{t}{D} \text{ and } D < 2t \text{ and } \alpha \leq \hat{\alpha} \\ \to \infty & \text{if } y < 1 - \frac{t}{D} \text{ and } D < 2t \text{ and } \alpha > \hat{\alpha} \\ \to \infty & \text{if } y < 1 - \frac{t}{D} \text{ and } D > 2t \end{cases}$$

with $\tilde{\beta}(\alpha)$ *defined by*

$$\theta^*(\alpha,\tilde{\beta},y) = y + \frac{1}{\sqrt{\alpha+\tilde{\beta}}}\Phi^{-1}\left(\frac{t}{D}\right) ,$$

$\tilde{\alpha}$ *defined by*

$$\theta^*(\tilde{\alpha},\tilde{\beta}(\tilde{\alpha}),y) = \theta^*(\tilde{\alpha},\beta^{min}(\tilde{\alpha}),y) ,$$

and $\hat{\alpha}$ *defined by*

$$1 - \frac{t}{D} = \Phi\left(\sqrt{2\pi}(1 - \frac{t}{D} - y) - \sqrt{\frac{1+2\pi}{\hat{\alpha}}}\,\Phi^{-1}\left(\frac{t}{D}\right)\right) .$$

[2] The sequence of solution steps is chosen due to simplicity reasons. The results do not change by first solving for the optimal α and then searching the optimal β given the already optimal risk.

Proof:
From (10.3), we know that the threshold value θ^* increases in precision β, whenever $\theta^*(\alpha, \beta, y) < y + \frac{1}{\sqrt{\alpha+\beta}}\Phi^{-1}(\frac{t}{D})$. In case that inequality (10.3) is satisfied, it is optimal to choose the lowest possible value of β. In contrast, if $\theta^*(\alpha, \beta, y) > y + \frac{1}{\sqrt{\alpha+\beta}}\Phi^{-1}(\frac{t}{D})$ holds, so that θ^* decreases in β, the optimal choice calls for an infinitely high value of β. The proof of proposition 10.1 therefore requires to analyze the influence of β on the left-hand-side (l.h.s.) and right-hand-side (r.h.s.) of inequality (10.3). Recall that for infinitely precise private signals, the equilibrium value θ^* (and as such the l.h.s. of (10.3)) converges to the constant $\theta_0^* = 1 - \frac{t}{D}$. For the r.h.s., we find that it converges to y for $\beta \to \infty$. Convergence is from above, whenever $\Phi^{-1}(\frac{t}{D}) > 0 \Leftrightarrow D < 2t$, and from below for $D > 2t$. We therefore need to distinguish four cases, defined by either combination of $y >$ [<] θ_0^* and $D <$ [>] $2t$, in order to find the value of β which minimizes θ^* for given α.

Case 1: $y > \theta_0^* = 1 - \frac{t}{D}$ and $D < 2t$.
This is the case of a good market sentiment and a low payoff from a successful attack on the fixed parity. Here, inequality (10.3) holds for large β, since for $\beta \to \infty$ the l.h.s. approaches θ_0^*, while the r.h.s. converges to y, with $y > \theta_0^*$. Reducing β, therefore, lowers threshold θ^*, while it increases the right hand side of (10.3). Hence, (10.3) holds for all β. Optimal information policy then is to choose the smallest β that guarantees a unique equilibrium:

$$\beta^*(\alpha) = \beta^{\min} := \frac{\alpha^2}{2\,\pi} \,.$$

This result can also be seen from Fig. 10.1. The vertical dashed line gives the minimum value of β, which is just sufficiently high to guarantee uniqueness of equilibrium.

Case 2: $y > \theta_0^* = 1 - \frac{t}{D}$ and $D > 2t$.
Again, we find (10.3) to hold for $\beta \to \infty$, so that for high values of β, θ^* increases in β. Yet, reducing β from high levels not only lowers threshold θ^*, but also reduces the r.h.s. of (10.3). This follows from $D > 2t$, so that the r.h.s. converges to y from below. If there is some $\tilde{\beta} > \beta^{min}$, at which (10.3) holds with equality, a further reduction in β would increase the threshold θ^*, while the r.h.s. would continue to fall. Since θ^* is continuous, $\tilde{\beta}$ must exist and is delineated in Fig. 10.2. The optimal precision of private information in case 2 is then given by

$$\beta^*(\alpha) = \max\left\{\tilde{\beta},\, \beta^{\min}\right\} \,.$$

However, $\tilde{\beta}$ is only feasible if the uniqueness condition is satisfied as well. Thus, whether $\tilde{\beta}$ is feasible depends on the value of α as follows: inserting (10.3) as equality into (10.1), we get

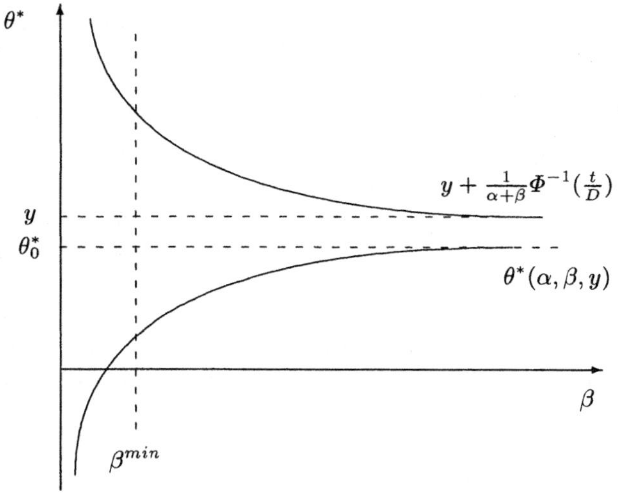

Fig. 10.1. Influence of β on θ^* for $y > 1 - \frac{t}{D}$ and $D < 2t$

$$y + \frac{\Phi^{-1}(\frac{t}{D})}{\sqrt{\alpha + \tilde{\beta}}} = \Phi\left(-\sqrt{\frac{\tilde{\beta}}{\alpha + \tilde{\beta}}}\,\Phi^{-1}(\frac{t}{D})\right) . \tag{10.9}$$

Total differentiation of (10.9) delivers

$$\frac{\partial \tilde{\beta}}{\partial \alpha} = \frac{\sqrt{\tilde{\beta}} + \tilde{\beta}\,\phi(\cdot)}{\alpha\,\phi(\cdot) - \sqrt{\tilde{\beta}}} . \tag{10.10}$$

Since the denominator of (10.10) is negative for $\tilde{\beta} > \beta^{\min}$, $\tilde{\beta}$ decreases in α. As β^{min} is increasing in α, there exists a unique $\tilde{\alpha}$, such that $\tilde{\beta}(\tilde{\alpha}) = \frac{\tilde{\alpha}^2}{2\pi}$. For $\alpha \geq \tilde{\alpha}$, the optimal precision of private information is then given by $\beta^{\min}$. For $\alpha < \tilde{\alpha}$ however, the optimum is at $\tilde{\beta}$.

Case 3: $y < \theta_0^* = 1 - \frac{t}{D}$ and $D < 2t$.
For $\beta \to \infty$, the r.h.s. of (10.3) approaches y from above and is smaller than θ^* in this case. Hence, θ^* decreases in β for large values of β. Reducing β from high levels, therefore, raises both sides of (10.3), so that eventually there may exist some $\hat{\beta} > \beta^{min}$, at which (10.3) holds with equality. A further reduction of β lowers threshold θ^*. As indicated by Fig. 10.3, the optimal information policy is then given either by the minimal precision required for uniqueness, $\beta^{\min}$ or by its highest possible value $\beta \to \infty$.

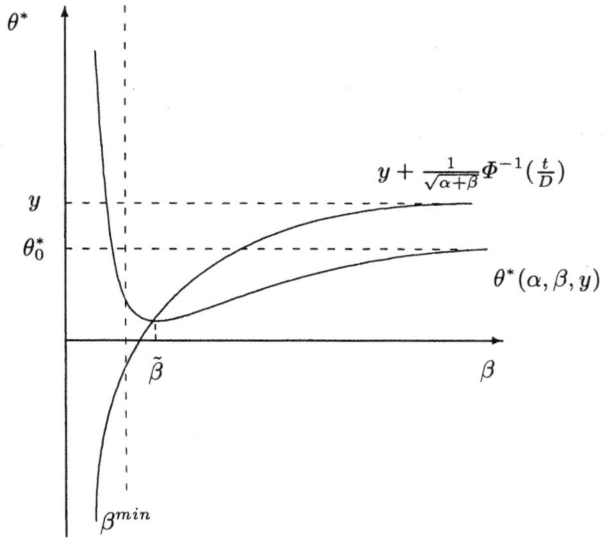

Fig. 10.2. Influence of β on θ^* for $y > 1 - \frac{t}{D}$ and $D > 2t$

Which of the two corner solutions yields the lower threshold θ^* depends on α. For $\beta \to \infty$, the threshold is given by θ_0^*. Choosing the lowest possible value, β^{min}, instead yields

$$\theta^*(\alpha, \beta^{\min}(\alpha), y) = \Phi\left(\sqrt{2\,\pi}\,(\theta^* - y) - \sqrt{1 + \frac{2\,\pi}{\alpha}}\,\Phi^{-1}(\frac{t}{D})\right) . \tag{10.11}$$

For $\alpha \to 0$, this threshold converges to $\Phi(-\infty) = 0$. But what happens for higher values of α? Total differentiation of (10.11) gives

$$\frac{\partial\,\theta^*(\alpha, \beta^{\min}(\alpha), y)}{\partial\,\alpha} = \frac{\phi(\cdot)\,\pi\,\sqrt{\alpha}}{\alpha^2\,\sqrt{\alpha + 2\,\pi}\,(1 - \sqrt{2\,\pi}\,\phi(\cdot))}\,\Phi^{-1}\left(\frac{t}{D}\right) . \tag{10.12}$$

Using the fact that $\phi(\cdot) \leq \frac{1}{\sqrt{2\,\pi}}$ with strict inequality almost everywhere, shows that $\theta^*(\alpha, \beta^{\min}(\alpha), y)$ increases in α. Hence, there must be a unique $\hat{\alpha}$, for which both corner solutions lead to the same threshold. For $\alpha \leq \hat{\alpha}$, optimal precision of private information is then given by $\beta^{\min}$. For $\alpha > \hat{\alpha}$, it is optimal to choose $\beta \to \infty$.

Case 4: $y < \theta_0^* = 1 - \frac{t}{D}$ and $D > 2\,t$.
In this case, (10.3) is violated for high values of β, since $y < \theta_0^*$. Reducing β raises threshold θ^* and lowers the r.h.s. of (10.3), since convergence to y is from below, as $D > 2t$. This can also be seen from Fig. 10.4. Threshold

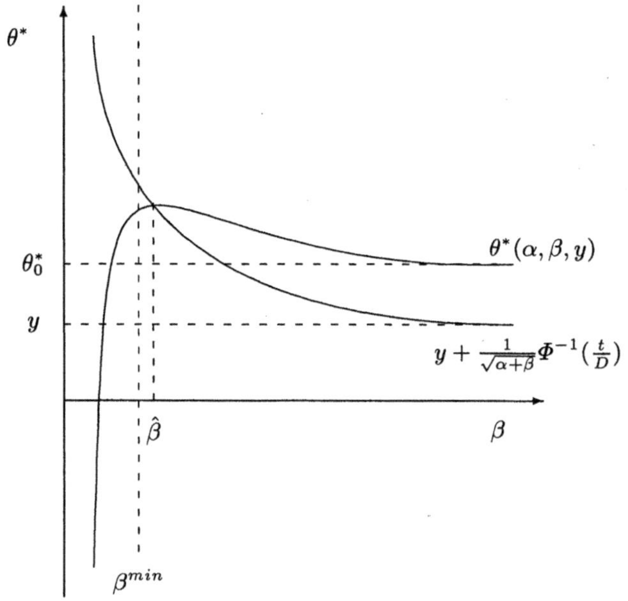

Fig. 10.3. Influence of β on θ^* for $y < 1 - \frac{t}{D}$ and $D < 2t$

θ^* unambiguously rises with decreasing precision of private information. In this case, the best information policy is to choose the highest possible β, i.e. $\beta^*(\alpha) \to \infty$. □

In the following we will give an informal reasoning for the solution to the optimal information precision according to the various cases that must be distinguished. Quite clearly, in order to characterize optimal information policy we have to differentiate between prior fundamentals being good, i.e. $y > \theta_0^* = 1 - \frac{t}{D}$, or bad, i.e. $y < \theta_0^* = 1 - \frac{t}{D}$. Additionally, we have to take account of the ratio of payoff from a successful attack to twice the cost of this action. For $D > 2t$, there is a high prior incentive to attack the fixed parity. In this case, even with equal probability of an attack being successful or unsuccessful, speculators would always want to attack. For $D < 2t$, however, the prior incentive to attack is rather low.

From (10.8) we know that precision parameter β can only influence the probability of a currency crisis through its effect on the threshold value θ^*, but has no impact on the distribution of θ. Speculators will attack the fixed parity, whenever they expect the actual fundamental state to be lower than the switching value θ^*. Based on their information, speculators believe the fundamental value to be equal to

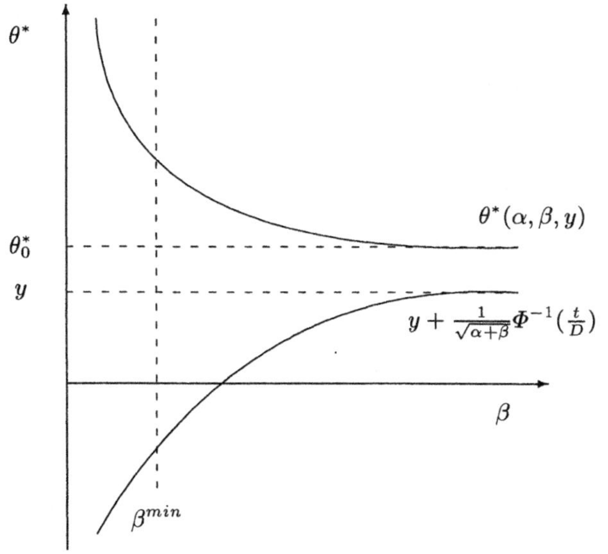

Fig. 10.4. Influence of β on θ^* for $y < 1 - \frac{t}{D}$ and $D > 2t$

$$E(\theta|x_i) = \frac{\alpha}{\alpha+\beta}y + \frac{\beta}{\alpha+\beta}x_i \; . \tag{10.13}$$

The higher the precision β of private information, the more weight speculators will attach to their private signals and the less weight to the common prior y. Denote this as the "weight-effect" of β. The sign of this weight-effect follows from inequality (10.3), i.e. it depends on whether $\theta^* > (<) y + \frac{1}{\sqrt{\alpha+\beta}}\Phi^{-1}(\frac{t}{D})$.

In case 1 with good prior fundamentals and a low prior incentive to attack ($y > 1 - \frac{t}{D}$ and $D < 2t$), the optimal information policy constitutes of disseminating private information with the lowest possible precision, just sufficiently high to guarantee uniqueness of equilibrium. By choosing the minimum value for β, the government tries to incite speculators to only take into account their good prior information when deciding on their optimal action. Since the incentive to attack is low in this case, it is optimal to make speculators neglect even potentially good private signals.

In case 2 with good priors but a high incentive to attack ($y > 1 - \frac{t}{D}$ and $D > 2t$), this reasoning no longer always holds. Since the prior incentive to attack is rather high in this case, the central bank will want to take into account a possible usage of private information. Whether it is reasonable to disseminate private information of a higher-than-minimal precision, depends on the chosen risk, respectively the chosen precision of public information. Whenever α is high, so that the fundamental state will be quite close to the commonly expected level y, it is again optimal to make speculators neglect their private information. Here, public information is good enough and precise enough to make speculators refrain from attacking. However, if a large risk has been chosen and α is low, optimal information policy requires a specific non-minimum value of β being chosen. This precision of private information allows speculators to better infer the true fundamental state from their signals than in the case with minimal β, so that they will only want to attack for really bad signals.

Case 3 with bad prior fundamentals and a low incentive to attack ($y < 1-t/D$ and $D < 2t$) presents a similar problem for choosing the optimal precision of private information. With bad expected fundamentals, the government should quite generally want to disseminate very precise private information in order to make speculators neglect their bad prior information. This line of reasoning holds whenever the chosen risk is low, i.e. if α is high. Then, the true fundamental state will be close to the commonly expected value, so that indeed the probability of a currency crisis can be reduced by making speculators rely almost exclusively on their private signals, which might be good even for a bad prior. However, if the chosen risk is high (α is low), the realized fundamental state might not be too bad, so that the central bank does not want speculators to put too much weight on their private signals, which may always turn out to be bad. In this case, the optimal value for β is the minimum value that just guarantees uniqueness of equilibrium.

In case 4 with bad prior fundamentals and a high incentive to attack ($y < 1-\frac{t}{D}$ and $D > 2t$), it is intuitive from the above reasoning that the government should want to disseminate infinitely precise private signals. Since this case displays the highest overall incentive to attack, following from both the high payoff and the bad expected fundamental state, it is optimal for the central bank to induce speculators to completely neglect their bad prior information. Instead, when speculators rely on their private information exclusively, they will refrain from attacking at least if they receive good private signals.

In order to fully solve the optimization problem (10.6), we next look for the precision of the fundamental's distribution that minimizes the probability of a speculative attack, given that information policy has been adjusted to $\beta^*(\alpha)$. Here, we minimize over α

$$\min_{\alpha} \text{prob}(\theta < \theta^*(\alpha, \beta^*(\alpha), y) = \Phi\left(\sqrt{\alpha}\,[\theta^*(\cdot) - y]\right) , \tag{10.14}$$

subject to the conditions required for a unique threshold θ^*. Note that

$$\frac{\partial \text{prob}(\theta < \theta^*(\cdot))}{\partial \alpha} = \phi\left(\sqrt{\alpha}\,[\theta^* - y]\right) \left(\frac{1}{2\sqrt{\alpha}}\,[\theta^* - y] + \sqrt{\alpha}\,\frac{\partial \theta^*}{\partial \alpha}\right) . \tag{10.15}$$

Thus, in contrast to β, risk parameter α does not only influence the probability of a currency crisis by affecting θ^*, which corresponds to the last term in parenthesis, but also by changing directly the variance of the distribution of fundamentals. This second effect is reflected by the first term in parenthesis and will be seen to be very important for the overall effect of α on the danger of a crisis. The overall solution to optimization problem (10.6) is given by the following proposition.

Proposition 10.2. (Heinemann and Metz, 2002)
Optimal risk taking behavior and associated optimal precision of private information that minimize the probability of a crisis are

$$\alpha^* = \begin{cases} \to \infty & \text{if } y > 1 - \frac{t}{D} \\ \to 0 & \text{if } y < 1 - \frac{t}{D} \end{cases}$$

and

$$\beta^*(\alpha^*) = \begin{cases} \frac{\alpha^2}{2\pi} & \text{if } y > 1 - \frac{t}{D} \text{ or } D < 2t \\ \to \infty & \text{if } y < 1 - \frac{t}{D} \text{ and } D > 2t\,. \end{cases}$$

Proof:
To solve equation (10.6), we look for the risk parameter α (respectively $\frac{1}{\alpha}$) that minimizes the probability of a speculative attack, conditional on information policy being given by $\beta^*(\alpha)$. Thus we minimize (10.14) over α, subject to the uniqueness condition $\beta \geq \frac{\alpha^2}{2\pi}$. From the derivative of (10.14) with respect to α, as given by equation (10.15), we see that the optimal value of α is not only contingent on the influence of α on the threshold θ^*, but also on whether θ^* is higher or lower than y. If both terms in parenthesis are negative (positive), optimal policy requires the government to choose the highest (lowest) possible α, i.e. the lowest (highest) possible risk. Again, since the government can always approach θ_0^* by choosing to disseminate infinitely precise private information, $\theta^*(\alpha, \beta^*(\alpha), y)$ can never exceed θ_0^*.

Case 1: $y > \theta_0^* = 1 - \frac{t}{D}$ and $D < 2t$.
In this case, we have $\beta^*(\alpha) = \beta^{\min}$. As has been shown above, $\theta^*(\alpha, \beta^{\min}(\alpha), y)$ rises in α for $D < 2t$. For $\alpha \to 0$, this threshold converges to zero. From (10.14) we see that for $\alpha \to 0$, the probability of a successful attack approaches $\frac{1}{2}$. For positive α, in contrast, there is a positive probability for a successful attack that converges to zero if $\alpha \to \infty$, since θ^* can never exceed θ_0^*, which is smaller than y in this case. Hence, both expressions in parenthesis in (10.15) are negative, so that the government should avoid any risks and choose $\alpha^* \to \infty$.

Case 2: $y > \theta_0^* = 1 - \frac{t}{D}$ and $D > 2t$.
In this case, the optimal precision of private information is given by $\beta^{\min}$ for $\alpha < \tilde{\alpha}$ and $\tilde{\beta}(\alpha)$ otherwise. As $\Phi^{-1}\left(\frac{t}{D}\right) < 0$ in this case, (10.12) shows that $\theta^*(\alpha, \beta^{\min}(\alpha), y)$ is decreasing in α. Using the implicit function theorem, we find that

$$\frac{\mathrm{d}\,\theta^*(\alpha, \tilde{\beta}(\alpha), y)}{\mathrm{d}\,\alpha} = \left.\frac{\partial \theta^*(\alpha, \beta, y)}{\partial \alpha}\right|_{\beta = \tilde{\beta}(\alpha)} = \frac{\phi(\cdot)}{\sqrt{\tilde{\beta}} - \alpha\,\phi(\cdot)}\,\frac{\Phi^{-1}(t/D)}{2\sqrt{\alpha + \tilde{\beta}}}\,, \quad (10.16)$$

which is negative for $\tilde{\beta} > \beta^{\min}$, i.e. for $\tilde{\beta}$ being feasible. Thus, for both $\tilde{\beta}$ and β^{min}, increasing α reduces θ^*, so that the second term in parenthesis in (10.15) is negative. Furthermore, $\theta^* \leq \theta_0^* < y$. Hence, (10.15) implies that the probability of a speculative attack is decreasing with rising α, and optimal government policy is given by minimizing economic risks and choosing $\alpha \to \infty$.

Case 3: $y < \theta_0^* = 1 - \frac{t}{D}$ and $D < 2t$.
Here, β^* is either minimal or as large as possible. For $\beta \to \infty$, the threshold value converges to $\theta_0^* = 1 - \frac{t}{D}$, which is independent of α. Thus, $\frac{\partial\theta^*}{\partial\alpha} = 0$. Since $y < \theta_0^*$ in this case, (10.15) is positive, so that the optimal α associated with an infinitely high precision is given by $\alpha \to 0$. The probability of a currency crisis is then given by

$$\text{prob}(\theta < \theta^*(\alpha \to 0, \beta \to \infty, y)) = \Phi(0) = \frac{1}{2}\,. \tag{10.17}$$

However, recall that the maximal value for β is only optimal for large values of α, i.e. for $\alpha > \hat{\alpha}$. Hence, the combination of infinitely precise information and maximal risk cannot be optimal in this case. For the second option, $\beta \to \beta^{min} = \frac{\alpha^2}{2\pi}$ and $D < 2t$, we know that $\theta^*(\alpha, \beta^{\min}(\alpha), y)$ rises in α. For the overall influence of α on the probability of a currency crisis, we have to analyze the whole expression in parenthesis in (10.15), however. As long as $\frac{1}{2\sqrt{\alpha}}[\theta^* - y] + \sqrt{\alpha}\frac{d\theta^*}{d\alpha}$ is positive, the optimal α associated with minimal β is zero. If the expression is negative, the largest possible α should be chosen. Thus, $\alpha \to 0$ is optimal, whenever $y < \theta^*(\alpha, \beta^{min}, y) + 2\alpha\frac{\partial\theta^*}{\partial\alpha}$. This condition indeed is satisfied for $\alpha \to 0$, since $\theta^*(\alpha \to 0, \beta^{min}, y) = 1 - \frac{t}{D} > y$ and $\frac{\partial\theta^*}{\partial\alpha} = 0$. In contrast, $\alpha \to \infty$ would be optimal for $y > \theta^*(\alpha, \beta^{min}, y) + 2\alpha\frac{\partial\theta^*}{\partial\alpha}$. For $\alpha \to \infty$, this condition cannot be satisfied, though. Hence, the probability of a speculative attack is rising in α, and the government should gamble for resurrection by choosing the highest possible risk, i.e. $\alpha^* \to 0$. The associated crisis probability is given by $\frac{1}{2}$, which is the best the government can achieve in this case with bad priors and a low prior incentive to attack.

Case 4: $y < \theta_0^*$ and $D > 2t$.
In this case it is optimal to choose the highest precision of information, $\beta^*(\alpha) \to \infty$. This leads to the critical threshold being given by θ_0^*, which is independent of α. The probability of a successful attack is then given by $\text{prob}(\theta < \theta_0^*)$. For $y < \theta_0^*$, this probability exceeds $\frac{1}{2}$, and decreases with rising variance of fundamentals $\frac{1}{\alpha}$. Again, the government will gamble for resurrection and choose $\alpha^* \to 0$. □

At this point, again, let us give an informal interpretation of the solution to (10.6). Before going through the four different cases, be reminded of the various effects that α and β have on the probability of a crisis. As described earlier, precision parameter β influences the danger of a currency crisis through the weight-effect only. The more precise private information is, the higher the weight will be that agents attach to their private signals in determining the expected value of fundamentals.

From (10.13), it follows that α exerts a weight-effect as well, which follows the same reasoning as described above. Here, the sign of the effect stems from inequality (10.4), i.e. α has a positive (negative) impact on θ^*, if $\theta^*(\alpha, \beta, y) > (<) y + \frac{1}{2\sqrt{\alpha+\beta}} \Phi^{-1}(\frac{t}{D})$. Yet, a change in α additionally influences the distribution of fundamentals around the prior mean y. As such, even with speculators keeping the weights of their information parts constant, an increase in α can make a currency crisis more or less likely, simply by making the distribution of θ more dense around its mean. The sign of this "distribution-effect" is contingent on whether the threshold θ^* lies to the right or to the left of the common prior y. Whenever $\theta^* < y$, increasing α will decrease the probability of fundamentals being realized which are worse than θ^* (and which would therefore lead to a successful attack). However, for $\theta^* > y$, higher values of α are associated with a higher probability of a currency crisis, due to the higher density of the distribution function. As we will see, the weight- and the distribution-effect of α may have opposite signs, which makes the determination of optimal risk-taking rather difficult.

For good priors, $y > \theta_0^* = 1 - \frac{t}{D}$, it is always optimal to minimize risk ($\alpha \to \infty$) and to disseminate as imprecise private information as possible ($\beta \to \beta^{min} = \frac{\alpha^2}{2\pi}$). For good priors, the central bank obviously tries to incite speculators to attach the largest possible weight to their good prior information. Due to the weight-effect, the threshold θ^* will therefore decrease. Additionally, by choosing a low risk, the central bank tries to lock-in the good state. The distribution-effect of α decreases the probability of a crisis, since with a high α the distribution of fundamentals will be very dense around the good expected fundamental state, while the switching value of $\theta^*(\alpha, \beta, y)$ will be very low. For good prior expectations, therefore, a lower risk (i.e. high α) minimizes the probability of a currency crisis through both the distribution- and the weight-effect.

The influence of information precision in the case of good priors is equally unequivocal. Here, it is optimal to disseminate information with minimal precision. This policy strengthens the weight-effect of α additionally, since speculators will tend to neglect private information in calculating the posterior expected fundamental value and rely almost exclusively on the good prior information y. Minimizing the precision of private information is necessary in this case, since even with good priors, there might exist bad private signals with positive probability, which would induce speculators to attack rather than to abstain from attacking.

For bad prior expectations, $y < \theta_0^* = 1 - \frac{t}{D}$, however, deriving the optimal combination of risk and information precision is more complicated. This is due to the fact that for bad priors, the weight- and the distribution-effect of α not necessarily have to bear the same sign. Additionally, we have to distinguish between a high prior incentive to attack, caused by a high payoff from a successful attack relative to twice the costs of this action, and a low prior incentive to attack.

In the case of bad prior expectations and high payoff, i.e. $y < \theta_0^* = 1 - \frac{t}{D}$ and $D > 2t$, speculators have the highest incentive to attack and the fixed parity is therefore very vulnerable. Without any prior information and with Laplacian beliefs,[3] speculators will be likely to attack. This is due to the fact that with equal probability of an attack being successful or not, the expected payoff from attacking is always higher than the costs of doing so. Concerning the optimal risk taking, it is intuitive to see that the government will certainly want to maximize fundamental risk (i.e. minimize α). Since for extremely bad prior expectations θ^* will be higher than y, the probability of fundamentals lower than θ^* being realized can be reduced by decreasing the density of their distribution function, i.e. by decreasing α. Due to the distribution-effect, therefore, the highest possible risk should be chosen, so that the central bank simply gambles for success. Additionally, speculators will tend to neglect the bad prior information for very low values of α, following the weight-effect. For bad priors and a high prior incentive to attack, both effects of α therefore have the same positive effect on the probability of a crisis, so that $\alpha \to 0$ should be chosen.

Concerning information policy, we find that in this case of bad prior beliefs and a high payoff from attacking, it is optimal to disseminate private signals with highest possible precision ($\beta \to \infty$). The intuition behind this result refers to the aforementioned Laplacian beliefs. Due to the high payoff from a successful attack, speculators would certainly attack if they had no or only diffuse prior information about the fundamental state. Thus, an attack might be prevented by endowing them with rather precise private information, since even for bad priors there is a positive probability that private signals might turn out to be quite good. Hence, if speculators are (better) able to infer the true fundamental state from their information, they will refrain from attacking, at least for good signals. Optimal information policy therefore induces speculators to attach the highest possible weight to their private information.

For bad priors and a low prior incentive to attack, i.e. $y < \theta_0^* = 1 - \frac{t}{D}$ and $D < 2t$ exactly the reverse effects hold for the analysis of optimal information. Since with Laplacian beliefs speculators would abstain from attacking, it is optimal to disseminate very imprecise private information. Otherwise, speculators would be able to infer the true state from their signals and attack whenever they perceive the true fundamental state to be bad. Since bad signals may occur with positive probability, it is better for the central bank to keep speculators completely in the dark informationwise. As such, it is optimal to choose minimal precision of private information that is just sufficient to guarantee a unique equilibrium.

[3] Agents hold Laplacian beliefs, if they attach equal probability to all possible states.

With respect to the optimal risk taken in this case, we find that due to the weight-effect the central bank should decide on a very high risk, i.e. a low α, so that speculators tend to neglect the bad priors. Together with completely imprecise private information, agents are then almost completely in the dark about the economic state. Since the prior incentive to attack is low in this case, speculators can be expected to indeed refrain from attacking. However, the distribution-effect is not completely in line with the weight-effect in this case. Whereas it is always optimal to decrease α due to the weight-effect, a lower α will partially increase the danger of a crisis whenever threshold θ^* is lower than y. If this distribution-effect were strong enough to offset the weight-effect, the optimal policy in this case would be to take the lowest possible risk, $\alpha \to \infty$. The distribution effect is strongest when θ^* is close to y, i.e. only slightly lower than y. Decreasing α due to the weight-effect, however, reduces the threshold θ^*, so that the impact of the distribution-effect loses its importance. Thus, the weight-effect may be expected to dominate for all constellations of parameters, so that optimal policy requires to choose the highest possible risk. By letting $\alpha \to 0$, speculators are forced to neglect their bad prior information. Since optimal private signals are not very informative either, agents are kept completely in the dark about the fundamental state, so that they will attack or refrain from attacking with equal probability. The overall likelihood of a crisis is then given by $\frac{1}{2}$.

10.3 Conclusion

A summary of the results for optimal risk taking and optimal information policy can be found in Fig. 10.5. As can be seen, the central bank can only try to completely prevent a speculative attack on the fixed parity through optimal policy, if the market sentiment is sufficiently good, i.e. if $y > 1 - \frac{t}{D}$. From cases 1 and 2 it can be concluded that, whenever speculators commonly believe the fundamental state of the economy to be sufficiently strong, the central bank can strengthen this belief by choosing minimal risk and minimal precision of private information. Following this policy, fundamentals will be believed ex-post to be very close to the good prior mean, while at the same time individual private signals are considered as worthless. Hence, speculators are very much inclined to coordinate on the "not-attack" equilibrium. The probability of a currency crisis is reduced to a level of zero. Note that this result always holds for good prior expectations concerning θ, irrespective of a high prior incentive to attack ($D > 2t$) or a low incentive ($D < 2t$).

However, this minimum probability of a crisis is not attainable for the central bank in the case of a bad market sentiment. If $y < 1 - \frac{t}{D}$, the central bank can only decrease the danger of a crisis down to a 50:50-chance. This result again holds for both a high and a low incentive to attack. However, the optimal policy mix underlying this result is very different in the case of $D > 2t$ as compared to $D < 2t$.

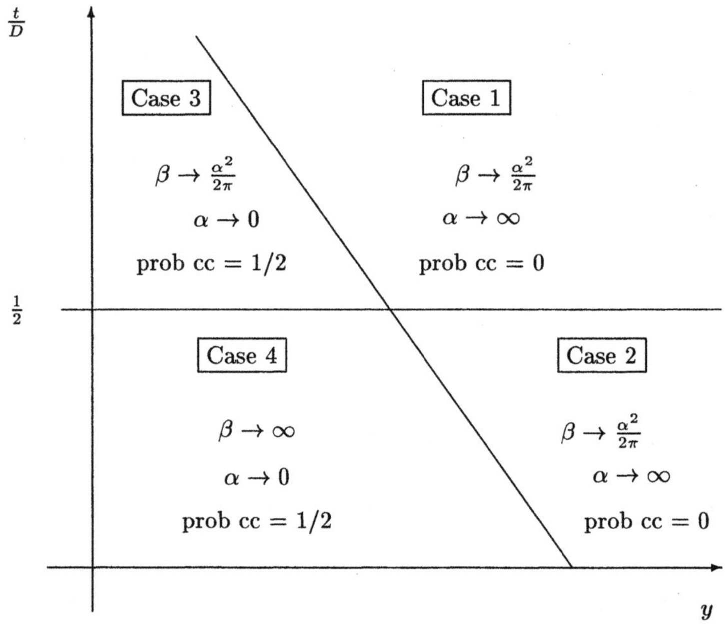

Fig. 10.5. Optimal risk and information policy with associated crisis probabilities

For a high prior incentive to attack the currency, combined with a weak expected fundamental state, the central bank has to choose both maximal fundamental risk and maximal precision of private information in order to minimize the likelihood of a crisis. In case of a low incentive for an attack on the peg combined with a bad market sentiment, however, optimal policy calls for the highest possible risk but the lowest possible precision of private information.

Following from our results, we can draw the conclusion that a central bank trying to minimize the danger of a speculative attack on the fixed parity has to be very careful in selecting the optimal strategy. It is of utmost importance to always bear in mind the common belief on the market about the fundamental state of the economy. In order to illustrate the impact of an incorrect perception of the market sentiment, consider the following example, where the parity is presumed to be very vulnerable due to a high payoff. Assume that the central bank mistakes the market sentiment to be in favor of economic fundamentals and decides to minimize risk and disseminates very imprecise private information. If the market, however, is very pessimistic, i.e. $y < 1 - \frac{t}{D}$, then the chosen combination of risk and information policy may increase the probability of a currency crisis up to a level of 100 per cent, so that the fixed parity will be devalued almost certainly. In contrast, if the central bank had chosen the "correct" policy combination, as appropriate to the case of a pessimistic common belief towards economic fundamentals, she would have decided on a more risky strategy and would have endowed speculators with very precise information. Due to this "correct" risk- and information-policy, the probability of a crisis could have been reduced to a level of $\frac{1}{2}$.

Summarizing, we have to state that even with a low potential payoff from attacking the fixed parity, the central bank is not immune against speculative attacks. The low incentive to attack notwithstanding, a crisis may be triggered by a bad market sentiment concerning the fundamental state, so that the central bank has to be careful to choose the appropriate policy measurements. However, in the case of a low incentive to attack, it is always optimal to disseminate rather imprecise private information.

This no longer holds for the case of a high incentive to attack. This case is especially important, since in countries with an impending currency crisis the fixed exchange rate typically is so strongly overvalued that speculators have a lot to gain from a successful attack on the parity. For the case of such a vulnerable parity, it is therefore crucial that the central bank chooses the correct policy mix in order to minimize the danger of a crisis. Applying the preliminary results of Chap. 9 concerning optimal policy measurements, we moreover find that these predictions have indeed been substantiated by the current chapter's analysis for the case of a vulnerable currency peg. Whenever the market sentiment y is low, the central bank should disseminate completely precise private information and select the largest possible fundamental risk, thereby minimizing the precision of public information. In contrast, for a good prior mean y, the optimal policy requires disseminating very imprecise private information and choosing the lowest possible fundamental risk, so that public information is completely precise.

Part IV

Informational Aspects of Speculators' Size and Dynamics

11

Introduction

The currency crisis models of parts II and III of this book considered only the most basic aspects of currency crises and the influence of information therein. The following chapters will undertake a more comprehensive study of currency crisis situations by taking into account additional aspects. In this respect, we will concentrate on the following issues: heterogeneity of speculators and a dynamic sequence of actions. In each case, we will place special emphasis on possible effects of information.

Chapter 12 is concerned with currency crisis models where speculators are no longer homogeneous as in the previous parts of this study, but may be either "small" or "large". In order to keep the analysis simple, we concentrate on the case where there is only one large trader and a continuum of small speculators on the foreign exchange market. The basic approach of analyzing the impact of a large trader in a currency crisis stems from the work by Corsetti, Dasgupta, Morris and Shin (2001). Empirical evidence for a similar model has been found by Corsetti, Pesenti and Roubini (2001). In the following chapter, we will review these approaches and analyze the impact of a large trader on a fixed exchange rate parity in a global game. In contrast to the model by Corsetti, Dasgupta et al. (2001), however, we assume normally distributed noise parameters, whereas the original model investigated into the general case of non-specific noise distributions. It can be shown that the large trader's influence strongly increases in his size as well as in his possible informational advantage. The intuitive results of the model by Corsetti, Dasgupta et al. (2001) notwithstanding, their model displays several shortcomings concerning the model setup. In order to overcome these difficulties, we therefore present a different model in Sect. 12.2, which also analyzes the influence of a large trader on a currency crisis. This model has been taken from Metz (2002b) and is derived from the original model by Corsetti, Dasgupta et al. (2001) by assuming a slightly different time structure. In this modified approach, we find that the large trader's impact generally depends on the market sentiment. Whenever the market is pessimistic regarding economic fundamentals, it will become even more so, if there is a large trader on the market. The market will get even more aggressive, if the large trader is known to have very precise information about the fundamental state of the economy. The results from both types of models therefore weakly substantiate the widespread belief that large traders may indeed render markets more aggressive and hence increase the danger of a currency crisis. However, they also show that this does not necessarily have to be the case.

Chapter 13 deals with a quite different aspect. Up to now, the analyzed models always assumed that speculators have to decide on their respective actions at the same point in time, thereby independently making a choice on their strategy. Currency crisis situations in reality are no one-shot games, though. Most of the time, speculators seize the opportunity of observing their opponents' moves before acting themselves, although there might be a cost of waiting. Chapter 13 therefore analyzes a dynamic coordination game, in which speculators may delay their actions in order to observe their predecessors' choices. Although a large part of the literature on dynamic financial crises is concerned with informational aspects like herding behavior or informational cascades, only very recently have economists begun to relate these aspects to the framework of global games. After giving an introduction to the notion of herding and cascades, Sect. 13.1 presents the famous models by Banerjee (1993) and Bikhchandani, Hirshleifer and Welch (1992) in order to illustrate herding behavior on financial markets. Section 13.2 delineates one of the most recent models by Dasgupta (2001), which combines the earlier cascades and herding issues with the global games approach. In order to simplify comparisons, we will refer to the context of currency crises, although the original model by Dasgupta has been applied to liquidity crises. Section 13.3 finally combines the dynamic time setting with the analysis of heterogeneous traders in currency crises. The examination here again follows the approach by Corsetti, Dasgupta et al. (2001) and Corsetti, Pesenti et al. (2001). They show how a large trader may signal his "financial weight" and his potential informational advantage to other market participants in order to make them coordinate their actions on his.

12

Currency Crisis Models with Small and Large Traders

During the last years, the activities of large traders on financial markets such as hedge funds, major commercial banks and other highly leveraged institutions (HLIs) have strongly increased. Many analysts as well as policy makers have expressed their concerns that large players may have a disproportionate effect on markets and as such may trigger crises that are not fully justified by fundamentals, hence threatening the stability of the whole financial system.[1]

Following some prominent examples of larger traders' actions on foreign exchange markets and their aftermath (for instance the bitter fight between George Soros and Dr. Mahathir, prime minister of Malaysia, in 1998), the Financial Stability Forum (FSF) in 1999 established a study group on market dynamics to assess the 1998 market turmoil and the role of highly leveraged institutions. Although the group could only find controversial evidence of destabilizing effects on the part of HLIs, its report in 2000 made clear that large traders played a material role during several crisis episodes, among them the ERM crisis in 1992-93, the 1994-95 Mexican peso crisis, the attack on the Thai baht in 1997 and the Malaysian ringgit in 1997-98. Moreover, the last years showed that even in the absence of a crisis, large traders gained importance on financial markets (Chang, Pinegar and Schachter, 1997). In the United States, therefore, major foreign exchange market participants are required by law to regularly give reports on their holdings of foreign currency. Based on these Treasury Foreign Currency reports, it can be found that although the number of "large" traders as defined by the Treasury (an institution qualifies as "large", if it has more than \$50 billion equivalent in foreign exchange contracts in its books) declined, the net dealing positions of large traders have increased over time.

Against this background, theoretical analyses started to concentrate on the role of large speculators in financial crises, notably in currency crises. The

[1] An analysis by Kim and Wei (1997) suggests that large traders' currency speculation makes exchange rates more volatile. However, they conclude that this might be due to large speculators' trading on noise rather than on information.

most important questions that economists tried to answer concerned both the influence of a large trader's size as well as his information's precision. In the context of global games, these aspects have been analyzed extensively by Corsetti, Dasgupta, Morris and Shin (2001) and Corsetti, Pesenti and Roubini (2001). In Sect. 12.1, we will reconsider these approaches in a specific distributional setting. In this respect, we assume normally distributed parameters in order to facilitate comparisons between the two models analyzed in this chapter, but also to compare the results concerning informational influences to the findings of previous chapters. In accordance with the aforementioned authors it can be seen that the large trader's influence strongly depends on his size. Whenever the large speculator has sufficient financial power, the danger of a crisis increases as compared to the case of only small speculators in the market. The size parameter, however, becomes irrelevant, if the large trader is known to exclusively possess completely precise information about economic fundamentals. In the latter case, he always renders the market more aggressive, thereby increasing the probability of a currency crisis. Although the model as taken from Corsetti, Dasgupta et al. (2001) and Corsetti, Pesenti et al. (2001) delivers quite intuitive insights into the large trader's influence on the market, it nonetheless displays some major shortcomings. One of the most startling problems is the assumed asymmetry in the behavior of small and large speculators. Whereas the authors presume that the small traders take into account the behavior of the large agent when deciding on their optimal actions, the large trader is supposed to act irrespective of the rest of the market. This, however, is hard to be confirmed by actual observations. Especially in a dynamic context, any large trader would certainly take account of potential signalling effects of his actions, which might coordinate the actions of small traders. A second shortcoming of the mentioned approach is that it does not allow to solve for the equilibrium explicitly. Since it is not possible to derive closed-form solutions of the equilibrium values, comparative statics analyses become extremely cumbersome.

In order to overcome these difficulties, we additionally analyze the impact of a large trader on a fixed exchange rate parity in a similar but more simplified model in Sect. 12.2. This model is taken from Metz (2002b). Due to the slightly changed time structure as compared to the model by Corsetti, Dasgupta et al. (2001), we are able to treat both small and large speculators symmetrically. Furthermore, we can solve explicitly for the equilibrium values and hence easily conduct comparative statics on the influence of the large trader's size and informational position relative to the rest of the market. We find that the large trader's influence generally depends on the market sentiment. Whenever the market is sufficiently pessimistic with regard to economic fundamentals, the large speculator will coordinate the mass of small traders towards an attack. Surprisingly, we find that improving the precision of the large trader's private information will increase the probability of a crisis only if fundamentals are generally believed to be strong, while the reverse holds for a weak market sentiment.

The results as derived from the analyses in this chapter therefore not fully substantiate the generally expressed belief that the existence of large traders increases the probability of currency crises, but rather relativize this view. In this respect, the "Soroses" of the world may make the markets more aggressive, but they not necessarily have to do so.

12.1 The Basic Model with Small and Large Traders - Corsetti, Dasgupta, Morris and Shin (2001)

The basic setup of the model we analyze in this chapter has been taken from Corsetti, Dasgupta et al. (2001). They consider an economy in which the exchange rate is pegged to a fixed level by the central bank. There is a single large trader in the market with a trading limit of $\lambda < 1$, and a continuum of small speculators who together have a combined trading limit of $1 - \lambda$.

Short selling is assumed to consist of borrowing the domestic currency and selling it for foreign currency. The cost entailed in this action is denoted as t. However, if the attack on the currency peg is successful, each trader receives a fixed payoff of D.[2] The net payoff from not-attacking the currency is supposedly equal to zero.[3] Payoff and cost parameters are given per unit of domestic currency.

Moreover, it is assumed that the central bank defends the peg as long as the proportion of attacking speculators, l, is lower than the fundamental index, θ.[4] Hence, the central bank abandons the currency peg if $l \geq \theta$. Consequently, if fundamentals are sufficiently strong ($\theta > 1$) the central bank keeps the fixed parity, irrespective of the actions of the traders. However, if θ is sufficiently low ($\theta \leq 0$), the central bank will always abandon the peg. The interesting case therefore is for the fundamentals to lie in the interval $0 < \theta \leq 1$, since in this region there may be a speculative attack as well as financial stability.

In the following, our illustration differs from the basic set-up in Corsetti, Dasgupta et al. (2001) by presuming specific distribution functions for the parameters, whereas they stick to the general case of non-specific distributions. The choice of this specific type of distribution is supposed to facilitate comparisons with the model of Sect. 12.2. Concerning the structure of the game between central bank and speculators we consider the following. First, nature chooses the value of the fundamental index θ according to a normal distribution with mean y and variance $\frac{1}{\alpha}$. Both parameters are assumed to

---

2 It is assumed that $D \gg t$, so that the prior incentive to attack the fixed parity is high.

3 As in the models of the former chapters, opportunity costs are not taken into account.

4 This notation captures the usual interpretation that the central bank derives a positive, non-specified utility from defending the currency peg, which increases with strengthening fundamentals but decreases in the speculative mass attacking the peg. See also the explanation in Sect. 5.1.

be common knowledge and to be exogenous to the model. The prior mean y might be interpreted as the value of the fundamental state that is commonly expected by the whole market. Therefore, y may be thought of as the market sentiment. Concerning the exogeneity of α, we assume that the central bank is not allowed to influence the fundamental variance after observing the market sentiment y or the true fundamental state θ. In accordance with the literature, the commonly known distribution of θ is also referred to as public signal, with α denoted as the precision of this signal. The public signal hence represents the common priors of the economic fundamental state. The truly realized value of θ, however, is only known to the central bank. Additionally to public information, each speculator i individually receives a private signal $x_i = \theta + \varepsilon_i$. Noise value ε_i is supposed to be i.i. normally distributed with mean zero and variance $\frac{1}{\beta}$, and to be independent of the realized value of θ. The distributional parameters of ε_i are presumed to be common knowledge to all traders and the central bank. However, as long as variance $\frac{1}{\beta}$ is higher than zero, the small speculators can neither precisely establish the true value of θ, nor the private signals of their opponents. The large trader also receives a private signal $x_l = \theta + \nu$, with ν being i.i. normally distributed with mean zero and variance $\frac{1}{\gamma}$, independent of θ and ε_i. The distributional parameters of this second noise parameter are again supposed to be common knowledge. After receiving public and private information, speculators simultaneously have to decide whether to attack the currency peg or to refrain from doing so.[5] The central bank observes the fundamental state, θ, and the proportion of attacking speculators, l, and abandons the peg whenever $l \geq \theta$.

As has been demonstrated by Corsetti, Dasgupta et al. (2001), the model entails a unique equilibrium in trigger strategies, as long as private information is sufficiently precise relative to public. In the equilibrium, the small speculators follow a trigger strategy around x^*, i.e. each small speculator attacks the currency peg if his private signal is smaller than or equal to x^*. For any given fundamental index θ, the proportion of small traders attacking the peg is then given by the proportion of speculators receiving a private signal smaller than or equal to x^*. Due to the assumption of an i.i.d. noise parameter ε, the probability with which a single speculator receives a signal smaller than or equal to x^* is equal to the proportion of attacking speculators

$$\begin{aligned}\text{Prob}(x \leq x^*|\theta) &= \Phi\left(\frac{x^* - E(x|\theta)}{\sqrt{\text{Var}(x|\theta)}}\right) \\ &= \Phi(\sqrt{\beta}(x^* - \theta)) \,.\end{aligned}$$

[5] The case, where the large trader makes his decision first, while the small speculators may observe his choice before determining the optimal action themselves, will be analyzed in Chap. 13.

The speculative mass of small speculators attacking the fixed parity is given by

$$(1-\lambda)\Phi(\sqrt{\beta}(x^*-\theta))\ .$$

Let θ_1^* be the value of the fundamental index, which makes the central bank indifferent between abandoning and keeping the peg if only small speculators attack the currency. θ_1^* is therefore defined by the following indifference condition

$$\theta_1^* = (1-\lambda)\Phi(\sqrt{\beta}(x^*-\theta_1^*))\ . \tag{12.1}$$

Thus, for all values of θ below θ_1^*, an attack of small speculators is successful, irrespective of the action of the large trader. I.e. fundamental states below θ_1^* are so bad, that the speculative mass of the small speculators is sufficient to force a devaluation from the central bank.

If there were no large speculator in the model, i.e. for $\lambda = 0$, θ_1^* would give the unique trigger point for the fundamental values, so that the central bank would abandon the peg for all states below θ_1^* and keep the peg otherwise. If, however, the large trader decides to join the attack, the speculative pressure rises to

$$\lambda + (1-\lambda)\Phi(\sqrt{\beta}(x^*-\theta))\ .$$

Let the critical value of the fundamental index at which an attack is successful, if the large speculator joins the attack be denoted by θ_2^*, so that

$$\theta_2^* = \lambda + (1-\lambda)\Phi(\sqrt{\beta}(x^*-\theta_2^*))\ . \tag{12.2}$$

Clearly, $\theta_2^* \geq \theta_1^*$. Hence, for fundamental states above θ_2^*, an attack on the fixed currency peg can never be successful, even if the large trader joins the attack. For fundamentals between θ_1^* and θ_2^*, a devaluation can only be achieved if the large speculator decides to attack as well. For fundamental values worse than θ_1^*, the attack will be successful irrespective of the large trader's action.

The single large speculator, however, will only be willing to attack if his expected payoff from attacking is at least as high as the expected payoff from not-attacking, which is equal to zero. Hence, he is indifferent between his two actions if

$$D \cdot \text{Prob}(\text{success}|x_l) = t\ .$$

For the large trader, the probability of a successful attack is given by the probability that the fundamental index is lower than θ_2^*. His indifference condition can therefore be transformed to

$$\begin{aligned} D \cdot \text{Prob}(\theta \leq \theta_2^*|x_l) &= t \\ D \cdot \Phi\left(\frac{\theta_2^* - E(\theta|x_l)}{\sqrt{\text{Var}(\theta|x_l)}}\right) &= t \\ D \cdot \Phi\left(\sqrt{\alpha+\gamma}(\theta_2^* - \frac{\alpha}{\alpha+\gamma}y - \frac{\gamma}{\alpha+\gamma}x_l^*)\right) &= t\ . \end{aligned} \tag{12.3}$$

This equation then defines the switching value x_l^* of the large speculator's private signal. Whenever his signal is below x_l^*, he will attack the peg, but will refrain from doing so for $x_l > x_l^*$.

The small traders' switching signal x^* is defined by a similar condition of indifference

$$D \cdot \text{Prob}(\text{success}|x) = t\ .$$

However, according to Corsetti, Dasgupta et al. (2001), the probability of a successful attack for the small speculators does not only depend on the realized fundamental index, but also on the incidence of the large trader joining the attack or not, so that indifference for any small speculator is given by

$$D \cdot \text{Prob}(\theta \le \theta_1^*|x^*) + D \cdot \text{Prob}(\theta_1^* < \theta \le \theta_2^*|x^*) \cdot \text{Prob}(x_l \le x_l^*|\theta) = t\ .$$

This condition can be transformed to

$$D \cdot \Phi\left(\sqrt{\alpha+\beta}\left(\theta_1^* - \frac{\alpha}{\alpha+\beta}y - \frac{\beta}{\alpha+\beta}x^*\right)\right) +$$
$$D \cdot \left(\int_{\theta_1^*}^{\theta_2^*} \phi\left(\sqrt{\alpha+\beta}\left(\theta - \frac{\alpha}{\alpha+\beta}y - \frac{\beta}{\alpha+\beta}x^*\right)\right)\Phi\left(\sqrt{\gamma}(x_l^* - \theta)\right)d\theta\right) = t\ . \tag{12.4}$$

The first term on the left-hand-side (l.h.s.) of (12.4) describes the expected payoff from attacking if only small speculators join the attack, the second part gives the additional expected payoff if the large trader attacks as well. Whereas the first integral on the l.h.s. can be solved quite easily, this is not possible, however, for the second integral. Note that according to the approach by Corsetti, Dasgupta et al. (2001), the small traders explicitly take the action of the large trader into account, whereas the large agent does not decide explicitly contingent on the small traders' choices.[6]

As has been shown by Corsetti, Dasgupta et al. (2001), there is a unique solution to the small traders' condition of indifference, since the l.h.s. of (12.4) is strictly decreasing in x^*. Hence, for small values of the private signal, the expected gross payoff for a small speculator is higher than the cost t, whereas for sufficiently high values of x the expected payoff is lower than t.[7] Therefore, there must be exactly one value x^* of the small traders' private signals, for which the expected payoff to attacking is equal to the cost of this action. Given x^*, the switching values θ_1^* and θ_2^* can be determined from (12.1) and (12.2). Subsequently, the trigger signal for the large trader, x_l^*, follows from

[6] For an analysis of when agents may be treated as "negligible", see Levine and Pesendorfer (1995).

[7] For the proof that trigger strategies are optimally chosen by speculators, so that the unique equilibrium is one in trigger strategies, we refer to Corsetti, Dasgupta et al. (2001).

(12.3).[8] Thus, with a large trader on the foreign exchange market, there are two thresholds for the fundamental state instead of a single one as in the model with small speculators only. Note, that the distance between θ_1^* and θ_2^* is not equal to the large trader's size, λ.

Since it is not possible to solve explicitly for the equilibrium values in this model, the conduct of comparative statics becomes slightly cumbersome. The following section therefore analyzes the influence of the different parameters on the unique equilibrium by using the approach of Corsetti, Dasgupta et al. (2001) and Corsetti, Pesenti et al. (2001). They explore the parameters' impact in the limit, as both the small speculators' private signals and the large trader's private signal become completely precise.

After deriving the equilibrium values from (12.1)–(12.4), we can now ask questions concerning the impact of the large trader. Since the benchmark case of the model with small speculators only is given by (x^*, θ_1^*), it is quite easy to see whether the large trader has an influence on the fragility of the exchange rate peg by comparing the new equilibrium with the benchmark case.

The main questions we want to analyze in this section are the following: first, does the large trader have an influence on the incidence of a currency crisis? I.e. does he change the trigger value of the fundamental index at which the central bank switches from abandoning to keeping the peg? And second, does the small traders' behavior change due to the existence of the large speculator? This question relates to the switching value x^* of the small speculators' private signals. If x^* increases due to the large trader's existence, the small speculators can be characterized as being more aggressive than before. As has been pointed out by Corsetti, Dasgupta et al. (2001) and Corsetti, Pesenti et al. (2001), in analyzing these questions we have to disentangle two different measures by which the large trader may exert an influence on the equilibrium: his impact may either be due to his size, as represented by λ, or to his informational advantage (or disadvantage) relative to the small traders, $\frac{\gamma}{\beta}$.

[8] Note that (x^*, θ_1^*), gives the equilibrium for the currency crisis model with only small speculators, i.e. for $\lambda = 0$. The model with only a single large trader, $\lambda = 1$, in contrast, reduces the game to a single person decision problem with a trivial solution: the large trader attacks whenever his expected net payoff from attacking is positive. This is the case for

$$D \cdot \text{Prob}(\theta \leq \lambda | x_l) > t$$

$$D \cdot \Phi(\sqrt{\alpha + \gamma}(\lambda - \frac{\alpha}{\alpha + \gamma} y - \frac{\gamma}{\alpha + \gamma} x_l)) > t \, .$$

This means that the single large trader will attack the fixed parity whenever his signal is low enough, i.e. for

$$x_l < \frac{\alpha + \gamma}{\alpha} \lambda - y - \frac{\sqrt{\alpha + \gamma}}{\gamma} \Phi^{-1}(\frac{t}{D}) \, .$$

Note that in this case there is no need for a "critical mass condition" as equivalent to (12.2).

Since it is not possible to solve for the equilibrium values explicitly, one way of finding the answers to the above questions is provided by analyzing the different parameters' influence in the limit, as both the small and the large trader's private signals become completely precise:

$$\beta \to \infty, \ \gamma \to \infty, \text{ and } \frac{\gamma}{\beta} \to r \ .$$

Hence, it is assumed that both types of speculators have very precise information but the precision of the large trader's signal relative to the small traders' signals tends to r. r can take on values from 0 (in which case the small traders have arbitrarily more precise information) to ∞ (so that the large trader possesses more precise information).

For the limiting case, where all private signals are very precise, Corsetti, Dasgupta et al. (2001) find, that the switching values of the private signals must converge to the value of the fundamental index at which the peg switches from being abandoned to being kept. This is exactly the case for $\theta = \theta_2^*$. For values higher than θ_2^*, the exchange rate peg can always be maintained by the central bank. If the large trader's private signal becomes completely precise, i.e. for $\gamma \to \infty$, the switching value of the private signal, x_l^*, has to converge to θ_2^*, as can be seen from (12.3). With a completely precise private signal, the conditional variance $\text{Var}(\theta|x_l)$ approaches zero, so that x_l^* has to converge to θ_2^*. Otherwise the indifference condition cannot be satisfied, since the l.h.s. of (12.3) in any other case converges to either zero or one, rather than t. Thus, in the limit the large speculator always attacks the fixed parity at states worse than θ_2^*, but refrains from attacking for better states. For the small traders the same argument holds, so that in the limit with very precise private signals, the switching signal x^* converges to θ_2^* as well. Thus, in the limit it holds that $x^* = x_l^* = \theta_2^*$, and a devaluation occurs with certainty for all fundamental states lower than θ_2^*. Moreover, with very precise private information the large trader obeys the same strategy rule as the small speculators. The action they decide on after θ has been realized, however, depends on whether their respective private signals lie to the right or to the left of θ_2^*.

The question of the large trader having an influence on the probability of a currency crisis in the limit hence simplifies to the issue whether θ_2^* is higher or lower than the threshold value of the game with small speculators only, θ_1^*. In order to elaborate on this point, consider Fig. 12.1. The upper curve in Fig. 12.1 represents the incidence of an attack with large trader, the lower curve without large trader. In the limit, the large trader always attacks for states worse than θ_2^*, but abstains from an attack to the right of θ_2^*. Hence, the overall incidence of attack follows the upper curve for values lower than θ_2^*, but jumps down to the bottom curve for states to the right of θ_2^*. With decreasing noise, both curves become steeper and converge to a step function around θ_2^*. Hence, the small traders switch their actions at θ_2^* as well: $x^* \to \theta_2^*$. However, following Corsetti, Dasgupta et al. (2001), we have to differentiate between the cases of $\theta_2^* > 1 - \lambda$ and $\theta_2^* \leq 1 - \lambda$. In the latter case, both curves

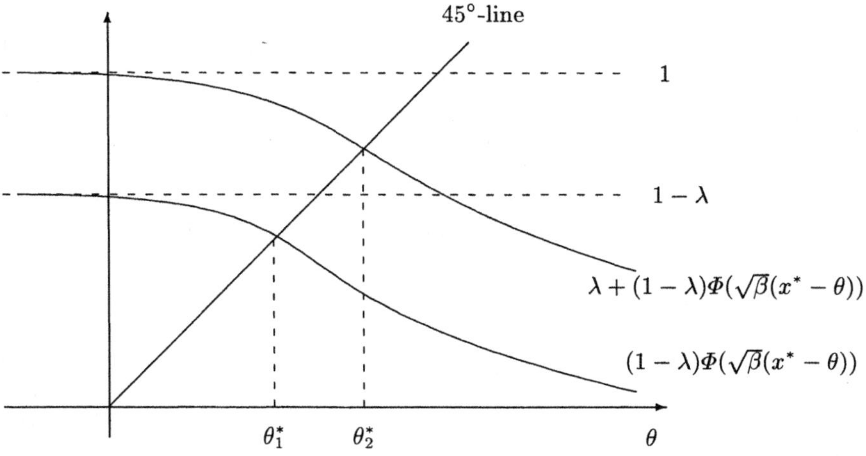

Fig. 12.1. Critical Mass Conditions

intersect with the 45°-line at the same point, so that $\theta_1^* = \theta_2^*$. Consequently, the prior probability of a crisis with infinitely precise information does not change due to the large trader. For $\theta_2^* > 1 - \lambda$, in contrast, we find that $\theta_2^* > \theta_1^*$, since in the limit the step function of the bottom curve will intersect with the 45°-line at its horizontal portion in this case, so that $\theta_1^* = 1 - \lambda$, which is lower than θ_2^*. In this case, the existence of the large trader increases the probability of a currency crisis, since the parity will be abandoned for all fundamental states lower than θ_2^*, which gives a larger interval of states than the benchmark case with small speculators only.

Proposition 12.1. (Corsetti, Dasgupta et al., 2001)
In the limit as noise vanishes, so that

$$\beta \to \infty,\ \gamma \to \infty,\ \textit{and}\ \frac{\gamma}{\beta} \to r\ ,$$

the large trader increases the ex-ante probability of a currency crisis, whenever $\lambda > 1 - \theta_2^*$. *In this case, the probability of a crisis moreover increases in* λ.

For a complete proof of proposition 12.1, we refer to Corsetti, Dasgupta et al. (2001). Since in the limit with completely precise private information, we have that $x^* = x_l^* = \theta_2^*$, another implicit result follows from proposition 12.1, which concerns the large trader's influence on the behavior of small speculators.

Proposition 12.2. *In the limit with vanishing noise, the large trader makes the mass of small speculators more aggressive whenever he is sufficiently large, i.e.* $\lambda > 1 - \theta_2^*$.

The proof of this proposition simply follows from the fact that with completely precise private signals, the threshold values for the signals are always equal to the threshold value for the fundamentals. Hence, if the threshold of the fundamental index increases in the case of $\theta_2^* > 1-\lambda$, then x^* must rise as well, so that if accompanied by the large trader, small speculators will attack the fixed parity for higher signal values than before. □

In contrast to the influence of the large trader's size λ, the model does not yet allow any clear-cut statements about the influence of the large trader's informativeness. According to Corsetti, Pesenti et al. (2001), however, it is possible to at least indirectly derive a result for the large trader's informational position by assuming the large trader's information to be arbitrarily more precise than that of the rest of the market. They show that for $r \to \infty$, the large trader always makes small speculators more aggressive, thereby increasing the incidence of a currency crisis. In the following, we will illustrate their finding in the introduced normal setting.

In the context of the model laid-out above, consider the following: If the large trader's information is completely precise and small speculators know this, they will attach a probability of one to the incidence of an attack by the large speculator for all fundamental states worse than θ_2^* and zero otherwise. Hence, equation (12.4) simplifies to

$$D \cdot \int_{-\infty}^{\theta_2^*} \phi\Big(\sqrt{\alpha+\beta}(\theta - \frac{\alpha}{\alpha+\beta}y - \frac{\beta}{\alpha+\beta}x_i)\Big)\, d\theta = t$$

$$D \cdot \Phi\Big(\sqrt{\alpha+\beta}(\theta_2^* - \frac{\alpha}{\alpha+\beta}y - \frac{\beta}{\alpha+\beta}x^*)\Big) = t\,. \tag{12.5}$$

In this case, therefore, the equilibrium values are given by

$$\theta_2^* = \lambda + (1-\lambda)\Phi(\frac{\alpha}{\sqrt{\beta}}(\theta_2^* - y) - \sqrt{\frac{\alpha+\beta}{\beta}}\Phi^{-1}(\frac{t}{D}))\,, \tag{12.6}$$

$$x^* = \frac{\alpha+\beta}{\beta}\theta_2^* - \frac{\alpha}{\beta}y - \frac{\sqrt{\alpha+\beta}}{\beta}\Phi^{-1}(\frac{t}{D})\,, \tag{12.7}$$

$$x_l^* = \frac{\alpha+\gamma}{\gamma}\theta_2^* - \frac{\alpha}{\gamma}y - \frac{\sqrt{\alpha+\gamma}}{\gamma}\Phi^{-1}(\frac{t}{D})\,. \tag{12.8}$$

From this analysis, the subsequent proposition follows quite obviously:

Proposition 12.3. (Corsetti, Pesenti et al., 2001)
In the limit as noise vanishes, while the large trader's private information becomes arbitrarily more precise than the small traders' information, so that

$$\beta \to \infty,\ \gamma \to \infty,\ \textit{and}\ \frac{\gamma}{\beta} \to r\ \textit{with}\ r \to \infty\,,$$

the large trader makes the small speculators more aggressive and raises the ex-ante probability of a currency crisis, i.e. x^* *and* θ_2^* *increase in* λ.

Proof:

$$\frac{\partial \theta_2^*}{\partial \lambda} = \frac{1 - \Phi(\cdot)}{1 + \lambda \phi(\cdot) \frac{\alpha}{\sqrt{\beta}}} > 0$$

$$\frac{\partial x^*}{\partial \lambda} = \frac{\alpha + \beta}{\beta} \frac{\partial \theta_2^*}{\partial \lambda} > 0$$

Through the increase in θ_2^*, the switching value of the small traders' private signal x^* increases as well. □

Hence, what follows from the analysis of the approaches by Corsetti, Dasgupta et al. (2001) and Corsetti, Pesenti et al. (2001) is that whenever both large and small speculators possess very precise information, the large trader makes the market more aggressive and thereby increases the danger of a crisis, if he has sufficient financial power as stated by propositions 12.1 and 12.2. In this case, his size outweighs the lacking dominance of superior information. In contrast, whenever the large trader possesses superior information, the small traders simply follow his actions irrespective of his size (proposition 12.3). In the latter case, the large trader always increases the probability of a crisis.[9]

Yet, the analysis thus far is rather unsatisfactory concerning the influence of the large trader's informativeness on the equilibrium. In order to elaborate on the informational aspects in more detail, we will in the following section consider a modified model by Metz (2002b), which enables answering these questions.

12.2 Simplified Model

In this section, we will delineate a similar but more simplified model by Metz (2002b), as compared to the approach by Corsetti, Dasgupta et al. (2001) and Corsetti, Pesenti et al. (2001). In this respect, a slightly different time structure is assumed. Whereas in the former model it has been presumed that the central bank can observe the number (or proportion l) of attacking speculators before deciding on whether to abandon the peg or not, in this section it is supposed that she has to come to a decision at an earlier time. Therefore, she cannot make her choice contingent on the observed value of l, but has to base her decision on the expected value of l. Hence, she will abandon the peg, whenever $E(l|\theta) > \theta$. This assumption helps to smooth the indifference condition for the central bank, so that the model entails a continuous speculative mass condition, which is in contrast to the model of the previous section.

The structure of the model by Metz (2002b) is then the following. In a first stage, nature selects the fundamental state θ from a normal distribution

[9] For an analysis of the parameters' influence away from the limit, see Corsetti, Dasgupta et al. (2001).

with mean y and variance $\frac{1}{\alpha}$. The central bank then observes the realized fundamental state, whereas speculators only get to know the distribution of θ, which becomes common knowledge. The small speculators receive their private signals, x_i, the large speculator his private signal, x_l, in the third stage of the game. They all simultaneously have to decide whether or not to attack the fixed parity. The central bank at the same time has to decide whether or not to abandon the peg, based on her observation of θ and on her knowledge about the speculators' information.

There might be an additional stage of the game, if the central bank at first did not decide to abandon the peg, the speculative mass l, however, turned out to be too large to withstand a devaluation. Since a crisis is inevitable should this stage come into play, we will in the following abstract from this problem and rather analyze the large trader's influence on a "premature" crisis.

As a motivation for the changed time structure, consider the fact that in currency crises of the past, central banks often gave up the fixed parity at an earlier point in time than justified by the means still available for defending the peg (usually the amount of international reserves). This observation might be attributed to the cost of waiting. If the costs from an ongoing defence of the peg suddenly shoot up and largely exceed the benefit from this action, it might be better for the central bank to have given up the peg before this event, in order to at least save a last part of reputation. This effect clearly becomes relevant when there is a single or a small number of large traders on the foreign exchange market. If they decide to speculate against the parity, the costs of defending the peg are rising so strongly, that the central bank might indeed be better off, if she decides on an early devaluation, based on her expectation of the large trader's joining the attack. This process is exactly captured by the above delineated time structure.

12.2.1 The Derivation of Equilibrium

Both small and large speculators will want to attack the fixed parity whenever the payoff from this action is higher than the payoff from not-attacking. Hence, they are indifferent between their two actions, if

$$D \cdot \text{Prob}(\text{success}|x_l) = t$$

and

$$D \cdot \text{Prob}(\text{success}|x_i) = t \ .$$

Moreover, all traders know that the central bank will only abandon the fixed exchange rate, if she expects the speculative mass attacking the peg to be large: $E(l|\theta) \geq \theta$. The better the fundamental state of the economy, θ, the higher this expected speculative mass has to be. On the basis of private and public information, each player therefore has to try to establish the realized but unobservable fundamental state and the information of his opponents and their subsequent actions. Given the assumed distribution of noise, it can be found that, similar to the model with homogeneous traders of Chap. 9, a small speculator with private signal x_i expects the unknown fundamental index to take on a value of

$$E(\theta|x_i) = \frac{\alpha}{\alpha+\beta}y + \frac{\beta}{\alpha+\beta}x_i ,$$

with a variance of

$$\mathrm{Var}(\theta|x_i) = \frac{1}{\alpha+\beta} .$$

The more precise private and public information are, the closer will the fundamental state be to the expected value conditional on the respective signals (posterior mean). Moreover, it holds that $E(\theta|x_i) = E(x_j|x_i) = E(x_l|x_i)$. Hence, each individual small speculator expects his opponents' private signals to be equal to his posterior of θ. However, the variance that the trader ascribes to his opponents' private signals is higher than the conditional variance of the fundamental state

$$\mathrm{Var}(x_l|x_i) = \frac{\alpha+\beta+\gamma}{\beta(\alpha+\gamma)} > \frac{1}{\alpha+\beta}$$

and

$$\mathrm{Var}(x_j|x_i) = \frac{\alpha+2\beta}{\beta(\alpha+\beta)} > \frac{1}{\alpha+\beta} .$$

Similarly, it holds for the large trader that

$$E(\theta|x_l) = \frac{\alpha}{\alpha+\gamma}y + \frac{\gamma}{\alpha+\gamma}x_l \quad \text{and} \quad \mathrm{Var}(\theta|x_l) = \frac{1}{\alpha+\gamma} .$$

Again, the large trader expects the small speculators to receive private signals equal to his posterior of θ: $E(x_i|x_l) = E(\theta|x_l)$. However, he also reckons his opponents' private signals to have a higher variance than the fluctuations he ascribes to the fundamental state

$$\mathrm{Var}(x_i|x_l) = \frac{\alpha+\beta+\gamma}{\gamma(\alpha+\beta)} ,$$

which is higher than $\mathrm{Var}(\theta|x_l) = \frac{1}{\alpha+\gamma}$. This feature is what drives the result of a unique equilibrium in this model. Although for certain values of the private signal an individual speculator will be sure that fundamentals are so weak that an attack on the fixed parity should almost certainly be successful, he cannot be sure that his opponents know this as well. What is more, even if he believes his opponents' signals to be sufficiently low, he still does not know whether they believe him to know what they know, etc.

In this model it can now be shown that there is exactly one value of the fundamental index, θ^*, which generates a distribution of private signals, so that a small speculator receiving signal x^* is indifferent between attacking and not-attacking, and the large speculator is indifferent between these two actions if he receives a signal of x_l^*. Moreover, for $\theta = \theta^*$, the central bank is indifferent between abandoning and keeping the peg.

In order to derive the unique equilibrium, consider the indifference condition for the central bank first. The central bank is indifferent, if the expected speculative mass attacking the fixed parity, $E(l|\theta)$, is exactly equal to the observed fundamental state, θ. When it is higher the central bank will always devalue the peg, when it is lower she will be able to defend the peg. In the following, it is assumed that the speculators optimally follow a trigger strategy around signals x^*, respectively x_l^*.[10] Due to the newly defined structure of events, we find that in contrast to the model of Sect. 12.1, the speculative mass condition is now continuous: the central bank is indifferent between abandoning and keeping the peg, if

$$\begin{aligned}\theta^* &= E(l|\theta^*)\\ &= (1-\lambda)\cdot\{\text{proportion of attacking small traders}|\theta^*\}\\ &\quad +\lambda\cdot\text{Prob}(\text{large trader attacks}|\theta^*)\\ &= (1-\lambda)\cdot\text{Prob}(x\le x^*|\theta^*)+\lambda\cdot\text{Prob}(x_l\le x_l^*|\theta^*)\\ &= (1-\lambda)\cdot\Phi\Big(\sqrt{\beta}(x^*-\theta^*)\Big)+\lambda\cdot\Phi\Big(\sqrt{\gamma}(x_l^*-\theta^*)\Big)\,. \end{aligned} \tag{12.9}$$

Whereas the first term on the r.h.s. of (12.9) gives the proportion of attacking small speculators, characterized as those who observe signals smaller than or equal to x^*, the second expression gives the probability with which the large speculator attacks the currency peg.

Note that for the model with homogeneous (i.e. only small) speculators, it does not matter whether the central bank makes her choice before or after observing the number of actually attacking traders. Thus, for $\lambda = 0$, we get back to the model of Chap. 9. This interesting finding follows from the fact that in the model with a continuum of small traders and independently distributed noise parameters, in equilibrium the expected proportion of attacking speculators is equal to the actual proportion of attacking traders. Hence, for a continuum of traders, there is no aggregate uncertainty.[11] In the model with heterogeneous traders, however, the newly defined time structure is required to smoothen the speculative mass condition for equilibrium.

Assuming this specific time structure also partly changes the equilibrium behavior of the traders. Whereas the indifference condition of the large speculator stays the same as before

$$\begin{aligned} D\cdot\text{Prob}(\theta\le\theta^*|x_l) &= t\\ D\cdot\Phi\Big(\sqrt{\alpha+\gamma}\Big(\theta^*-\frac{\alpha}{\alpha+\gamma}y-\frac{\gamma}{\alpha+\gamma}x_l\Big)\Big) &= t\,, \end{aligned} \tag{12.10}$$

[10] For the proof of the trigger strategy being the only optimal strategy for the speculators, we refer to Corsetti, Dasgupta et al. (2001).

[11] For this point, see also Morris and Shin (1998) or Metz (2002a).

the condition of indifference for the small speculators is different from the one of the previous section. Since the structure of the game is common knowledge, speculators know that the speculative mass condition is no longer a step function, jumping up by λ if the large trader decides to join the attack. Instead, they know that the probability of a successful attack is contingent only on whether the realized fundamental state is lower than the threshold value θ^*. The small speculators' indifference condition is therefore given by

$$D \cdot \text{Prob}(\theta \leq \theta^* | x_i) = t$$

$$D \cdot \Phi(\sqrt{\alpha + \beta}(\theta^* - \frac{\alpha}{\alpha + \beta} y - \frac{\beta}{\alpha + \beta} x_i)) = t \,. \tag{12.11}$$

By smoothing the indifference condition for the central bank, it is possible to derive a unique switching value for the fundamental index up to which the fixed parity will always be abandoned and unique switching values for the private signals, x_l^* and x^*, up to which each speculator will attack the fixed parity.

In order to prove the uniqueness of equilibrium, it has to be shown that there exists only one combination of signals and fundamentals that simultaneously makes the central bank and the speculators indifferent between their respective actions. In contrast to the model of Chap. 9, the uniqueness condition is given as a three-dimensional problem. However, since only the central bank's indifference condition contains all three dimensions, the task reduces to showing that there is only one intersection point of the central bank's indifference curve with each of the speculators' indifference curves.

Consider the simultaneous indifference situation of central bank and small speculators first. Solving the central bank's indifference condition (12.9) for x^*, yields

$$x^{*CB} = \theta^* + \frac{1}{\sqrt{\beta}} \Phi_a^{-1} \left(\frac{\theta^* - \lambda \Phi_b(\sqrt{\gamma}(x_l^* - \theta^*))}{1 - \lambda} \right) , \tag{12.12}$$

with Φ_a denoting the first cumulated normal density on the right hand side in equation (12.9) and Φ_b denoting the second. The small speculators' indifference condition follows from (12.11) as

$$x^{*SPs} = \frac{\alpha + \beta}{\beta} \theta^* - \frac{\alpha}{\beta} y - \frac{\sqrt{\alpha + \beta}}{\beta} \Phi^{-1} \left(\frac{t}{D} \right) . \tag{12.13}$$

Fig. 12.2 shows the two indifference curves in the (θ, x)-plane. We can see that there is exactly one intersection of the two curves, if the small speculators' indifference curve has a lower slope throughout the whole range of values. The slope of the central bank's indifference curve is given by

$$\frac{\partial x^{*CB}}{\partial \theta^*} = 1 + \frac{1}{\sqrt{\beta}} \phi_a^{-1}(\cdot) \Big(\frac{1}{1 - \lambda} - \frac{\lambda}{1 - \lambda} \phi_b(\cdot) (\sqrt{\gamma} \frac{\partial x_l^*}{\partial \theta^*} - \sqrt{\gamma}) \Big) .$$

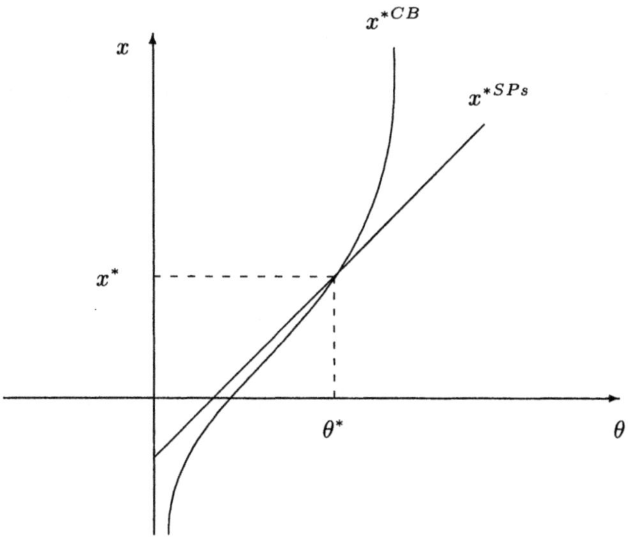

Fig. 12.2. Unique equilibrium - central bank and small speculators

For the small speculators' indifference curve it is given by

$$\frac{\partial x^{*SPs}}{\partial \theta^*} = \frac{\alpha + \beta}{\beta} .$$

Thus, a unique intersection point of the central bank's and the small speculators' indifference curve is guaranteed if

$$1 + \frac{1}{\sqrt{\beta}} \phi_a^{-1}(\cdot) \Big(\frac{1}{1-\lambda} - \frac{\lambda}{1-\lambda} \phi_b(\cdot) (\sqrt{\gamma} \frac{\partial y^*}{\partial \theta^*} - \sqrt{\gamma}) \Big) > \frac{\alpha + \beta}{\beta} .$$

Bearing in mind that the smallest value of $\phi^{-1}(\cdot)$ is equal to the reciprocal of the largest value of $\phi(\cdot)$, which is given at the mean μ, $\frac{1}{\phi(\mu)} = \frac{1}{\frac{1}{\sigma\sqrt{2\pi}}}$ with σ denoting the standard deviation, whereas the smallest value of $\phi(\cdot)$ is simply given by zero, a sufficient condition for uniqueness of equilibrium is described by

$$1 + \frac{1}{\sqrt{\beta}} \frac{1}{\frac{1}{(1-\lambda)\sqrt{2\pi}}} \left(\frac{1}{1-\lambda} - 0 \right) > \frac{\alpha + \beta}{\beta}$$

$$\Rightarrow \quad \beta > \frac{\alpha^2}{2\pi} . \tag{12.14}$$

Analyzing the simultaneous indifference situation for the central bank and the single large trader in the same way, the second sufficient condition results in

$$1+\frac{1}{\sqrt{\gamma}}\frac{1}{\frac{1}{(1-\lambda)\sqrt{2\pi}}}\left(\frac{1}{1-\lambda}-0\right)>\frac{\alpha+\gamma}{\gamma}$$

$$\Rightarrow \quad \gamma>\frac{\alpha^2}{2\pi}\,. \tag{12.15}$$

A unique equilibrium in our model is thus guaranteed, if the precision of both types of private information is high relative to the precision of public information. Whenever this condition is satisfied, the equilibrium switching values (θ^*, x^*, x_l^*) divide the strategy space into two intervals, so that for all $\theta \leq \theta^*$, strategy "abandon the peg" dominates the strategy to keep the peg, and for all signals x_i and x_l smaller than or equal to the switching values x^* and x_l^*, strategy "attack the peg" dominates strategy "do not attack".

In order to analyze comparative statics in the next section, the equilibrium values for the signals and the fundamental state remain to be derived. From (12.9)–(12.11) these are given as:

$$\theta^* = (1-\lambda)\Phi_1\left(\frac{\alpha}{\sqrt{\beta}}\theta^* - \frac{\alpha}{\sqrt{\beta}}y - \sqrt{\frac{\alpha+\beta}{\beta}}\Phi^{-1}\left(\frac{t}{D}\right)\right)$$
$$+\lambda\Phi_2\left(\frac{\alpha}{\sqrt{\gamma}}\theta^* - \frac{\alpha}{\sqrt{\gamma}}y - \sqrt{\frac{\alpha+\gamma}{\gamma}}\Phi^{-1}\left(\frac{t}{D}\right)\right)\,, \tag{12.16}$$

$$x^* = \frac{\alpha+\beta}{\beta}\theta^* - \frac{\alpha}{\beta}y - \frac{\sqrt{\alpha+\beta}}{\beta}\Phi^{-1}\left(\frac{t}{D}\right)\,, \tag{12.17}$$

and

$$x_l^* = \frac{\alpha+\gamma}{\gamma}\theta^* - \frac{\alpha}{\gamma}y - \frac{\sqrt{\alpha+\gamma}}{\gamma}\Phi^{-1}\left(\frac{t}{D}\right)\,. \tag{12.18}$$

12.2.2 Comparative Statics

After deriving the equilibrium values, the influence which the different parameters exert on the equilibrium can be analyzed. Herein, we are mostly interested in the parameters' impact on the ex-ante or prior probability of a currency crisis. Since a devaluation will take place for all fundamental values lower than or equal to θ^*, each parameter that increases θ^* subsequently raises the ex-ante probability of an attack. By analyzing the influence on θ^*, it is assumed that the conditions for uniqueness of equilibrium are satisfied, i.e. we presume the private signals to be sufficiently precise relative to public information.

Proposition 12.4. (Metz, 2002b)
The probability of a currency crisis increases in payoff D and decreases in cost t.

Proof:
The partial derivatives of θ^* with respect to t and D are given by

$$\frac{\partial\theta^*}{\partial t} = -\frac{(1-\lambda)\phi_1(\cdot)\sqrt{\frac{\alpha+\beta}{\beta}}\frac{\partial\Phi^{-1}(\frac{t}{D})}{\partial t}}{1-(1-\lambda)\phi_1(\cdot)\frac{\alpha}{\sqrt{\beta}}-\lambda\phi_2(\cdot)\frac{\alpha}{\sqrt{\gamma}}} - \frac{\lambda\phi_2(\cdot)\sqrt{\frac{\alpha+\gamma}{\gamma}}\frac{\partial\Phi^{-1}(\frac{t}{D})}{\partial t}}{1-(1-\lambda)\phi_1(\cdot)\frac{\alpha}{\sqrt{\beta}}-\lambda\phi_2(\cdot)\frac{\alpha}{\sqrt{\gamma}}} < 0$$

and

$$\frac{\partial\theta^*}{\partial D} = +\frac{(1-\lambda)\phi_1(\cdot)\sqrt{\frac{\alpha+\beta}{\beta}}\frac{\partial\Phi^{-1}(\frac{t}{D})}{\partial D}}{1-(1-\lambda)\phi_1(\cdot)\frac{\alpha}{\sqrt{\beta}}-\lambda\phi_2(\cdot)\frac{\alpha}{\sqrt{\gamma}}} + \frac{\lambda\phi_2(\cdot)\sqrt{\frac{\alpha+\gamma}{\gamma}}\frac{\partial\Phi^{-1}(\frac{t}{D})}{\partial D}}{1-(1-\lambda)\phi_1(\cdot)\frac{\alpha}{\sqrt{\beta}}-\lambda\phi_2(\cdot)\frac{\alpha}{\sqrt{\gamma}}} > 0\,.$$

Bearing in mind that the maximum values for the standard normal density are given by $\frac{1}{\sqrt{2\pi}}$, the denominator is always positive in the unique equilibrium case, since then $1 > (1-\lambda)\phi_1(\cdot)\frac{\alpha}{\sqrt{\beta}} - \lambda\phi_2(\cdot)\frac{\alpha}{\sqrt{\beta}}$. Hence, the partial derivative of θ^* with respect to transaction costs t (payoff D) is negative (positive). □

Proposition 12.5. (Metz, 2002b)
The ex-ante expected fundamental value y (prior mean) exerts a negative influence on the probability of a currency crisis. The negative influence of y increases in the size λ of the large trader, if the precision of the large trader's information is sufficiently low relative to the precision of the small traders' information.

Proof:

$$\frac{\partial\theta^*}{\partial y} = -\frac{(1-\lambda)\phi_1(\cdot)\frac{\alpha}{\sqrt{\beta}}+\lambda\phi_2(\cdot)\frac{\alpha}{\sqrt{\gamma}}}{1-(1-\lambda)\phi_1(\cdot)\frac{\alpha}{\sqrt{\beta}}-\lambda\phi_2(\cdot)\frac{\alpha}{\sqrt{\gamma}}} < 0$$

and

$$\frac{\partial\frac{\partial\theta^*}{\partial y}}{\partial\lambda} = \frac{\phi_1(\cdot)\frac{\alpha}{\sqrt{\beta}}-\phi_2(\cdot)\frac{\alpha}{\sqrt{\gamma}}}{[1-(1-\lambda)\phi_1(\cdot)\frac{\alpha}{\sqrt{\beta}}-\lambda\phi_2(\cdot)\frac{\alpha}{\sqrt{\gamma}}]^2}$$

The last partial derivative is positive, whenever $\sqrt{\gamma} > \sqrt{\beta}\frac{\phi_2(\cdot)}{\phi_1(\cdot)}$. □

Hence, the stronger the commonly expected fundamental state, i.e. the higher y, the lower is the probability of a currency crisis and vice versa. The large trader increases this negative influence of the prior mean on θ^*, if his private information is sufficiently imprecise relative to the small traders' private information. If, instead, the large speculator is very precisely informed about the fundamental state of the economy, i.e. γ is high relative to β, the negative effect of y on θ^* is reduced. In other words, the large trader cannot change the sign of the effect of the commonly expected fundamental index on the probability of a currency crises. But he will increase the extent of the effect if he is only poorly informed relative to the continuum of small speculators. However, if the precision of his signal is high, the negative effect of y on the probability of crisis decreases.

From this analysis, it can easily be seen that the large trader may coordinate the actions of his opponents. Whenever the large trader's information is commonly known to be only poorly precise, small speculators can be sure that the large agent will mostly base his decision of whether or not to attack on the common prior y, instead of his private information. A high prior mean y and a low precision γ therefore not only make small speculators more optimistic about the fundamental state θ, but they are then also sure that the large trader will hold a very similar belief concerning θ. Hence, following from a strong common prior, the market will tend to refrain from attacking, so that θ^* decreases. Of course, the opposite holds for a pessimistic market belief about fundamentals, i.e. low y.

Proposition 12.6. (Metz, 2002b)
If $\theta^* > \max(y + \frac{1}{2}\frac{1}{\sqrt{\alpha+\beta}}\Phi^{-1}(\frac{t}{D}), y + \frac{1}{2}\frac{1}{\sqrt{\alpha+\gamma}}\Phi^{-1}(\frac{t}{D}))$, the precision of the public signal α has a positive influence on the probability of a currency crisis. If $\theta^* < \min(y+\frac{1}{2}\frac{1}{\sqrt{\alpha+\beta}}\Phi^{-1}(\frac{t}{D}), y+\frac{1}{2}\frac{1}{\sqrt{\alpha+\gamma}}\Phi^{-1}(\frac{t}{D}))$, the precision of the public signal α has a negative influence on the probability of a currency crisis. In both cases, the influence of α on the crisis probability is strengthened by the large player's size λ.

Proof:

$$\frac{\partial\theta^*}{\partial\alpha} = \frac{(1-\lambda)\phi_1(\cdot)\left(\frac{1}{\sqrt{\beta}}\theta^* - \frac{1}{\sqrt{\beta}}y - \frac{1}{2\beta}\sqrt{\frac{\beta}{\alpha+\beta}}\Phi^{-1}(\frac{t}{D})\right)}{1-(1-\lambda)\phi_1(\cdot)\frac{\alpha}{\sqrt{\beta}} - \lambda\phi_2(\cdot)\frac{\alpha}{\sqrt{\gamma}}} + \frac{\lambda\phi_2(\cdot)\left(\frac{1}{\sqrt{\gamma}}\theta^* - \frac{1}{\sqrt{\gamma}}y - \frac{1}{2\gamma}\sqrt{\frac{\gamma}{\alpha+\gamma}}\Phi^{-1}(\frac{t}{D})\right)}{1-(1-\lambda)\phi_1(\cdot)\frac{\alpha}{\sqrt{\beta}} - \lambda\phi_2(\cdot)\frac{\alpha}{\sqrt{\gamma}}}$$

The partial derivative of θ^* with respect to α is positive, whenever $\theta^* > y + \frac{1}{2}\frac{1}{\sqrt{\alpha+\beta}}\Phi^{-1}(\frac{t}{D})$ and $\theta^* > y + \frac{1}{2}\frac{1}{\sqrt{\alpha+\gamma}}\Phi^{-1}(\frac{t}{D})$. However, it is negative, whenever $\theta^* < y + \frac{1}{2}\frac{1}{\sqrt{\alpha+\beta}}\Phi^{-1}(\frac{t}{D})$ and $\theta^* < y + \frac{1}{2}\frac{1}{\sqrt{\alpha+\gamma}}\Phi^{-1}(\frac{t}{D})$. Note that these conditions for the influence of α on θ^* are sufficient but not necessary for the influence being positive or negative respectively.

For the influence of the large player's size on the impact of the precision of public information, it holds that

$$\frac{\partial \frac{\partial \theta^*}{\partial \alpha}}{\partial \lambda} = \phi_1(\cdot)\phi_2(\cdot) \cdot \left(\frac{1}{\sqrt{\gamma}}\theta^* - \frac{1}{\sqrt{\gamma}}y - \frac{1}{2\gamma}\sqrt{\frac{\gamma}{\alpha+\gamma}}\Phi^{-1}(\frac{t}{D})\right) \cdot \frac{\left(\frac{1}{\sqrt{\beta}}\theta^* - \frac{1}{\sqrt{\beta}}y - \frac{1}{2\beta}\sqrt{\frac{\beta}{\alpha+\beta}}\Phi^{-1}(\frac{t}{D})\right)}{[1-(1-\lambda)\phi_1(\cdot)\frac{\alpha}{\sqrt{\beta}} - \lambda\phi_2(\cdot)\frac{\alpha}{\sqrt{\gamma}}]^2}$$

This partial derivative is positive, whenever $\theta^* > \max(y + \frac{1}{2}\frac{1}{\sqrt{\alpha+\beta}}\Phi^{-1}(\frac{t}{D}), y + \frac{1}{2}\frac{1}{\sqrt{\alpha+\gamma}}\Phi^{-1}(\frac{t}{D}))$ or $\theta^* < \min(y + \frac{1}{2}\frac{1}{\sqrt{\alpha+\beta}}\Phi^{-1}(\frac{t}{D}), y + \frac{1}{2}\frac{1}{\sqrt{\alpha+\gamma}}\Phi^{-1}(\frac{t}{D}))$. Again, these conditions are sufficient but not necessary. □

Consequently, whenever the switching value of the fundamental state, θ^*, turns out to be sufficiently high, the danger of a currency crisis will be the higher the more precise public information is. In contrast, if the switching value is very low, the probability of a crisis will be the lower the higher the chosen precision of public information. Note, that this result is very similar to the finding in the model of Chap. 9 with homogenous speculators. Hence, for low values of the prior mean, θ^* will be very likely to be higher than the respective threshold function and the precision of public information will exert a positive influence on the danger of a crisis. For a good market sentiment, i.e. for high values of y, the reverse holds. The argument behind this result follows the explanation of Chap. 9. The higher the precision of public information, the larger the weight that both small and large traders will place on this type of information in calculating the possible value of θ. Good prior means therefore will decrease the incentive to attack, so that the danger of a currency crisis is reduced. In case of bad prior means, in contrast, the danger of a crisis rises in the precision of public information.

Moreover, we find that the influence of the public information's precision on the danger of a crisis is the stronger, the more market power the large trader possesses. In contrast to the influence of the prior mean, however, the impact of the large trader's size is not linked to the precision of his information.

Proposition 12.7. (Metz, 2002b)
The precision of the small speculators' private information, β, exerts a negative influence on the probability of a currency crisis, if $\theta^* > y + \frac{1}{\sqrt{\alpha+\beta}}\Phi^{-1}(\frac{t}{D})$. If $\theta^* < y + \frac{1}{\sqrt{\alpha+\beta}}\Phi^{-1}(\frac{t}{D})$, the precision of small speculators' information has a positive influence on the probability of a crisis. The influence of the precision of small traders' information moreover decreases in the size of the large trader.

Proof:

$$\frac{\partial \theta^*}{\partial \beta} = \frac{(1-\lambda)\phi_1(\cdot)\left(-\frac{\alpha}{2\sqrt{\beta^3}}\theta^* + \frac{\alpha}{2\sqrt{\beta^3}}y + \frac{\alpha}{2\beta^2}\sqrt{\frac{\beta}{\alpha+\beta}}\Phi^{-1}(\frac{t}{D})\right)}{1-(1-\lambda)\phi_1(\cdot)\frac{\alpha}{\sqrt{\beta}} - \lambda\phi_2(\cdot)\frac{\alpha}{\sqrt{\gamma}}}$$

The partial derivative of θ^* with respect to β is negative, whenever $\theta^* > y + \frac{1}{\sqrt{\alpha+\beta}}\Phi^{-1}(\frac{t}{D})$, but positive if θ^* is lower than the threshold function. Additionally, it is obvious to see that $\frac{\partial \frac{\partial \theta^*}{\partial \beta}}{\partial \lambda} < 0$, so that indeed the influence of β on θ^* decreases in the size of the large speculator. □

Hence, if the switching value θ^* is sufficiently high, the danger of a currency crisis is the lower, the more precise the small speculators' private information is. In the opposite case of a very low switching value θ^*, however, the probability of a crisis is the lower, the less precise the private information held by the mass of small speculators is. Note that since θ^* is a decreasing function in y, as follows from proposition 12.5, there must be a value of the prior mean which leads to equality of $\theta^*(y)$ and the threshold function $y + \frac{1}{\sqrt{\alpha+\beta}}\Phi^{-1}(\frac{t}{D})$. Let this value be denoted by y_β. Thus, for all prior means lower than y_β, the probability of a currency crisis decreases in the precision of small speculators' private information, whereas for all prior means above y_β, the probability of a crisis increases in β. The interpretation of this finding again follows the fact that speculators will only want to attack, if they expect the fundamental state to be sufficiently bad. The more precise their private information is, the more weight they will attach to this part of information in order to calculate $E(\theta|x_i)$. Whenever the prior mean y is low, speculators will naturally tend to attack the fixed parity. However, if private information is very precise relative to public information, they might neglect this bad prior information, so that the incentive to attack decreases and therefore also the probability of a crisis is diminished. The opposite holds for a good market sentiment, i.e. for high values of y.

Furthermore, it is easy to see that the influence of β on the equilibrium value θ^* increases in the speculative mass $(1-\lambda)$ that can be built up by the small speculators. Since for high values of β, only the small speculators with a mass of $(1-\lambda)$ will neglect their prior information, whereas the large trader might still take y into account for his optimal action, the influence of β on θ^* is very much influenced by the size λ of the large trader. Hence, the more market power the large trader possesses, i.e. the higher λ, the less pronounced is the influence of β on the danger of a crisis.

Similarly to proposition 12.7, the following holds for the precision of the large trader's private signal:

Proposition 12.8. (Metz, 2002b)
The precision of the large trader's private information, γ decreases the probability of a currency crisis, if $\theta^* > y + \frac{1}{\sqrt{\alpha+\gamma}}\Phi^{-1}(\frac{t}{D})$. If $\theta^* < y + \frac{1}{\sqrt{\alpha+\gamma}}\Phi^{-1}(\frac{t}{D})$, the precision of large trader's information exerts a positive influence on the probability of a crisis. Moreover, the influence of the precision γ on θ^* increases in the size of the large trader.

Proof:

$$\frac{\partial\theta^*}{\partial\gamma} = \frac{\lambda\phi_2(\cdot)\left(-\frac{\alpha}{2\sqrt{\gamma^3}}\theta^* + \frac{\alpha}{2\sqrt{\gamma^3}}y + \frac{\alpha}{2\gamma^2}\sqrt{\frac{\gamma}{\alpha+\gamma}}\Phi^{-1}(\frac{t}{D})\right)}{1-(1-\lambda)\phi_1(\cdot)\frac{\alpha}{\sqrt{\beta}} - \lambda\phi_2(\cdot)\frac{\alpha}{\sqrt{\gamma}}}$$

For values of θ^* above $y + \frac{1}{\sqrt{\alpha+\gamma}}\Phi^{-1}(\frac{t}{D})$, this partial derivative is negative, so that the probability of a crisis decreases in the precision of the large trader's information. For $\theta^* < y + \frac{1}{\sqrt{\alpha+\gamma}}\Phi^{-1}(\frac{t}{D})$, however, the partial derivative is positive and the opposite holds. For the influence of λ on the partial derivative, it is obvious that $\frac{\partial\frac{\partial\theta^*}{\partial\gamma}}{\partial\lambda} > 0$, so that the influence of the large trader's information's precision is strengthened by his size. □

The influence of the precision of the large trader's private information, γ, is similar to the influence of β. Again, we can define a value of the prior mean which leads to equality of $\theta^*(y)$ and the threshold function $y + \frac{1}{\sqrt{\alpha+\gamma}}\Phi^{-1}(\frac{t}{D})$. Let this value be denoted by y_γ. If the commonly expected value of the fundamental state is worse than y_γ, the danger of a currency crisis decreases in the precision of the large trader's private information. In contrast, if the prior mean is higher than y_γ, the reverse holds and the crisis probability increases in the precision γ of the large trader's information. The interpretation of this result is the same as for the influence of β. Of course, the effect of γ on θ^* is the stronger, the larger the financial power λ of the single trader is.

Lastly, the pure influence of the large trader's size, λ, on the probability of a currency crisis remains to be analyzed. This is done by proposition 12.9.

Proposition 12.9. (Metz, 2002b)
If $\theta^* > y + \frac{\sqrt{\beta(\alpha+\gamma)}-\sqrt{\gamma(\alpha+\beta)}}{\alpha(\sqrt{\beta}-\sqrt{\gamma})}\Phi^{-1}(\frac{t}{D})$, the large speculator's size, λ, has a positive influence on the probability of a currency crisis.

Proof:

$$\frac{\partial\theta^*}{\partial\lambda} = \frac{\Phi_2(\cdot) - \Phi_1(\cdot)}{1-(1-\lambda)\phi_1(\cdot)\frac{\alpha}{\sqrt{\beta}} - \lambda\phi_2(\cdot)\frac{\alpha}{\sqrt{\gamma}}}$$

This partial derivative of θ^* with respect to λ is positive, if $\Phi_2(\cdot) > \Phi_1(\cdot)$. This implies that θ^* has to be higher than $y + \frac{\sqrt{\beta(\alpha+\gamma)}-\sqrt{\gamma(\alpha+\beta)}}{\alpha(\sqrt{\beta}-\sqrt{\gamma})}\Phi^{-1}(\frac{t}{D})$. □

Hence, the large trader's size has a positive influence on the danger of a crisis, if the switching value θ^* is sufficiently high. Denote as y_λ the value of the prior mean for which $\theta^*(y_\lambda) = y_\lambda + \frac{\sqrt{\beta(\alpha+\gamma)}-\sqrt{\gamma(\alpha+\beta)}}{\alpha(\sqrt{\beta}-\sqrt{\gamma})}\Phi^{-1}(\frac{t}{D})$. Whenever the commonly expected fundamental state is better than y_λ, the probability of a crisis decreases in the size of the large trader, for a prior mean below y_λ the reverse holds. Hence, even irrespective of his informativeness, the large trader may make the market more aggressive. However, this only holds, if the market is already quite pessimistic about the fundamental state of the economy, i.e. if the market sentiment y is sufficiently low. In the opposite case of the commonly expected fundamentals being good, the large speculator on the contrary will increase the incidence of a "do not attack" equilibrium.

12.3 Conclusion

The different theoretical models on the influence of large traders on the foreign exchange market have some results in common: They show that a large trader may indeed make the rest of the market more aggressive towards attacking the fixed parity and as such trigger a crisis earlier than in the absence of a single large speculator, although he does not necessarily have to. However, the different models point to several varying details, which are worthwhile exploring.

If the models take into account that the speculative mass jumps up by the whole financial power of the large trader whenever he decides to join the attack, it can be found that his influence strongly depends on his size. The probability of a currency crisis increases only if the large trader is sufficiently "large", i.e possesses financial power above a certain threshold. Otherwise, his influence is not significant. This, however, changes if the large trader is known to exclusively have completely precise information about the fundamental state of the economy. In this latter case, the large trader will always make the market more aggressive and as such increase the danger of a currency crisis.

The results are different, if the models assume that the central bank reacts as early as even to only the expectation of the large trader's joining the attack, so that the speculative mass function becomes smooth. In this case, the large trader's influence depends on the market sentiment. Whenever the market commonly believes fundamentals to be bad, the probability of a currency crisis increases in the large trader's size. However, if the market sentiment is good, the existence of the large trader will rather lead to a coordination on the "do not attack" equilibrium, so that the danger of a crisis decreases in the large speculator's size. Quite the opposite holds for the large trader's informativeness. The danger of a crisis rises in the precision of the large trader's private information only if the market sentiment is good. Additionally to these direct effects, the large trader also strengthens or weakens the impact of other parameters on the event of a crisis. In this respect, we find that the effects of a changing precision of public information as well as of the large speculator's private information are strengthened by the large trader's size, whereas the opposite holds for the impact of the small traders' private information precision. Moreover, the negative influence of the prior mean on the probability of a currency crisis decreases in the large trader's size, if his information is sufficiently precise relative to that of the small speculators. From this analysis, it can clearly be seen that optimal decisions of speculators on the foreign exchange market are based on complex situations, which do not always allow to disentangle the influence of single parameters such as a speculator's size or his precision of information. Consequently, we can deduct from the model of Sect. 12.2, that the existence of a large trader not necessarily makes the market more aggressive. However, the model also clearly tells that the worst case for a central bank trying to prevent a speculative attack on the fixed parity is a large uninformed trader acting on a generally pessimistic market.

Several of the theoretical results are substantiated by empirical analyses of currency crisis situations, especially in the case of emerging markets. As Corsetti, Pesenti et al. (2001) point out, often large traders have privileged access to policy makers and as such to special information on the economic state. Therefore, large traders quite generally are believed to have superior information as compared to the rest of the market. This view is also taken by the FSF (2000) study, which suggests that in the 1990s, a number of macro hedge-funds had built up a very strong reputation in terms of information gathering, processing and of forecasting economic developments. Anecdotal evidence even shows that a large number of financial institutions stood ready to provide hedge-funds with all necessary resources in order to track down their investment strategies.

Moreover, according to Corsetti, Pesenti et al. (2001) it should be noted that even though the actual size of large traders on foreign exchange markets does not always appear to be terribly influential during normal times, their relative size may increase significantly during periods of financial turmoil. This is due to the fact that in crisis periods market liquidity severely shrinks. This effect is magnified under institutionalized fixed exchange rate regimes, since these limit the overall degree of liquidity in the system.

Although the results from empirical analyses concerning the influence of large traders in currency crisis situations are mixed, there are several cases in which single major institutions obviously did have a large impact on financial turmoil. For the Asian crisis during the latter half of the 1990s, several analyses corroborate the superior influence of hedge-funds on the collapse of a number of currencies. Especially for the Thai baht, Fung, Hsieh and Tsatsaronis (2000) estimated that a large part of the short positions against the currency was in the hands of only a few major institutions. The FSF (2000) report came to a similar conclusion for the Malaysian ringgit. Also for Hong Kong it was reported that large traders played a major role in triggering the devaluation of the currency.

Summing up, we may state that several of the recent currency crises point to an important role of large traders on financial markets. Theoretical analyses identify different effects through which large speculators may possibly influence the market outcome. Although some part of the theoretical models comes to the conclusion that the large trader's size and his potential informational advantage may have separate influences on the probability of a crisis, we find from a simplified approach as delineated in Sect. 12.2, that the impact of these two parameters cannot be completely disentangled. This result mirrors the high complexity on financial markets but shows nonetheless how large traders may coordinate the decision processes on a whole market towards either a crisis or financial stability. This finding highlights the importance of monitoring the actions of large and influential market participants, especially of those who may use informational channels to strengthen their influence.

13

Informational Cascades and Herds: Aspects of Dynamics and Time

The currency crisis models of the last chapters necessarily assumed that speculators have to decide at the same point in time whether or not to attack the fixed exchange rate parity. The models therefore analyzed currency crises as static coordination games. In reality, however, market participants are free to decide when, if ever, to short-sell the domestic currency, thereby attacking the fixed peg. Such a setting is inherently dynamic, encompassing several time periods. Even though a very important aspect, questions of dynamic coordination games in currency crisis models have only recently attracted scholarly attention. However, there exists a vast theoretical literature on dynamic aspects of financial markets in general.[1] Typically, these models allow for backward-looking behavior, analyzing the decisions of agents who can observe their predecessors' actions. At the center of attention in these models is the question whether market participants act according to their own private information, or if they are willing to completely neglect their individual information and base their decisions solely on the observed behavior of their predecessors. The emphasis therefore is on aspects of herding behavior and informational cascades. Market observers on financial markets frequently note excessively optimistic or pessimistic behavior of market participants. Often it is suspected that decision makers simply imitate the behavior of others, obviously making no effort to gather and process information about underlying fundamentals. In December 1996, Alan Greenspan referred to such herding behavior as "irrational exuberance", thereby criticizing markets for not efficiently using available information. Theoretical work on this kind of behavior, however, emphasized that herding not necessarily has to be irrational. Rather, it has been found that, once stuck in an informational cascade, agents rationally decide to neglect their information. The rationality question notwithstanding, the market outcome will most certainly be inefficient, since herding behavior is characterized by the fact that market participants can no longer learn from their predecessors' choices. Hence, the amount of information ag-

[1] For an overview, see for instance Shiller (1995) or Gale (1996).

gregated by the market process remains at a constant level, so that the market outcome is very likely to be inefficient at some point.

On foreign exchange markets, large traders in particular have been accused of acting as leaders for a herd of speculators. This accusation mostly draws upon the fact that a large trader's behavior by definition is clearly "visible" to the market. In the case of currency crisis situations, therefore, large traders are often suspected of taking advantage of their influence and triggering an otherwise avoidable devaluation. However, even without particularly large market participants, foreign exchange markets may be accused of displaying herding behavior. In this respect, think of the so-called "dollar-bubble" in the mid-1980s. The increase of the dollar value was obviously driven by a large mass of overly optimistic speculators, acting all in the same direction and buying dollars.

In the following, we will analyze these aspects in more detail. Section 13.1 will present the two pioneering papers analyzing herding behavior: the models by Banerjee (1993) and Bikhchandani, Hirshleifer and Welch (1992). By briefly depicting these seminal models, we aim at pointing out the main characteristics of herding behavior and informational cascades on financial markets. These earlier models, however, typically neglected several aspects which have been proven to be important for the analysis of currency crisis models. Most importantly, they do not take into account strategic complementarities among the actions of market participants. The first models trying to resolve this shortcoming of dynamic models, stem from work by Dasgupta (2000, 2001). By taking account of strategic complementarities, the work by Dasgupta additionally displays forward-looking behavior, since agents become concerned about the signals, which their actions send to their successors. Although the model by Dasgupta (2001) has been applied to liquidity crises originally, we will depict his approach in Sect. 13.2 in the context of currency crises. As will be seen, his model is a natural extension of the static currency crisis models analyzed in the previous chapters of this book. Additionally to the case of homogeneous traders on the foreign exchange market, we will also present a model analyzing the role of a single large trader in a dynamic coordination game in Sect. 13.3. The illustration herein follows the results by Corsetti, Dasgupta et al. (2001) and Corsetti, Pesenti et al. (2001) and is a direct extension of the model of Sect. 12.1.

13.1 Herding Behavior and Informational Cascades

13.1.1 The Model by Banerjee (1993)

The model by Banerjee (1993) is a very simple case of a sequential decision game in which each decision maker observes the actions of previous market participants. The model results in showing that rational individuals may optimally decide to neglect their own information, so that optimizing behavior leads to herding.

In order to give a rationale for herding behavior, Banerjee (1993) considers a simple example. Next to each other, there are two restaurants A and B, for which it is know that with a prior probability of 51 percent restaurant A is the better one. Assume that 100 people sequentially arrive at the restaurants and have to decide on either of the two, after observing their predecessors' choices. Additionally to the prior probabilities, people receive private signals which tell them that either A or B is better. Suppose now that of the 100 agents, 99 observe a signal that favors restaurant B, but that the first person to choose is the one with a signal for A. Of course, this first person will decide on restaurant A. The second person observes this and knows that the first person must have received a signal favoring A. Her signal, however, tells her that B is better. Since both signals are of the same quality, they offset each other. Hence, the second person has to make her choice based only on the prior information. Consequently, she will choose restaurant A, regardless of her own signal. Note that her choice provides no new information to the people later in the line. Therefore, the third person's decision problem is the same as that of the second person. Again, she will decide on restaurant A, even if her private signal told her not to do so. Thus, everyone in the line ends up choosing restaurant A, effectively disregarding their individual information. According to Banerjee, the second person's decision to neglect her information and join the herd, imposes a negative externality on the rest of the group. If she had used her own information, her decision would have provided new information to the rest of the population, which would have encouraged them to use their information as well.

Banerjee (1993) formalizes this idea in the following model. Consider a number N of agents, who try to maximize identical risk-neutral von Neumann-Morgenstern utility functions. Utility is defined on the space of asset returns. There is a continuum of assets, indexed by $i \in [0,1]$. Asset $a(i)$ delivers a return of $z(i) \in \mathbb{R}$. Assume that there is a unique asset i^*, such that $z(i) = 0$ for all $i \neq i^*$ and $z(i^*) > 0$. Priors on the assets are uniform, so that no one ex-ante knows which asset to invest in. Suppose now that with a probability of p each agent receives a signal telling that the true i^* is i'. However, with a probability of $1 - q$, the signal is false. Additionally, it is assumed that false signals are uniformly distributed on $[0,1]$. The decision process is sequential: one person is randomly chosen and has to take the first decision. The next agent observes the predecessor's choice and afterwards has to decide herself and so on. After everyone has made a choice, the true asset i^* is revealed, and all the agents that decided on this asset receive their payoff $z(i^*)$.

The structure of the game and Bayesian rationality are common knowledge. In order to search for the Bayesian Nash equilibrium in this game, a few more assumptions are necessary. Following Banerjee (1993), these assumptions are made in order to minimize the possibility of herding, as will become obvious during the course of the game. Assumption 1: Whenever an agent has no signal and all the other players have chosen $i = 0$, she will also choose $i = 0$. Assumption 2: In case of indifference between following the own signal and following someone else's choice, an agent always follows her own signal. Assumption 3: In case of indifference between following more than one of the previous agents' choices, an agent always decides on following the one with the highest value of i.

Let us now consider the course of the game which leads to the equilibrium. The first agent will clearly make her decision contingent on whether she received a signal or not. If she has no signal, she will choose $i = 0$, according to assumption 1, otherwise she will follow her signal. If the second decision maker has no signal, she will follow the choice of her predecessor. However, if she receives a signal and the first agent chose $i \neq 0$ with i unequal to her own signal, she knows that her predecessor has received a signal which is as likely to be correct as hers. Hence, she is indifferent between following her own signal and her predecessor's choice. In this case, assumption 2 comes into play, so that the second agent will follow her own signal.

The third agent may observe one of four different situations. Either both of her predecessors chose $i = 0$, which tells her that they both did not receive a signal. In this case, she will either follow her own signal, or choose $i = 0$ as well, if she did not observe a signal. If only one of her predecessors decided on $i = 0$, she should follow the other one if she herself did not receive a signal, and follow her own signal otherwise. If both predecessors chose $i \neq 0$ but did not agree, the third agent is indifferent, if she did not receive a signal. In this case, assumption 3 holds and she decides to follow the person with the highest i. However, if she did receive a signal, she will follow her own signal, unless both of her predecessors decided on the same asset. Whenever the third person's signal matches one of the choices of her predecessors, she can be sure that her signal tells her the correct asset and hence will follow her signal. This follows from the fact that in this model the probability of two people receiving the same signal and yet both signals being wrong is zero.

What ensues from this analysis is that whenever one option has been chosen by more than one person, as long as this is not the option with the highest i, each successor will optimally choose the same asset. This is due to the fact that clearly the first of these two agents must have received a signal. The second person, however, is very likely to have received the same signal which is a substantial support for the correctness of this signal. Hence, for all subsequent agents it is optimal to follow their choice. Consequently, once one option has been chosen by more than one person, the next decision maker should always select this option as well, unless her signal matches one of the options that have already been chosen. In this case, her signal will undoubtedly be correct and she should follow her own signal.

Hence, from the third decision maker on, there is a high positive probability of an informational cascade, in which agents rationally neglect their own information. The first person always follows her signal whenever she observes one, and so does the second agent due to assumption 2. However, the third agent may be the first to decide solely based on the observation of her predecessors' choice, irrespective of her own signal. Of course, there is a high probability that herding is on the wrong option. Generally, herding on the wrong action may spring off two different histories: Either the first k agents received wrong signals, therefore chose different wrong options, and agent $k+1$ did not observe a signal and hence decided on one of her predecessors' actions, thereby triggering a cascade. Or the first k agents did not receive any signals, afterwards j agents received wrong signals and agent $k+j+1$ did not receive a signal and selected one of her predecessors' options, thereby leading the herd.

Actually, the probability that no one in the whole population chooses the correct option is the sum of the two histories. The probability of the first part as described above, is given by

$$(p(1-q))^k+(p(1-q))^{k-1}(1-p)+(p(1-q))^{k-2}(1-p)1+...+p(1-q)(1-p)1 .$$

This probability can be transformed to

$$(p(1-q))^k+p(1-q)(1-p)[1+p(1-q)+(p(1-q))^2+...+(p(1-q))^{k-2}]$$
$$=(p(1-q))^k+p(1-p)(1-q)\sum_{j=0}^{k-2}(p(1-q))^j .$$

For $k \to \infty$, we find that this probability converges to

$$\frac{p(1-p)(1-q)}{1-p(1-q)} . \tag{13.1}$$

The second part of the history can be formalized as follows

$$(1-p)\frac{p(1-p)(1-q)}{1-p(1-q)}+(1-p)^2\frac{p(1-p)(1-q)}{1-p(1-q)}+...+(1-p)^k 1$$
$$=\frac{p(1-p)(1-q)}{1-p(1-q)}(1-p)\sum_{j=0}^{k}(1-p)^j+(1-p)^k .$$

Again, for an infinitely large population, $k \to \infty$, this probability approaches a value of

$$\frac{(1-p)(1-p)(1-q)}{1-p(1-q)} . \tag{13.2}$$

The probability that no one in the whole population chooses the correct option is then given as the sum of (13.1) and (13.2)

$$\frac{p(1-p)(1-q)}{1-p(1-q)}+\frac{(1-p)(1-p)(1-q)}{1-p(1-q)}=\frac{(1-p)(1-q)}{1-p(1-q)} .$$

Intuitively, this probability is decreasing in the likelihood of receiving a signal, p, and in the likelihood of the signal being correct, q. For q sufficiently low, this probability will be very close to one. Note, that if agents were not allowed to observe their predecessors' choices, the probability that someone eventually chooses the correct option converges to pq, so that the probability of no one selecting the right asset is close to $1 - pq$.

Additionally to the fact that agents rationally decide to follow the cascade-path, it is important to recognize that it is not the observability of the history of the game which renders informational cascades. Rather it is the lack of invertibility from actions to signals. In the model by Banerjee, it is not possible to tell from the mere observation of choices, which information the decision has been based on. If agents were able to observe their predecessors' signals instead of only their actions, there would be no herding in the model.

13.1.2 The Model by Bikhchandani, Hirshleifer and Welch (1992)

The model by Bikhchandani et al. (1992) is more similar to the typical case of a financial market crisis than the rather stylized model by Banerjee (1993). However, since we only want to present the basic characteristics of herding behavior, we will illustrate only the most basic aspects of the rather complex and extendable model by Bikhchandani et al. (1992).

Consider a sequence of individuals $i = 1, 2, ..., n, ...$. They each have to decide whether to adopt or reject an option. Before making their choice, they can observe their predecessors' behavior. There is a cost of adoption, C, and a gain V, which are the same for all agents. Gain V takes on a value out of a set $v_1 < v_2 < ... < v_S$, with $v_1 < C < v_S$, so that the decision problem is non-trivial.

In contrast to the currency crisis context that we are going to analyze in the sections to follow, Bikhchandani et al. (1992) assume that an individual's payoff does not depend on the actions chosen by later agents. Hence, there is no incentive to deviate and make an out-of-equilibrium move in order to influence later individuals. Consequently, the model does not take into account any strategic complementarities.

Each agent observes one out of a set of private signals, which are conditionally independent and identically distributed, taken from the sequence $x_1 < x_2 < ... < x_R$. Denote by p_{ql} the probability that an individual observes a signal x_q, given a true gain from adoption of v_l. Let J_i be the set of signal realizations which incite player i to adopt. From his decision, followers may then conjecture whether player i observed a signal from set J_i or from its complement. However, if J_i contains the whole set of possible signals or is empty, individual i's decision does not contain any information about his signal for the following agents.

According to the definition by Bikhchandani et al. (1992), an individual is in a cascade, if his action does not depend on his private signal. Hence, if a person is in a cascade, then his action does not deliver any information to the individual next in line. Consequently, all subsequent decision makers are in a cascade. A cascade once started will last forever, unless signals are no longer given with the same quality (i.e. taken from the same distribution).

Let a_i give the action (adopt or reject) chosen by individual i and let $A_i = (a_1, a_2, ..., a_i)$ denote the history of actions taken up to individual i. Let $J_i(A_{i-1}, a_i)$ be the set of signals which incite individual i to choose action a_i after observing history A_{i-1}. Then, individual $n+1$'s expectation of the gain from adopting V, conditional on his signal x_q and history A_n, is given by

$$V_{n+1}(x_q; A_n) = E[V|X_{n+1} = x_q, X_i \in J_i(A_{i-1}, a_i), \text{for all}\, i \leq n] .$$

Individual $n+1$ will choose to adopt whenever $V_{n+1}(x_q; A_n) \geq C$, and reject otherwise. Hence, individual $n+2$ can draw the following inference from observing agent $n+1$'s choice:

$$J_{n+1}(A_n, \text{adopt}) = \{x_q \text{ such that } V_{n+1}(x_q; A_n) \geq C\}$$
$$J_{n+1}(A_n, \text{reject}) = \{x_q \text{ such that } V_{n+1}(x_q; A_n) < C\}$$

In order to determine the equilibrium behavior of agents, Bikhchandani et al. (1992) imposed two more regularity conditions to facilitate the analysis. First, they assumed that the conditional distributions of signals given gain V are ordered by the monotone likelihood ratio property.[2] This means that an individual observing a higher signal realization may infer that the gain from adopting is higher. Hence, the conditionally expected gain from adopting increases in the observed signal realization. From this, it follows that if agent i is not in a cascade and adopts, later individuals infer that $X_i \geq x_q$ for some q, whereas if i rejects, later individuals conclude that $X_i < x_q$. Secondly, it has to be assured that there are no long-run ties, i.e. $v_l \neq C$ for all l. Thus, if agents learn enough from observing their predecessors' choices, they are not indifferent between adopting and rejecting.

Instead of deriving the equilibrium of this very complex model, let us in the following rather interpret the results and state the differences between the models by Banerjee (1993) and Bikhchandani et al. (1992). The two major results that Bikhchandani et al. (1992) derive from their model are that eventually a cascade will start, and that with an increasing number of agents the probability of a cascade approaches one. Additionally, they find that cascades are often wrong. For a complete conduction of the proof, we refer to Bikhchandani et al. (1992).

The almost certainty of arriving at an informational cascade in the model by Bikhchandani et al. (1992) is intriguing. This is even more so, since the set-up of the model concerning signals and payoffs is very complex and as such should allow agents to distinguish sufficiently precisely between and value the informational content of their own information and that of their predecessors. However, as has been stated above, this conclusion is obviously not correct. Again, the underlying reason is that from observing his predecessors' choices, an individual agent is not able to conjecture their information. Hence, the

[2] For a more detailed illustration of the monotone likelihood ratio property, we refer to Milgrom (1981).

lack of invertibility from actions to signals triggers an inevitable cascade. This finding has also been emphasized by Vives (1996), who shows that herding on an incorrect option requires indivisibilities in terms of a discrete action space as well as signals of bounded precision.

What is interesting in this context moreover is that although the probability of a cascade increases in the number of agents, the process of rationally neglecting private information is rather fragile. In other words, the "depth" of a cascade does not necessarily increase in the number of agents adopting the herding behavior. Instead, the arrival of new public information after a cascade has started can easily destroy herding behavior, even if this public signal is less informative than the neglected private signals. This result is intuitive, since a cascade only aggregates the information of a few early individual actions. Hence, public information disseminated later has to offset only the information conveyed by the last decision maker before the cascade started. This is irrespective of the number of imitating agents in the informational cascade. From this finding, it is also easy to see that individuals with high-precision information, who have to decide late in the sequence, can also break a cascade.[3]

The results of the model by Bikhchandani et al. (1992) are more complex than the findings by Banerjee (1993), since the former model allows a much more refined decision structure. Although agents still have to choose between only two actions, the information structure underlying the decision is much finer than in the previous section. Note, that a large number of variations and applications followed the two pioneering papers on herding behavior and informational cascades. One aspect of a generalization concerns the sequence of agents. Whereas in the hitherto presented models, the sequencing was given exogenously, the models by Chamley and Gale (1994), Chari and Kehoe (2000) and Gul and Lundholm (1995) allow the sequence to arise endogenously by assuming costs to delay the choice. Avery and Zemsky (1998), Lee (1993), Scharfstein and Stein (1990), and Welch (1992) apply the herding models to several aspects of the financial literature, for instance to investment decisions in order to explain one-sided movements in asset prices. Lux (1995) analyzes both herding behavior and bubbles as causes for financial market crashes, thereby combining various forms of anomalies on financial markets. An overview of the recent literature on herding behavior and informational cascades is provided by Bikhchandani, Hershleifer and Welch (1998). What is important to note in our context is that all these models neglect any strategic payoff-complementarities. This, however, is an important feature of the decision whether or not to attack a fixed exchange rate parity. The model by Dasgupta (2001), as delineated in the next section, therefore takes into account both backward- and forward-looking behavior of agents. In this model, agents do not receive a prespecified gain from adopting the "attack-strategy".

[3] Note that this requires signals of different quality, which has not been assumed for the general case above, where a cascade once started lasts forever.

Rather, the payoff depends on the number of opponents who choose the same strategy.

13.2 Currency Crises as Dynamic Coordination Games - Dasgupta (2001)

The model by Dasgupta (2001) analyzes general coordination problems on financial markets, complicated by dynamics and social learning. Hence, agents in this model do not only display backward-looking behavior, since they are allowed to observe their predecessors' actions and learn from them, but the model also takes account of forward-looking behavior, as coordination problems make an agent's payoff contingent on his successors' actions. Additionally to combining aspects of both herding behavior and strategic complementarities, the model also derives signalling behavior, i.e. incentives to signal certain information to later agents, thereby trying to influence their choices and hence one's own payoffs. Dasgupta (2001) considers these aspects in the setting of a typical coordination situation on financial markets: an investment problem. Agents may decide to invest in a risky project or a safe option at several points in time, with a cost of delaying their decision. Since the decision problem for the investment project is similar to the decision of whether or not to attack a fixed parity, we will place the illustration of the model by Dasgupta directly into a currency crisis context. This modification of background does not change the general structure of the model and allows to adopt a similar methodology and notation as in the models of previous chapters.

As Dasgupta (2000, 2001) points out, dynamic coordination games, like their static counterparts, display multiple equilibria whenever the state of the game is common knowledge. It is, however, possible to show that under certain conditions equilibria can be eliminated iteratively, so that a unique equilibrium in the formerly defined sense prevails. Dasgupta (2001) does so by extending the equilibrium selection results by Carlsson and van Damme (1993) and Morris and Shin (1998) to a dynamic setting. For the context of currency crises, the method of working with a unique equilibrium strongly facilitates comparisons between the static currency crisis models of Chaps. 5–12 and the dynamic model. Moreover, uniqueness of equilibrium again allows to analyze the role of information in the dynamic case.

Transformed to a currency crisis setting, the model by Dasgupta (2001) considers the following: a mass of agents has to decide whether or not to run an attack on the fixed exchange rate parity. Each agent disposes of one unit of the domestic currency. There are two periods in which a speculator may attack, t_1 and t_2. Fundamentals of the economy are summed up in an index θ, which is unknown to the speculators. The success of an attack depends both on fundamentals and on the actions chosen by the agents. An attack will be successful, if the proportion l of attackers is at least as high as θ. A successful attack in period t_1 pays off a value of D. However, attacking is also costly as denoted by parameter t. The payoff from a successful attack in period t_2 is lower than in the first period and is denoted by $D - k$. Costs of attacking, in contrast, stay the same in both periods.

In this model, the stages of the game are the following: First, nature chooses the fundamental state θ according to an improper prior distribution over the real line.[4] In contrast to the central bank, speculators cannot observe the chosen value of θ. However, they receive private signals $x_i = \theta + \sigma\varepsilon_i$ about it, with ε being distributed standard normal and independent of θ. After receiving private information, there are four different courses for the game to carry on: Either all agents decide at time t_1 whether or not to attack, or they all wait and make their choice at time t_2. These two cases can be represented by simple static coordination games in the style of Morris and Shin (1998). Another possibility is given by an exogenous sequencing, so that an arbitrarily chosen proportion λ of speculators has to decide at time t_1, whereas the rest, $1-\lambda$, waits until period t_2 to decide on an action. Lastly, it might be up to the agents to decide both on whether to attack, and, if at all, when. This game is denoted as a dynamic coordination game with endogenous order of actions. After the last speculators made their decisions, the central bank observes the proportion of attacking traders, l, and devalues the peg whenever $l \geq \theta$. In the following, we will illustrate Dasgupta's (2001) model by delineating the four cases as depicted above and comparing the results.

13.2.1 The Static Benchmark Case

In accordance with Dasgupta (2001) we denote the static coordination games as $\Gamma_{st,1}$ and $\Gamma_{st,2}$, with $\Gamma_{st,1}$ referring to the case where all speculators have to decide at time t_1 whether or not to attack, whereas in game $\Gamma_{st,2}$ the time of decision is t_2. Note that payoffs are given as follows.

Table 13.1.

	success	no success
attack	$D-t$	$-t$
no attack	0	0

for t_1 in $\Gamma_{st,1}$

[4] Note that this improper prior assumption may be interpreted as speculators having diffuse expectations about fundamentals. Formally, it poses no difficulties as long as we are concerned with conditional probabilities only. See also Hartigan (1983).

Table 13.2.

	success	no success
attack	$D-k-t$	$-t$
no attack	0	0

for t_2 in $\Gamma_{st,2}$

Again, we look for monotone equilibria[5] as in the former models by Morris and Shin (1998) and Metz (2002a). It can be shown that for each of the static games, there exists a unique equilibrium in trigger strategies, whenever noise is sufficiently small. Hence, speculators receiving signals below a certain threshold signal will attack, but refrain from doing so for higher signals. Likewise, the central bank will abandon the parity, whenever the fundamental index is lower than a unique threshold value and keep the peg otherwise. Let us first consider the static game at period t_1. It can be shown that the following proposition holds:

Proposition 13.1. (Dasgupta, 2001)
$\Gamma_{st,1}$ displays a unique equilibrium if $\sigma < \sqrt{2\pi}$. For $\sigma \to 0$, it is given by

$$x^*_{st,1} = \theta^*_{st,1} = 1 - \frac{t}{D}.$$

Proof:
The marginal speculator with signal $x^*_{st,1}$ has to be indifferent between attacking and not-attacking, which is the case if

$$D \cdot \text{Prob}(\theta \leq \theta^*_{st,1} | x^*_{st,1}) = t \ .$$

Due to the assumed distribution of noise, we find that $\theta | x_i \sim N(\frac{x_i}{1+\sigma^2}, \frac{\sigma^2}{1+\sigma^2})$. Hence, the speculators' indifference condition can be written as:

$$D \cdot \Phi\left(\frac{\sqrt{1+\sigma^2}}{\sigma}(\theta^*_{st,1} - \frac{x_i}{1+\sigma^2})\right) = t \ ,$$

which yields

$$x^*_{st,1} = (1+\sigma^2)\theta^*_{st,1} - \sigma\sqrt{1+\sigma^2}\Phi^{-1}(\frac{t}{D}) \ . \tag{13.3}$$

The central bank is indifferent between abandoning the peg and keeping the parity, whenever the proportion of attacking speculators is exactly equal to the fundamental index:

$$\text{Prob}(x \leq x^*_{st,1} | \theta^*_{st,1}) = \theta^*_{st,1} \ .$$

Taking into account that $x_i | \theta \sim N(\theta, \sigma^2)$, the critical mass condition can be written as

[5] An equilibrium is in monotone strategies, if higher signals incite agents to choose "higher" actions.

$$\Phi\left(\frac{x^*_{st,1} - \theta^*_{st,1}}{\sigma}\right) = \theta^*_{st,1} \,.$$

Substituting for $x^*_{st,1}$ delivers

$$\theta^*_{st,1} = \Phi\big(\sigma\theta^*_{st,1} - \sqrt{1+\sigma^2}\Phi^{-1}(\tfrac{t}{D})\big) \,. \tag{13.4}$$

Uniqueness of equilibrium requires that only one value of $\theta^*_{st,1}$ exists, which satisfies equation (13.4). This is the case whenever $\frac{\partial\Phi(\cdot)}{\partial\theta^*_{st,1}} < 1$, from which it follows that $\sigma\phi(\cdot) < 1$ and hence $\sigma < \sqrt{2\pi}$.

For vanishing noise, i.e. $\sigma \to 0$, it is easy to see from equation (13.3) that $x^*_{st,1} \to \theta^*_{st,1}$ and from (13.4) that $\theta^*_{st,1} \to \Phi(-\Phi^{-1}(\frac{t}{D})) = 1 - \frac{t}{D}$, which concludes the proof of proposition 13.1. □

Symmetry of arguments delivers that for game $\Gamma_{st,2}$ in period t_2, the trigger values are given as

$$x^*_{st,2} = (1+\sigma^2)\theta^*_{st,2} - \sigma\sqrt{1+\sigma^2}\Phi^{-1}(\frac{t}{D-k}) \tag{13.5}$$

and

$$\theta^*_{st,2} = \Phi\big(\sigma\theta^*_{st,2} - \sqrt{1+\sigma^2}\Phi^{-1}(\frac{t}{D-k})\big) \,. \tag{13.6}$$

Again, uniqueness of equilibrium holds as long as $\sigma < \sqrt{2\pi}$. For $\sigma \to 0$, the equilibrium values converge to

$$x^*_{st,2} = \theta^*_{st,2} = 1 - \frac{t}{D-k} \,.$$

These results may serve as a benchmark case for the dynamic modelling of the crisis-problem. The next subsection deals with the simplest case of a dynamic coordination game, where the sequence of agents deciding on an action is given exogenously.

13.2.2 Dynamic Game with Exogenous Order

In this type of game, denoted by Γ_{ex}, it is assumed that speculators are exogenously subdivided into two groups: agents $i \in [0,\lambda]$ have to make their decision whether to attack or not at time t_1, whereas speculators $i \in (\lambda, 1]$ have to select an action at time t_2. Payoffs are given as before, with agents attacking at time t_1 receiving a net payoff of $D-t$ if the attack is successful, while agents short-selling at time t_2 can only receive a net gain of $D-k-t$ in case of success.

In order to allow for social learning, Dasgupta (2001) additionally assumes that agents deciding in the second period can observe a statistic based on their predecessors' chosen actions in the first period. Thus, traders $(\lambda, 1]$ receive an additional signal $w_i = \Phi^{-1}(l_1) + \tau\delta_i$, with δ being distributed according to a standard normal, independent of ε and θ. This supplementary signal represents noisy private information about the proportion of attacking agents at time t_1, denoted as l_1. Note that complete information about past actions is given for $\tau \to 0$. In the general case of $\tau \neq 0$, speculators cannot exactly observe their predecessors' choices. This is in contrast to the models by Banerjee (1993) and Bikhchandani et al. (1992). However, it represents a very realistic modelling of the situation on financial markets, where indeed market participants cannot directly observe the actions taken by their opponents. Rather, they try to infer them from verifiable statistics, for instance the movement of prices.

Hence, players $[0, \lambda]$, who have to take a decision at the earlier point in time t_1, only observe one private signal x_i, whereas speculators $(\lambda, 1]$ receive two private signals: x_i and w_i. Let $s(x, w)$ denote a sufficient statistic for these two signals. According to Dasgupta (2001), an equilibrium in this type of dynamic game then contains three variables $(x^*_{ex}, s^*_{ex}, \theta^*_{ex})$, so that speculators $[0, \lambda]$ attack iff $x_i \leq x^*_{ex}$, speculators $(\lambda, 1]$ attack iff $s_i \leq s^*_{ex}$, and the attack is successful iff $\theta \leq \theta^*_{ex}$.

In the same way as in the static game, speculators receiving the equilibrium signals have to be indifferent between their respective actions. Thus, agents $[0, \lambda]$ after receiving signal x^*_{ex} are indifferent between attacking and not-attacking if

$$D \cdot \text{Prob}(\theta \leq \theta^*_{ex} | x^*_{ex}) = t \ ,$$

whereas traders $(\lambda, 1]$ after receiving s^*_{ex} are indifferent if

$$(D - k) \cdot \text{Prob}(\theta \leq \theta^*_{ex} | s^*_{ex}) = t \ .$$

The critical mass condition, which makes the central bank indifferent between devaluing and keeping the peg, is given by

$$\lambda \cdot \text{Prob}(x \leq x^*_{ex} | \theta^*_{ex}) + (1 - \lambda) \cdot \text{Prob}(s \leq s^*_{ex} | \theta^*_{ex}) = \theta^*_{ex} \ .$$

In solving for the equilibrium values, statistic s first has to be subdivided into its two parts: x and w. Since the proportion of speculators attacking at t_1 is given by $l_1 = \Phi(\frac{x^*_{ex} - \theta}{\sigma})$, the supplementary private signal for traders deciding in period t_2 can be transformed to

$$\begin{aligned} w_i &= \Phi^{-1}(l_1) + \tau\delta_i \\ &= \frac{x^*_{ex} - \theta}{\sigma} + \tau\delta_i \ . \end{aligned}$$

For simplicity, Dasgupta (2001) defines $z_i = -\sigma w_i + x^*_{ex}$, so that

$$z_i = \theta - \sigma\tau\delta_i \ .$$

This auxiliary signal has a conditional distribution of $z_i | \theta \sim N(\theta, \sigma^2\tau^2)$. It then follows that

$$\theta|x_i, z_i \sim N\left[\frac{\frac{1+\sigma^2}{\sigma^2}\frac{x_i}{1+\sigma^2} + \frac{1}{\sigma^2\tau^2}z_i}{\frac{1+\sigma^2}{\sigma^2} + \frac{1}{\sigma^2\tau^2}}, \frac{1}{\frac{1+\sigma^2}{\sigma^2} + \frac{1}{\sigma^2\tau^2}}\right],$$

which gives the distribution of the fundamental state for a speculator in period 2 with private signal x_i and transformed signal z_i. Substituting z_i by definition with $-\sigma w_i + x^*_{ex}$, delivers

$$\theta|x_i, w_i \sim N\left[\frac{x_i - \frac{\sigma}{\tau^2}w_i + \frac{1}{\tau^2}x^*_{ex}}{1+\sigma^2 + \frac{1}{\tau^2}}, \frac{\sigma^2}{1+\sigma^2+\frac{1}{\tau^2}}\right].$$

Following Dasgupta (2001), it is comfortable to define

$$s_i = \frac{x_i - \frac{\sigma}{\tau^2}w_i + \frac{1}{\tau^2}x^*_{ex}}{1+\sigma^2+\frac{1}{\tau^2}},$$

so that

$$\theta|x, w \;\equiv\; \theta|s \sim N\left[s, \frac{\sigma^2}{1+\sigma^2+\frac{1}{\tau^2}}\right].$$

Equivalently, it can be seen that

$$s_i|\theta \sim N\left[\frac{1+\tau^2}{1+\tau^2+\sigma^2\tau^2}\theta, \frac{\sigma^2\tau^2(1-\tau^2)}{(1+\tau^2+\sigma^2\tau^2)^2}\right],$$

since s is given as a linear combination of the two normally distributed variables x and w.[6]

Consequently, the equilibrium conditions can be represented as follows: speculators $[0, \lambda]$ are indifferent after receiving signal x^*_{ex} if

$$x^*_{ex} = (1+\sigma^2)\theta^*_{ex} + \sigma\sqrt{1+\sigma}\Phi^{-1}(\frac{t}{D}).$$

Note that this condition did not change from the static coordination game, since speculators in period 1 still decide based on the same information. For traders $(\lambda, 1]$ it holds that they are indifferent if

$$(D-k)\cdot\Phi\left(\frac{\theta^*_{ex} - s^*_{ex}}{\sqrt{\frac{\sigma^2}{1+\sigma^2+\frac{1}{\tau^2}}}}\right) = t,$$

which leads to a trigger value for statistic s of

$$s^*_{ex} = \theta^*_{ex} - \frac{\sigma}{\sqrt{1+\sigma^2+\frac{1}{\tau^2}}}\Phi^{-1}\left(\frac{t}{D-k}\right).$$

The central bank is indifferent if

[6] For the derivation of conditional probabilities, see Greene (2000), Hamilton (1994) or Galambos (1995).

$$\lambda \cdot \Phi\left(\frac{x^*_{ex} - \theta^*_{ex}}{\sigma}\right) + (1-\lambda) \cdot \Phi\left(\frac{s^*_{ex} - \frac{1+\tau^2}{1+\tau^2+\sigma^2\tau^2}\theta^*_{ex}}{\sqrt{\frac{\sigma^2\tau^2(1-\tau^2)}{(1+\tau^2+\sigma^2\tau^2)^2}}}\right) = \theta^*_{ex} \, .$$

Rearranging yields

$$\lambda\Phi\left(\sigma^2\theta^*_{ex} + \sqrt{1+\sigma^2}\Phi^{-1}\left(\frac{t}{D}\right)\right)$$

$$+(1-\lambda)\Phi\left(\frac{\sigma\tau}{\sqrt{1+\tau^2}}\theta^*_{ex} - \sqrt{\frac{\tau^2+\sigma^2\tau^2+1}{1+\tau^2}}\Phi^{-1}\left(\frac{t}{D-k}\right)\right) = \theta^*_{ex}$$

Similar to the static games of the last subsection, it can be showed that the equilibrium is unique, if the noise parameters in the private signals x and w satisfy a certain condition, as given in the following proposition:

Proposition 13.2. (Dasgupta, 2001)
For $\sigma < \frac{\sqrt{2\pi}}{\lambda + (1-\lambda)\frac{\tau}{\sqrt{1+\tau^2}}}$, the dynamic game Γ_{ex} has a unique equilibrium, which in the limit for $\sigma \to 0$ converges to

$$x^*_{ex} = s^*_{ex} = \theta^*_{ex} = \lambda(1 - \frac{t}{D}) + (1-\lambda)(1 - \frac{t}{D-k}) \, .$$

Note that the equilibrium of the game with exogenous order of actions is not fundamentally different from the static game. This does not come as a surprise, since essentially the dynamic game has been compounded as a "weighted average" of the two static games at times t_1 and t_2. Hence, for $\lambda \to 0$, all speculators have to decide in the second period whether or not to attack, so that naturally $\theta^*_{ex} \to \theta^*_{st,2}$. Similarly, for $\lambda \to 1$, all speculators have to make their choice in the first period, so that the equilibrium value θ^*_{ex} converges to $\theta^*_{st,1}$. Thus, forcing speculators to decide on an attack with an exogenously given sequence is equivalent to forcing them to play two static games at times t_1 and t_2. However, there is no sign of herding behavior yet. Up to now, speculators still decided on both their individual private signals x_i as well as their (noisy) observation of their predecessors' behavior as represented by w_i.

Additionally to the delineated analysis above, Dasgupta (2001) questions the influence of learning in the dynamic game. In contrast to the static game $\Gamma_{st,2}$, speculators in the dynamic game have superior information, since they can observe their predecessors' choices through the signal w_i. As Dasgupta succeeds to show, speculators in the dynamic game indeed do better than their counterparts in the static game. He proves this by showing that if the attack is successful and learning is sufficiently accurate, i.e. τ falls below a certain critical level, the proportion of attacking speculators at time t_2 in Γ_{ex} is higher than in $\Gamma_{st,2}$. Equivalently, if the attack is unsuccessful, the proportion of traders refraining from an attack at t_2 is higher in Γ_{ex} than in $\Gamma_{st,2}$. Hence, the dynamic game demonstrates that learning from history enables agents to improve their choices.[7]

13.2.3 Dynamic Game with Endogenous Order

Presenting a currency crisis model as a dynamic coordination game with endogenous sequence of actions, denoted as Γ_{en}, is clearly the most realistic, but also the most complex case. In the following, we will not go through all the steps of the proof by Dasgupta (2001), but rather delineate only the most important aspects. For a detailed description, we refer to Dasgupta (2001) and Dasgupta (2000), where a similar topic is raised in a more general setting.

Payoff and information structure are given as in the former section. Additionally, it is assumed that speculators not only have to decide whether or not to attack, but also when, if at all. Again, traders in period 1 have their private signals x_i solely to base their decision on. If they wait one more period, they receive additional information w_i about their predecessor's choices. However, this further information comes at the cost of a lower possible gain, which is reduced from D for a successful attack at period t_1, to $D - k$ at t_2.

For this game an equilibrium can be derived, which displays the following characteristics: speculators attack the fixed parity at time $t = t_1$ if $x_i \leq x^*_{en}$. Otherwise they wait. If period $t = t_2$ is reached, a speculator will attack if $s_i \leq s^*_{en}$.

Note that in contrast to the previously analyzed games Γ_{st} and Γ_{ex}, the fact that agents follow monotone strategies, i.e. choose "higher" actions for higher signals, does not automatically guarantee the existence of a unique trigger value of the fundamental state θ. However, as shown by Dasgupta (2001), there still exists a unique equilibrium in the model as described above. Given that the equilibrium is given in trigger strategies, the necessary conditions for uniqueness are the following: conditional on arriving at period 2, speculators are indifferent between attacking and not-attacking, if

$$(D - k) \cdot \text{Prob}(\theta \leq \theta^*_{en} | s^*_{en}) = t \,,$$

which can be transformed to

$$s^*_{en} = \theta^*_{en} - \frac{\sigma}{\sqrt{1 + \sigma^2 + \frac{1}{\tau^2}}} \Phi^{-1}\left(\frac{t}{D - k}\right) . \tag{13.7}$$

Note that this condition is the same as in the dynamic game with exogenous ordering. This is due to the fact that speculators in period 2 in both cases possess the same information, x_i and w_i, and have to make a choice between the same alternatives: either attack at $t = t_2$ or refrain from attacking. In

[7] Vives (1993) comes to a similar result concerning learning effects. However, he concludes that learning in a model where the market price is informative about the unknown fundamental variable through the actions of agents is rather slow.

period 1, however, the conditions for making a decision crucially changed. At t_1, traders have to decide whether to attack or not, or whether to delay the decision one more period. This massively changes the indifference condition as we will see below.

The critical mass condition to guarantee indifference of the central bank is given by

$$\mathrm{Prob}(x \leq x^*_{en}|\theta^*_{en}) + \mathrm{Prob}(x > x^*_{en}, s \leq s^*_{en}|\theta^*_{en}) = \theta^*_{en} \ , \tag{13.8}$$

where the first expression on the l.h.s. of (13.8) gives the proportion of attacking traders at t_1. The second expression on the l.h.s. shows the proportion of attackers at t_2. Their private signals x_i have not been weak enough to incite them to attack at the earlier period, but they are convinced to attack after observing the number of attackers at t_1, i.e. after receiving signal w_i. Substituting (13.7) into (13.8) delivers

$$\mathrm{Prob}(x \leq x^*_{en}|\theta^*_{en}) + \mathrm{Prob}(x > x^*_{en}, s \leq \theta^*_{en} - M|\theta^*_{en}) = \theta^*_{en} \ ,$$

with $M = \frac{\sigma}{\sqrt{1+\sigma^2+\frac{1}{\tau^2}}}\Phi^{-1}(\frac{t}{D-k})$.

According to Dasgupta (2001), the indifference condition for speculators in period t_1 has to satisfy

$$\begin{aligned} D \cdot \mathrm{Prob}(\theta \leq \theta^*_{en}|x^*_{en}) - t = {} & (D-k-t) \cdot \mathrm{Prob}(\theta \leq \theta^*_{en}, s \leq s^*_{en}|x^*_{en}) \\ & - t \cdot \mathrm{Prob}(\theta > \theta^*_{en}, s \leq s^*_{en}|x^*_{en}) \ . \end{aligned} \tag{13.9}$$

The expression on the l.h.s. of equation (13.9) gives the expected net payoff from attacking at t_1, the r.h.s. in contrast shows the expected net gain from attacking at t_2, both expectations based on the information at period t_1, i.e. on x_i.

As Dasgupta (2001) demonstrates, it is not possible to solve for the equilibrium values $(x^*_{en}, s^*_{en}, \theta^*_{en})$ in closed form, although the condition for uniqueness of equilibrium can easily be derived to be given as

$$\sigma < \frac{\sqrt{2\pi}}{1 + \frac{\tau}{\sqrt{1+\tau^2}}} \ .$$

However, the equilibrium may be analyzed in the limit, as noise becomes small. In contrast to the case of an exogenous sequencing of action, for the case of an endogenous order it has to be assumed that both $\tau \to 0$ and $\sigma \to 0$. Hence, speculators have almost complete information about their predecessors' choices and about the fundamental state of the economy (without θ becoming common knowledge).

For $\tau \to 0$, equation (13.8) simplifies to

$$x^*_{en} = \theta^*_{en} + \sigma\Phi^{-1}\left(\frac{D-k}{t}(1-\theta^*_{en})\right) \ ,$$

while the indifference condition of speculators at $t = t_1$, as given by equation (13.9), reduces to

$$\Phi\left(\frac{\theta^*_{en} - \frac{x^*_{en}}{1+\sigma^2}}{\frac{\sigma}{\sqrt{1+\sigma^2}}}\right) = 1 - \frac{k}{t+k} .$$

Substituting the expression for x^*_{en} into this last equation delivers

$$\Phi\left(\frac{\sigma\theta^*_{en}}{\sqrt{1+\sigma^2}} - \frac{\Phi^{-1}(\frac{D-k}{t}(1-\theta^*_{en}))}{\sqrt{1+\sigma^2}}\right) = 1 - \frac{k}{t+k} .$$

Taking the limit of $\sigma \to 0$, the unique trigger value for the fundamental state is given by

$$\theta^*_{en} = 1 - \frac{t^2}{(t+k)(D-k)} .$$

Hence, in the endogenous order game the following proposition holds:

Proposition 13.3. (Dasgupta, 2001)
For $\tau \to 0$ and $\sigma \to 0$, game Γ_{en} entails a unique equilibrium consisting of the following values:

$$x^*_{en} = s^*_{en} = \theta^*_{en} = 1 - \frac{t^2}{(t+k)(D-k)} .$$

Note, that if we abstract from any costs of delay, so that $k = 0$, the equilibrium trigger value of the fundamental state converges to $1 - \frac{t}{D}$, which is the same as in the static game $\Gamma_{st,1}$. Dasgupta (2001) moreover shows that in this case x^*_{en} converges to zero, whereas s^*_{en} approaches $1 - \frac{t}{D}$ as well. Hence, if signals are completely precise and there are no costs of delaying one's decision, everybody will decide to wait until the second period to make their choice. In contrast, if the costs of delay become large, i.e. $k \to D - t$, again $\theta^*_{en} \to 1 - \frac{t}{D}$. This this time, however, $x^*_{en} \to 1 - \frac{t}{D}$ and $s^*_{en} \to 0$, so that no one will wait until the second period, but all will decide in the first period whether or not to attack the fixed parity.

Let us finally compare the threshold values for the fundamental state in the different games. In this respect, Dasgupta (2001) states the following:

Proposition 13.4. (Dasgupta, 2001)
As noise vanishes, i.e. $\tau \to 0$ and $\sigma \to 0$, we find that

$$\theta^*_{ex} < \max[\theta^*_{st,1}, \theta^*_{st,2}] < \theta^*_{en} .$$

This proposition holds for $D > k + t$, which is a necessary condition for the speculators to have an incentive to attack the fixed parity in the second period. Hence, from the dynamic modelling of currency crises as coordination games we find that, due to the possibility of herding behavior, currency crises may become more likely if speculators can observe their opponents' actions.

Whereas comparisons between θ^*_{ex} and θ^*_{st} gives evidence of possible learning effects on the part of the speculators, the difference between θ^*_{ex} and θ^*_{en} may be taken as a sign of coordination due to signalling effects. The possibility of observing the behavior of other market participants and signalling one's own information to the rest of the market obviously make traders more aggressive in this model. Thus, they coordinate more easily on the attack-strategy, thereby increasing the event of a currency crisis, since $\theta^*_{en} > \theta^*_{ex}$. Note, however, that the existence of "waiting-costs" prevents traders from displaying "strong herding" behavior (Dasgupta, 2000), in which case the trigger signals would take on values of either $-\infty$ or $+\infty$.

Since the analyses of the current and the previous chapter showed that both due to the existence of a large trader as well as following from the possibility of observing the opponents' behavior, traders on financial markets may become more aggressive and hence make a currency crisis more likely, one of the remaining questions is which influence a large trader will have in a dynamic time setting. This most realistic modelling of foreign exchange markets with a fixed exchange rate parity will be examined in the following section.

13.3 Large Traders in Dynamic Coordination Games

One of the major characteristics of large traders on financial markets is their "visibility". Since large traders typically have a large impact on the market outcome, their actions heavily influence prices and as such are easily observable by the rest of the market. Whereas the analysis of chapter 12 did not really capture this aspect, it is possible to fully take into account the large trader's role in a dynamic setting as laid out in the previous section.

The present section hence combines the features of the dynamic coordination game by Dasgupta (2001) as delineated in Sect. 13.2 with the analytical features of the model by Corsetti, Dasgupta et al. (2001) and Corsetti, Pesenti et al. (2001) of Sect. 12.1. Herein, we follow the approach by Corsetti, Dasgupta et al. (2001), who examined the role of a large player in a dynamic setting of a foreign exchange market. However, as has already been done in Chap. 12, we will apply their model to a normal setting in order to facilitate comparisons. If not otherwise mentioned, the assumptions of Sect. 12.1 apply.

The model considers the following framework: both the large trader and the small speculators can take speculative positions in one of two periods, t_1 and t_2. At the beginning of the first period, all traders receive private signals, denoted as x_l for the large speculator and x_i for the small speculators. After receiving private information and the common public signal y, each agent has to decide whether to attack, to refrain from attacking or to wait one more period. After deciding on the attack or not-attack option, a trader may not reverse his position. At the beginning of period 2, each trader observes the choices that other speculators made in period t_1. Consequently, agents can learn from the behavior of others and also signal their own information to their successors, as has been described in the previous section. In contrast to the model by Dasgupta (2001), however, Corsetti, Dasgupta et al. (2001) assume that there are no costs of delaying one's decision. Hence, when comparing the utilities following from different actions, speculators do not have to take into account a possible loss from waiting. Instead, agents just have to compare the net payoffs from attacking and not-attacking the peg, which simplifies the analysis as we will see in the following. Additionally, it is assumed that small speculators ignore any signalling effects of their behavior.[8] Payoffs D and costs t are again given exogenously, independent of the fundamental state. After all traders have built up their potential speculative positions, the chosen fundamental state θ is disclosed, and the central bank either devalues the peg if the proportion of attacking speculators l is at least as high as θ, or keeps the peg otherwise.

With respect to the dynamic setting of the game between speculators and central bank, Corsetti, Dasgupta et al. (2001) point out the following. Since small traders are of infinitesimal size, there is no reason for them to decide on an action in the first period.[9] Their individual trading positions are too small to have an influence on the market. Hence, they are not able to make use of the potential signalling effect of their choice. On the other hand, they can learn by waiting until the second period to make a decision. Since there are no costs to delaying an action, it is a weakly dominant action for small traders to refrain from taking a decision at $t = t_1$, and wait until period t_2. Exactly the opposite holds for the large trader. If he knows that small speculators will always wait until period t_2 before deciding whether to attack or not, he can never learn by waiting for the small agents' actions. However, the large speculator can try to signal his own information to the mass of small traders by moving early, thereby attempting to coordinate their actions on his. Thus, the large trader weakly prefers to move early.

As has been demonstrated by Corsetti, Dasgupta et al. (2001), there is a unique equilibrium in trigger strategies, so that the large trader attacks in period 1 if his signal x_l is lower than x_l^*. If he does not attack, a small trader in period 2 will nonetheless speculate against the parity if his private signal x_i is sufficiently weak, i.e. lower than a threshold x_1^*. However, if the large speculator does attack in period 1, then small traders in period 2 know that the currency is so weak that they are willing to attack for an even larger set of signals, i.e. for signals lower than x_2^*, with $x_2^* \geq x_1^*$. Due to the positive correlation of signals and fundamental states, the corresponding threshold values for θ are given as θ_2^* if the large trader participates in the attack, and

8 We will come back to this point in due time. For a rigorous justification of small traders' negligibility concerning signalling effects, we refer to Levine and Pesendorfer (1995).

9 Note that this conclusion by Corsetti, Dasgupta et al. (2001) hinges crucially on the neglect of the costs from delaying a decision.

θ_1^* if he does not, so that below these thresholds an attack will be successful in the respective cases. Note, that following from the dynamic structure of the model, the equilibrium consist of five values, since there are two different trigger values for the small speculators' private signals.

The equilibrium conditions are given as follows: the large trader in period 1 is indifferent between attacking and not-attacking, if both actions lead to the same expected net payoff, i.e.

$$D \cdot \text{Prob}(\theta \leq \theta_2^* | x_l^*) = t \, .$$

This condition can be transformed to yield the large trader's trigger signal x_l^*

$$x_l^* = \frac{\alpha + \gamma}{\gamma} \theta_2^* - \frac{\alpha}{\gamma} y - \frac{\sqrt{\alpha + \gamma}}{\gamma} \Phi^{-1}\left(\frac{t}{D}\right) . \tag{13.10}$$

The indifference condition for the small speculators in case that the large trader does not participate in the attack, is given by

$$D \cdot \text{Prob}(\theta \leq \theta_1^* | x_l > x_l^*, \, x_1^*) = t \, , \tag{13.11}$$

whenever a finite solution to this condition exists. In case that the l.h.s. of (13.11) is always larger than the r.h.s., attacking the fixed parity in the absence of the large trader is always optimal. Hence, the trigger value of the small traders' private signal then converges to $+\infty$. In the opposite case, where the l.h.s. of (13.11) is strictly lower than the r.h.s., the net payoff from attacking is always lower than the net payoff from not-attacking, so that small speculators will never attack, which is represented by a trigger value $x_1^* \to -\infty$.

Whenever the large trader has been observed to join the attack, the small speculators' indifference condition changes to

$$D \cdot \text{Prob}(\theta \leq \theta_2^* | x_l \leq x_l^*, \, x_1^*) = t \, . \tag{13.12}$$

Again, if no finite solution to this condition exists, then x_2^* converges to either $+\infty$ or $-\infty$, depending on whether the l.h.s. of (13.12) is higher or lower than the r.h.s. Note that the model displays strict herding in the sense of Dasgupta (2000), whenever the trigger values of the small traders' signals are not finite.

The threshold values for the fundamental state are determined by the following conditions

$$(1 - \lambda)\text{Prob}(x_i \leq x_1^* | \theta_1^*) = \theta_1^* \, ,$$

if the large trader does not participate in the attack, and by

$$\lambda + (1 - \lambda)\text{Prob}(x_i \leq x_2^* | \theta_2^*) = \theta_2^*$$

otherwise.

In order to describe the large trader's influence on a speculative attack in this dynamic setting, it is again useful to analyze behavior in the limit, as noise goes to zero. Let us first assume that the large trader's private information is arbitrarily more precise than the small traders' information, i.e. $\gamma \to \infty$, $\beta \to \infty$ and $\frac{\gamma}{\beta} \to \infty$. For this case of vanishing noise, Corsetti, Dasgupta et al. (2001) find the following results to hold

$$\begin{aligned} x_l^* &\to \theta_2^* \\ x_1^* &\to -\infty \\ x_2^* &\to +\infty \\ \theta_1^* &\to 0 \\ \theta_2^* &\to 1. \end{aligned}$$

For a rigorous proof of these results, we refer to Corsetti, Dasgupta et al. (2001). At this point, it should suffice to note that whenever the large trader is perceived to have completely precise information as compared to the rest of the market, the small traders follow him blindly. Hence, they fully disregard their own private information and attack the fixed parity whenever they observe the large trader to do so, but refrain from attacking whenever the large speculator does not attack. This is reflected by the respective trigger values of the small traders' private signals converging to $-\infty$ and $+\infty$. As a consequence, either the whole market joins the attack, or there is no attack at all. Note, that the large trader's size λ plays no role in this case. Hence, when the large trader possesses completely precise private information, his size becomes irrelevant.

A quite different result holds for $\frac{\gamma}{\beta} \to 0$, while still $\gamma \to \infty$ and $\beta \to \infty$. In this case, although both types of players have precise information, the large trader's private signal is arbitrarily less precise than the small speculators' private information. In this case, according to Corsetti, Dasgupta et al. (2001), the resulting threshold values for signals and states strongly depend on the large trader's size. The argument behind this finding is again intuitive. If the large trader is known to possess less accurate information than the small traders, he cannot hope to effectively influence the small traders' beliefs concerning θ. However, if he observes a weak signal and attacks, a smaller gap remains to be filled by the small speculators in order to force a devaluation from the central bank. Hence, even without superior information, the large agent can make the market more aggressive. However, this effect is contingent on the financial size of the large trader.

Comparing the large trader's influence in the static and in the dynamic context, we find that his impact in both types of models depends on his size and on his informational advantage. Since in the dynamic setting the large speculator may additionally use the signalling effect of his action, his influence on the behavior of the mass of small traders is even magnified. In the static model he may render the mass of small trader more aggressive if his financial power is sufficiently large, and most certainly increases the danger of a speculative attack if he possesses superior information. Whenever the large trader's actions can be observed by the rest of the market, however, the small speculators will follow him blindly if he is known to have arbitrarily more precise information about the fundamental state of the economy than they do. Even if he lacks superior information, the signalling effect of his action will make the market more aggressive. In this case, the large trader's influence on the probability of a currency crisis strongly depends on his financial power, i.e. on his size. This, however, is in contrast to the static case. Hence, the size effect may outweigh the information effect in the dynamic setting, so that large traders become even more dangerous to fixed-rate regimes.

Summing up, we may state that the influence of informational aspects is strongly emphasized in a dynamic setting of currency crisis models. In a dynamic sequencing of actions, it is not only the precision of the large trader's information being common knowledge that may lead to a coordination of speculators' actions towards the "attack"-equilibrium, but it is moreover the large trader's ability to additionally "signal" his information to speculators. By doing so, he enables them to verify not only the quality of his information, as represented by the precision, but also to closely establish the content of his information. Again, these findings call for the need of monitoring large traders' actions on foreign exchange markets in order to keep track of their decisions as well as the informational content which they convey.

Part V

Testing the Theoretical Results

14

Introduction

After discussing several aspects of coordinated behavior on foreign exchange markets on a theoretical level, the relevant question to be asked is whether the theoretical results can be tested and if so, whether the tests will corroborate or negate the models' findings. In this respect, apart from the various aspects that might require verification, we also have to take into account the different methods on how to do this. Whereas results from game-theory are usually tested by conducting experiments in laboratory situations, evidence for macroeconomic issues is most often found through econometric testing on empirical data. Since the topic of this book is concerned with game-theoretic predictions in a macroeconomic setting, the problem of finding an appropriate testing procedure is therefore quite momentous.

Let us first concentrate on the different results that have been derived throughout this book and that might require testing. From Chap. 5 we learned that multiplicity of equilibria in currency crisis models can be avoided by making traders' information slightly noisy. Note that noisy information in this case had to be private, for instance in the form of insider information, as compared to public information, which is common to the whole market. Chapter 5 then showed that if speculators' private information about economic fundamentals is slightly noisy, their strategies will unambiguously converge to a unique equilibrium in trigger strategies. Hence, each trader behaves according to the same rule: he attacks if his information tells him that the fundamental state of the economy is sufficiently bad, i.e below a certain threshold, and refrains from attacking if his information is better than the unique threshold level. From Chap. 6 we moreover learned that in a setting with only private information increasing transparency through more precise information diminishes the probability of a currency crisis. Chapters 9 and 10 investigated into the influence of different types of information, private and public, on the probability of a currency crisis. We found that more precise private information may have a completely different effect on the event of a speculative attack than more precise public information. Moreover, it was demonstrated that the informational influence strongly depends on the market belief. In this context, we were able to infer that in the relevant case of a fixed rate regime with a severely threatened parity,[1] the central bank should commit to disseminating very precise private information but very imprecise public information whenever the market generally believes fundamentals to be weak. However, if fundamentals are commonly expected to be strong, the opposite combination of information policy is optimal. Chapters 12 and 13 finally demonstrated that a large trader may have a significant influence on the aggressiveness of the market, which is positively affected by his size and his informational advantage. It was moreover shown that his impact is strengthened, whenever the market participants can observe the large trader's choice before deciding on their own actions.

Although several of these results are rather intuitive, whereas others are more intriguing and therefore call for verification of any form, it is not possible to test all of the above findings. This is mostly due to the fact that we are hardly able to isolate the influence of single parameters in such complex situations as real-life currency crises. However, in the following, we will derive and describe methods which try to at least find evidence of a tendency for several of the above delineated results.[2]

In this respect, we will first of all demonstrate, how the result of a unique equilibrium and hence of uniquely optimal strategies on the part of the speculators in a foreign exchange market can be tested. Chapter 15 presents experimental analysis on the question whether noisy private information indeed lets speculators' strategies converge to a unique equilibrium in trigger strategies. The delineated experiment has been conducted by Heinemann, Nagel and Ockenfels (2001), who, through several sessions in laboratory situations, faced subjects with a decision problem similar to the coordination problem of speculators on a foreign exchange market. Additionally to testing the uniqueness result, they also tried to find out how agents react to changes in the structure of information. Chapter 15 is hence concerned with the game-theoretic predictions as derived in Chaps. 5 and 6 of this book. From their experimental data, Heinemann, Nagel and Ockenfels (2001) conclude that indeed agents behave according to the findings of global games theory and adopt trigger strategies around a unique threshold signal. However, their experiment also suggests that the effects of increasing transparency are not as clear as predicted by theory.

Chapter 16 emphasizes the macroeconomic setting of the delineated currency crisis models. It presents the empirical methods of testing the theoretical results, using both data and descriptions from currency crises of the past. The

[1] This might be attributable to a highly overvalued exchange rate, so that speculators could achieve a high payoff relative to the costs from attacking, if the fixed parity were to be abandoned.

[2] Note that empirical evidence for a large trader's influence has already been mentioned in Chap. 12. However, to the current date none of the few tests of coordinated behavior on foreign exchange markets known to the author have been concerned with the role of a large speculator's informational position.

first section of chapter 16 describes an approach by Prati and Sbracia (2001), who tested on empirical data whether uncertainties in private and public information had an influence on speculators' behavior during the Asian crisis 1997–98. Additionally to laying out their testing procedure, we will depict the difficulties of finding appropriate aggregates for uncertainty parameters on foreign exchange markets and interpret their findings with regard to our theoretical results. Their empirical model is of special interest, since it presents a direct application of our findings concerning the role of information dissemination in currency crises as derived in Chap. 9 to real-life data. They find that indeed the precision of private and public information, respectively the uncertainty within these types of information, plays a major role for explaining the onset of a currency crisis.

The second section of Chap. 16 analyzes whether similar proof of informational influences can be found for the 1994–95 Mexican Peso crisis as well. In contrast to the empirical work by Prati and Sbracia (2001), it concentrates on the question whether central bank and government behaved as predicted by the results of Chap. 10 to prevent speculative attacks. In order to find evidence for our predictions, we will not use any data from this crisis but rather informally evaluate the literature at the time. These "soft" facts very strongly suggest that the Mexican authorities actually made use of their information policy measurements in the predicted way in order to diminish the danger of a currency crisis.

15

Experimental Evidence

In an experiment on coordination games, Heinemann, Nagel and Ockenfels (2001) test the predictions of global games theory concerning agents' behavior. Their experimental test design mimics the model of speculative attacks by Morris and Shin (1998). In order to find out whether agents' behavior changes due to the type of information they possess, they analyze artificial currency crisis situations once with private information, once with public information. In particular, they test the hypothesis that players coordinate on the strategies predicted by global games theory against alternative hypotheses, which propose the use of payoff dominant strategies, maximin strategies or so-called Laplacian strategies. In the following, we will briefly describe the structural design of their experiment and discuss the results.

The experiment by Heinemann, Nagel and Ockenfels (2001) has been conducted at the Universities of Frankfurt and Barcelona. In order not to exert a premature bias by hinting at a particular economic context, subjects are simply asked to decide between one of two actions, A and B. Action B is denoted as the risky action, delivering a payoff of Y if the number of persons deciding on B exceeds a certain hurdle-function given by $a(Y)$, with $\frac{\partial a(Y)}{\partial Y} < 0$. Otherwise the return to B is given by 0. Action A is introduced as the safe alternative, yielding a positive and constant payoff of T. This payoff can be interpreted as the transaction costs to attacking the fixed parity with the attack-action being denoted by B. Note, that due to the assumption of $\frac{\partial a(Y)}{\partial Y} < 0$, the order of states is reversed as compared to the hitherto delineated currency crisis models, so that higher values of Y represent worse states instead of better ones.

The experiment has been conducted with economics and business students participating at both universities. In all, there are 25 sessions out of which 13 are run with public (or common) information and 12 sessions with private information. 15 persons participate in each session. A session consists of two stages, each divided into 8 rounds. In each round, subjects are given 10 different and independent situations in which they have to decide on either option A or B.

The 10 situations are characterized by independent draws of the state variable Y. Y is randomly selected from a uniform distribution on $[10, 90]$. In sessions with public information, students are informed on the chosen value of Y. In sessions with private information, subjects individually receive private signals instead, which are randomly selected from a uniform distribution on $[Y - 10, Y + 10]$. The difference between the two stages in each game lies in the payoff to the safe action A, which is either first 20, then 50, or vice versa. Hence, the experiment differentiates between currency crisis situations with low transaction costs from attacking and therefore a highly vulnerable peg, and a rather stable parity due to high transaction costs from attacking. Additionally, the hurdle-function for option B delivering the positive payoff Y is being varied as well, with a low value of parameter Z representing a quickly declining, rather low function, and a high value of Z mirroring a slowly declining, high hurdle. The rules of the game are made commonly known to all participants.

Once all subjects have made their decisions in one round, the selected value of Y is disclosed to them and they are informed about how many people have chosen B, whether or not B has been successful, and on their individual payoff from this round. However, further information on their opponents' information and actions is not shared. At the end of each session, every participant is paid corresponding to the achieved cumulated payoff during the session.

Within the delineated experiment, Heinemann, Nagel and Ockenfels (2001) intend to find evidence for the prediction from global games theory, that agents endowed with sufficiently precise private information will coordinate on the risk-dominant equilibrium. In order to test this hypothesis against several alternative hypotheses, the authors account for the following equilibrium concepts:[1] i) payoff dominant equilibrium: the criterion of payoff dominance requires to choose the action, which potentially delivers the highest payoff, i.e. to choose B whenever $Y > T$; ii) risk dominant equilibrium: this is the equilibrium concept which global games theory prescribes for a coordination game with noisy private information. The equilibrium threshold is given as the state at which an agent is indifferent between A and B, if he beliefs his opponents to stick to the same (optimal) trigger strategy; iii) laplacian belief equilibrium: this equilibrium is given by the global games equilibrium when noise converges to zero; iv) maximin equilibrium: this strategy proposes to choose action B only if Y is so high, that the hurdle can be overcome even by one single agent, i.e. if $Y > \bar{Y}$ with $\bar{Y} = a^{-1}(1)$.

Following global games theory, we know that if endowed with noisy private information, agents should coordinate on the risk dominant equilibrium. Instead, in the case of public (common) information, it should not possible

[1] Note that all of the depicted equilibrium concepts present equilibria in trigger strategies.

to predict on which strategy agents coordinate, in case they coordinate their actions at all. Moreover, we know that in a game with private information, whenever noise vanishes the equilibrium should converge to the Laplacian belief equilibrium. Thus, in the limit with noise going to zero, agents should hold uniform beliefs over their opponents' actions. As compared to the former concepts, the maximin-strategy represents a very extreme equilibrium concept, since it is based on the worst beliefs of the opponents' choices (i.e. the expectation that no one else chooses the risky action B). The resulting threshold from a maximin strategy will therefore be very high compared to the other concepts' thresholds. According to Heinemann, Nagel and Ockenfels (2001), it is nonetheless reasonable to include this equilibrium concept into the set of alternative hypotheses, since overly pessimistic behavior by the participants might not be ruled out.

In order to test the different equilibrium concepts, Heinemann, Nagel and Ockenfels (2001) first of all try to verify whether the observed behavior during the course of the game complies with threshold strategies at all. Afterwards, they try to establish the threshold levels chosen by the subjects in order to find out whether or not the estimated threshold values are in accordance with one of the theoretical equilibria. In doing so, they differentiate between the experimental setting with private information on the one hand and public information on the other.

Concerning the existence of threshold strategies, they define a subject's behavior to be consistent with a threshold, if the highest signal (in the case of private information games) or state (in public information games) for which action A has been chosen, is lower than the smallest signal/state for which the same subject decided on action B. The experiment shows that from the second round on, most subjects behaved consistently with a threshold strategy. The number of students displaying rational behavior, i.e. not choosing any dominated actions, is moreover found to have increased over time. Although common sense requires agents to choose action B for high signals respectively states and A otherwise, this "rationality"-result is rather intriguing. As Heinemann, Nagel and Ockenfels (2001) point out, the employment of trigger strategies as optimal choice requires the structure of the game to be common knowledge. Hence, agents have to know that all their opponents know (and understand) the rules of the game and behave rationally, that their opponents know that they know and so on to infinity. Earlier experiments by Stahl and Wilson (1994) or Nagel (1995) demonstrated that subjects failed to reason more than three layers of beliefs over beliefs, so that the rules of the game did not become common knowledge in these experiments.

After verifying that agents indeed behave according to trigger strategies, Heinemann, Nagel and Ockenfels (2001) try to extract the respective thresholds from the observed actions. Although a rather difficult task due to the small number of data per subject, the authors find that most players choose a threshold value which coincides with one of the steps of the hurdle-function (the hurdle, as defined, is a function which decreases in Y in steps). Obviously, the hurdle-function seems to be a natural candidate for coordination. Out of 25 sessions, thresholds in 18 sessions can be identified as steps of the hurdle-function.

In order to achieve a better comparison between the games with private information on the one hand and public information on the other, Heinemann, Nagel and Ockenfels (2001) additionally estimate average thresholds for each session by using a logistic regression. They find significant influence of hurdle-function parameter Z, payoff T and the information scenario on the chosen thresholds: they demonstrate that the chosen threshold values are the higher, the higher the hurdle-function for the risky action B delivering the positive payoff Y, and the higher transaction costs T, i.e. the payoff from the safe action. Moreover they succeed in showing that in sessions with private information, the thresholds are usually higher than in sessions with public information. As Heinemann, Nagel and Ockenfels (2001) point out, this result is again very surprising, since earlier tests by Cabrales, Nagel and Armenter (2000), were not able to show any differences in behavior between games with private and public information. Heinemann, Nagel and Ockenfels (2001) attribute this finding to the continuous state and signal space of their experiment, which simplifies coordination in the case of public information.

After analyzing the influence of the experimental design on the threshold values for the participants' optimal actions, Heinemann, Nagel and Ockenfels (2001) finally test the hypotheses that the estimated mean thresholds comply with either of the theoretically derived equilibrium concepts. Quite clearly, they find that the hypothesis of the maximin equilibrium being played can be rejected, since average threshold values as observed are far below the trigger values predicted by maximin strategies. Similarly, the hypothesis of the Laplacian belief equilibrium can be rejected for most parameter constellations. For the games with public information, however, estimated threshold levels come close to the trigger values predicted by the payoff dominant equilibrium, especially in the cases of high transaction costs T. In these games, payoff dominance can only be rejected at the 5 percent level. A fact speaking against payoff dominance as the prevailing equilibrium concept, however, is the above mentioned finding that subjects' choice of threshold strongly depends on parameter Z, since the payoff dominant equilibrium is not contingent on Z. Concerning the risk dominant equilibrium, Heinemann, Nagel and Ockenfels (2001) find that it holds particularly well for private information games. Here, the threshold levels are close to the predictions by global games theory (which corresponds to the risk dominance concept), especially if low transaction costs have been chosen.

From their experimental results, Heinemann, Nagel and Ockenfels (2001) are able to draw the following conclusions for speculators' behavior in currency crisis situations. First, they find that indeed agents' behavior is different when endowed with private information as compared to public information. Secondly, they demonstrate that the thresholds for trigger strategies are significantly higher in the case of private information than with public information.

For the currency crisis context, their experiment therefore predicts that disseminating private information about economic fundamentals will decrease the probability of a speculative attack on the fixed parity, compared with a situation of public information only. This is due to the fact that with a higher threshold in the experimental setting, the range of states for which "attacking" (i.e. action B) will be chosen, becomes smaller. Note, again, that this follows from the reversed order of states as compared to the currency crisis model by Morris and Shin (1998). Finally, the authors conclude from the experimental findings, that the optimal and rather complex mode of information dissemination might not play that important a role in reality as predicted by theory. In particular, they claim that disseminating public information, instead of destabilizing agents' behavior, might rather reduce strategic uncertainty, so that agents more easily coordinate on the payoff dominant equilibrium, which has been observed in the experiment. Since in the currency crisis context the payoff dominant equilibrium usually coincides with the "attack"-strategy, disclosing information about the fundamental state of the economy publicly should therefore be expected to raise the danger of a speculative attack on the fixed parity. Since it is reasonable to assume that there will always be a certain amount of information in the market which is "common", the authors therefore argue that the central bank should try to reduce speculators' potential gains from a devaluation, for instance through realignments of the parity. By doing so, she can at least diminish the advantage of the payoff dominant equilibrium relative to the risk dominant equilibrium. Concerning the role of information disclosure on the part of the central bank or government, Heinemann, Nagel and Ockenfels (2001) suggest from their experimental findings to abstain from providing public information as long as the payoff from attacking is desirably high, since otherwise the prior probability of a successful speculative attack on the fixed parity will certainly rise.

The experiment by Heinemann, Nagel and Ockenfels (2001) as one of the few experiments on coordinated behavior in global games can be seen to largely substantiate the predictions derived from theory. Obviously, agents indeed coordinate on a unique trigger strategy when endowed with sufficiently precise information, which is a very important finding since it requires the rules of the game to become common knowledge. However, the experiment also suggests that the choice between disseminating either private or public information might not be as clear-cut as predicted by theory. Yet, it has to be kept in mind that the experiment distinguishes games with only private information on the one hand, and only public information on the other. Hence, it should not be expected to give evidence for the theoretical findings of chapter 9, where both private and public information have been included into the model. This aspect, however, will be analyzed in the following chapter.

16

Empirical Evidence

16.1 The Asian Crisis 1997–98 - Empirical Tests by Prati and Sbracia (2001)

A quite different approach to testing the results of global games theory for currency crisis models has been chosen by Prati and Sbracia (2001). They aim at verifying the effects of uncertainty about economic fundamentals on the incidence of a currency crisis, as derived in Chap. 9 of this book, by using empirical data from the Asian crisis during the latter half of the 1990s. Their paper is one of the first empirical analyses on the role of uncertainties during currency crises and as such of great interest to the whole branch of economics concerned with financial crises. The prevailing empirical work on currency crises, including Eichengreen, Rose and Wyplosz (1996), Berg and Patillo (1999) and Kaminsky and Reinhart (1999), generally neglects the importance of fundamental uncertainty for speculators' behavior.[1] Hence, the investigation by Prati and Sbracia plays an eminent role for empirically explaining the onset of currency crises in coordination games. Concerning the value of their analysis for this book, we gratefully acknowledge that it is a direct application of own theoretical work (Metz, 2002a) as delineated in Chap. 9 of this book. We will therefore put emphasis on closely presenting their empirical findings and evaluating the impact of the theoretically derived results for real-life currency crises, as a possibility of substantiating our theoretical predictions.

Prati and Sbracia (2001) analyze the influence of uncertainty about economic fundamentals in a set of forecast data of key macro variables for six Asian countries, as collected and provided by Consensus Economics. The dataset includes the period from January 1995 to May 2001 for the countries Thailand, Korea, Indonesia, Malaysia, Singapore and Hong Kong. Within

[1] One exception is the work by Goldfajn and Valdés (1997), who analyze the role of exchange rate expectations for explaining currency crises. However, their result suggests that expectations fail to anticipate crises in general.

the different macro variables that Consensus Economics provides, they concentrate on forecasts for GDP growth. In a first step, they conclude from the data that during the Asian crisis 1997–98 not only did expected GDP growth deteriorate, but additionally, the predictions also became more uncertain. Therefore, they address the question whether the increase in uncertainty can be shown to have influenced exchange rate pressure at the time of the crisis and whether this effect is additional to the impact of deterioration in the mean of expected fundamentals.

Although the issues they intend to verify are very similar to the statements of propositions 9.5, 9.6 and 9.7 in this book, where the influence of the speculators' prior mean (y) and of the precision of private and public information (β and α respectively) on the event of a currency crisis have been analyzed, their test is centered around a slightly different parameter. Instead of addressing the question whether the relevant parameters make a currency crisis more or less likely (i.e. influence θ^*), they study whether speculators become more or less aggressive through changes in y, β or α (i.e. influence x^*). In order to be able to interpret their empirical findings, we therefore first have to elaborate on the parameters' theoretical influence on x^* along the lines of Prati and Sbracia (2001).[2]

Consider the model of Chap. 9, where speculators have both public information about economic fundamentals (in the form of the distribution of fundamentals being common knowledge: $\theta \sim N(y, \frac{1}{\alpha})$) and receive private signals about θ, denoted as x_i with $x_i|\theta \sim N(\theta, \frac{1}{\beta})$. It is assumed that after receiving private and public information, speculators simultaneously have to decide whether or not to attack the fixed parity, whereas the central bank, after observing both the realized fundamental state and the proportion of attacking speculators, l, chooses to devalue the peg if $l \geq \theta$.

As is known from previous chapters, the depicted currency crisis model displays a unique equilibrium in trigger strategies, whenever private information is sufficiently precise relative to public information, i.e. for $\beta > \frac{\alpha^2}{2\pi}$. The threshold values for fundamentals and private signals are given as follows

$$\theta^* = \Phi\left(\frac{\alpha}{\sqrt{\beta}}(\theta^* - y) - \sqrt{\frac{\alpha+\beta}{\beta}}\Phi^{-1}\left(\frac{t}{D}\right)\right) \tag{16.1}$$

and

$$x^* = \frac{\alpha+\beta}{\beta}\theta^* - \frac{\alpha}{\beta}y - \frac{\sqrt{\alpha+\beta}}{\beta} \quad \Phi^{-1}\left(\frac{t}{D}\right). \tag{16.2}$$

Since an attack on the fixed parity will be successful for all fundamental states worse than θ^*, the comparative statics section of Chap. 9 analyzed the influence of the model's parameters on threshold θ^* as a proxy for the prior probability of a crisis. As has been stated in propositions 9.5–9.7, the

[2] The following description always refers to Prati and Sbracia (2001), unless otherwise stated.

commonly expected fundamental state, y, has a negative influence on θ^* and as such on the probability of a currency crisis. For the role of the precision parameters, it has been shown that precision α of public information increases (reduces) the danger of a crisis, whenever $\theta^* > (<)\ y + \frac{1}{2\sqrt{\alpha+\beta}}\Phi^{-1}(\frac{t}{D})$, whereas precision β of private information raises (decreases) the incidence of a crisis, if $\theta^* < (>)\ y + \frac{1}{\sqrt{\alpha+\beta}}\Phi^{-1}(\frac{t}{D})$.

In contrast to these findings, Prati and Sbracia concentrate on the parameters' influence on x^*, i.e. on the threshold value for the speculators' behavior. In the derived equilibrium, each speculator receiving a signal lower than x^* will attack the fixed parity, but will refrain from attacking after observing private information better than x^*. Prati and Sbracia decide on testing comparative statics on x^*, since there exists an empirical counterpart to this theoretical parameter which is given by the exchange rate pressure. As each trader will attack when receiving a private signal lower than x^*, $\text{Prob}(x \leq x^*|\theta)$ not only gives the probability that a single speculator attacks, but, due to the assumed distribution of noise, it is also equivalent to the proportion of attacking agents at fundamental state θ. Hence, the larger this expression, the higher the pressure on the fixed exchange rate parity, which can be measured by several representative indicators.

Concerning the impact of the different parameters on the switching value x^*, the model predicts the following: similar to the influence on the threshold for the fundamental state θ^*, Prati and Sbracia find that the prior mean y always has a negative effect on x^*, and that the precision of public information, α, increases (decreases) the private signals' threshold x^* whenever $\theta^* > (<)y + \frac{1}{2\sqrt{\alpha+\beta}}\Phi^{-1}(\frac{t}{D})$. However, the condition for the private signals' influence is slightly different. As Prati and Sbracia show, a higher precision β of private signals raises (reduces) x^* if

$$\theta^* \ < \ (>)\, y - \frac{\alpha^2\phi(\cdot) - 2\sqrt{\beta}\alpha - (\sqrt{\beta}^3)}{\alpha\sqrt{\alpha+\beta}((\alpha-\beta)\phi(\cdot) - 2\sqrt{\beta})}\Phi^{-1}(\frac{t}{D}) \ .$$

As can be seen, although the threshold function for β's influence has slightly changed, it still holds that for high values of the prior mean y, more precise private signals tend to have a positive influence on x^* and as such make speculators more aggressive, and vice versa for low y. Hence, precision of public and private information, α and β, have a mostly opposite influence not only on θ^*, but also on x^*.

However, the parameters' influence on x^* is only a first indicator for their influence on the overall pressure on the fixed exchange rate. Prati and Sbracia recognize that they do not have to test the parameters' unconditional influence on the threshold x^* of private signals, but on the share of speculators attacking the fixed parity given a certain fundamental state, $\text{Prob}(x \leq x^*|\theta)$, which in the model is given by

$$\text{Prob}(x \leq x^*|\theta) = \Phi\big(\sqrt{\beta}(x^* - \theta)\big) \ . \tag{16.3}$$

Differentiating this probability with respect to the parameters of interest delivers the following results:

Proposition 16.1. (Prati and Sbracia, 2001)
The share of attacking speculators decreases in the commonly expected value of fundamentals, y, and in the actual fundamental state, θ. The share of attackers increases (decreases) in the precision of public information, α, if $\theta^* > (<) y + \frac{1}{2\sqrt{\alpha+\beta}}\Phi^{-1}(\frac{t}{D})$. The proportion of attacking traders increases (decreases) in the precision of private signals, β, if $\frac{x^*-\theta}{2\sqrt{\beta}} + \sqrt{\beta}\frac{\partial x^*}{\partial \beta} > (<) 0$.

Note, that the influence of β on the share of attacking speculators is not necessarily opposite to the impact of α. This is due to the fact that the sign of β's impact is contingent not only on its influence on the threshold value x^*, which Prati and Sbracia denote as the "indirect" effect of β. Rather, there is an additional "direct" effect on $\text{Prob}(x \leq x^*|\theta)$, since β determines the variance of private signals around the actual fundamental index θ. In order to explain the direct effect of β, Prati and Sbracia consider the following example: assume that y is sufficiently good, so that β has a positive influence on threshold x^*. In this case, it may be expected that speculators would become more aggressive following an increased precision of private information. However, if the realized fundamental state is very good, so that $\theta > x^*$, a higher value of β lets an increasing number of traders receive very strong private signals. Speculators with signals $x_i > x^*$ will refrain from attacking. This "direct" effect on the share of attacking speculators might even be large enough to offset the first "indirect" effect on x^*. Due to the more precise private signals speculators' aggressiveness therefore diminishes. If the direct effect dominates, which tends to be the case if both θ and y are sufficiently good or both are sufficiently bad, then the precision of private information has the same influence as the precision α of public information. However, if the indirect effect prevails, both types of precision have an opposite effect on the share of attacking speculators.

Starting from these theoretical reflections, Prati and Sbracia establish an equation for testing the predictions from theory. In order to verify whether mean and variance of agent's expectations concerning economic fundamentals have a significant influence on exchange rate pressure, they use forecast data collected by Consensus Economics. The data set contains individual predictions of economic variables as calculated from a number of professional forecasters. In order to relate the data to the theory, it is reasonable to assume that individual forecasters announce their posterior mean to Consensus Economics. From theory, we know that the posterior probability distribution of fundamentals, conditional on information x_i, is given by

$$\theta|x_i \sim N\left(\frac{\alpha}{\alpha+\beta}y + \frac{\beta}{\alpha+\beta}x_i, \frac{1}{\alpha+\beta}\right).$$

The mean of the individual forecasts, denoted by $f^e(x_1,...,x_n)$, can then be calculated as

$$f^e(x_1,...,x_n) = \frac{\alpha}{\alpha+\beta}y + \frac{\beta}{\alpha+\beta}\frac{\sum x_i}{n} .$$

For a large number of agents, i.e. $n \to \infty$, this random variable converges to

$$f(\theta) = E[f^e(x_1,...,x_n)|\theta] = \frac{\alpha}{\alpha+\beta}y + \frac{\beta}{\alpha+\beta}\theta .$$

Hence, for a sufficiently large number of forecasts, the mean of individual forecasts is influenced by both y and θ. Moreover, since $E[f(\theta)] = y$, the mean of individual forecasts on average is equal to the commonly expected fundamental y, and does not depend on α or β. However, the precision parameters affect the variance of individual forecasts

$$[\sigma^e(x_1,...x_n)]^2 = \sum_i \frac{[f_i^e(x_i) - f^e]^2}{n} = \frac{\beta^2}{(\alpha+\beta)^2}\frac{\sum(x_i-\bar{x})^2}{n} ,$$

with $\bar{x} = \frac{\sum_i x_i}{n}$. For $n \to \infty$ the variance of forecasts approaches a value of

$$\sigma^2 = \frac{\beta}{(\alpha+\beta)^2} .$$

Hence, for a large number of forecasts, the dispersion of predictions only depends on the precision parameters: it decreases in α, whereas the influence of β is negative if $\beta > \alpha$, and positive for $\beta < \alpha$. This can be explained by the fact that although more precise private signals tend to be closer to the actual fundamental θ and as such decrease the variance of forecasts, a higher precision of private information also increases the weight that speculators attach to their private signals relative to public information. Forecasts are then more heterogeneous across traders. For their empirical analysis, Prati and Sbracia assume that $\beta > \max\{\alpha, \frac{\alpha^2}{2\pi}\}$, so that equilibrium is always unique and the precision of private information always exerts a negative influence on the variance of forecasts. Hence, precision of both private and public information reduces the dispersion of forecasts.

For testing the parameters' influence on exchange rate pressure, Prati and Sbracia estimate a specific form of the following general equation

$$ERP_t = \gamma_0 + \gamma_1 f_{t-1}^e + \gamma_2 \sigma_{t-1}^e \cdot (f_{t-1}^e - \underline{\gamma}) + \gamma_3 e_{t-1} + \varepsilon_t . \tag{16.4}$$

ERP represents a measure of exchange rate pressure, and $\underline{\gamma}$ corresponds to the threshold separating "good" from "bad" expected fundamentals. Hence, it is a proxy for the threshold functions of α and β's influence on x^*. e gives the actual exchange rate and ε the error term. In order to avoid a simultaneity bias, Prati and Sbracia use regressors lagged by one period.

From theoretical analysis, γ_1 is expected to take on only negative values, since better expected fundamentals should decrease the proportion of attacking speculators. The impact of standard deviation σ^e, however, is supposed to depend on expected fundamentals and on the source of uncertainty, i.e. whether it is private or public information that is too noisy. Thus, γ_2 should be positive if changes of σ^e are due to changes in the precision of public information, or if changes of β are underlying, while at the same time actual and expected fundamentals are either both sufficiently good or both sufficiently bad. However, γ_2 is expected to be negative, if changes in the precision of private information are at the origin of shifts in σ^e, and either the actual fundamental θ is good and the expected value y is bad or vice versa. Finally, the exchange rate has been included among the regressors to take account of the fact that the model to be tested is static by nature whereas the data is collected along the time-series dimension. Hence, the data may display changes in exchange rate pressure although fundamental forecasts neither deteriorated nor became more dispersed. These variations in exchange rate pressure can then be attributed to exchange rate changes.[3] Since the exchange rate is defined to increase if the currency appreciates, γ_3 is expected to be positive.

Concerning the data and index creation, Sbracia and Prati state the following. They generally follow Weymark (1998) on building an index of exchange rate pressure. However, they do not transform the index into a discrete zero-one-variable as is usually done in the literature to separate attack periods from tranquil periods. This is reasonable for the considered currency crisis model, since the proportion of attacking speculators can take on all values from the interval $[0, 1]$. Their index of exchange rate pressure (denoted as IND) then comprises three indicators: *i*) the percentage depreciation of the respective currency relative to the US dollar over the previous month, *ii*) the fall in international reserves over the previous month, represented as percentage of the 12-month moving average of imports, and *iii*) the three-month interest rate minus the annualized percentage change in consumer prices over the previous six months.

Forecast data from Consensus Economics is given as monthly data. In order to work with a constant forecast horizon of one year, Prati and Sbracia compute the weighted average of the current and following year forecast with weights of $\frac{11}{12}$ and $\frac{1}{12}$ in January, $\frac{10}{12}$ and $\frac{2}{12}$ in February etc.[4] Instead of the mean, they use the median of individual forecasts to reduce the influence of possible "outliers" in the data. Furthermore, although Consensus Economics delivers forecasts of a large number of economic variables, they decide to limit their study to GDP growth only. This is explained by the fact that the number of forecasts is highest for GDP growth, which makes mean and variance mea-

[3] Note, that the analyzed time interval includes periods of revaluations as well as of floating rates, so that exchange rate changes may be quite large.

[4] For using moving averages on seasonal adjustment see also Gourieroux and Monfort (1997).

sures highly reliable and by the finding that hardly any other forecast variable turned out to be significant in preliminary estimations when GDP growth was included. Lastly, they mention that working with the real exchange rate for e instead of the nominal exchange rate leads to a slightly better performance of estimates. Other variables, such as international reserves or the ratio of M2 to international reserves, are not found to be significant.

As a first step of empirically testing the influence of uncertainty on exchange rate pressure, they estimate a set of seemingly unrelated regressions (one for each country), with the following specification of equation (16.4)

$$IND_{j,t} = \hat{\gamma}_{0,t}+\hat{\gamma}_1 f^e_{GDP_j,t-1}+\hat{\gamma}_2\sigma^e_{GDP_j,t-1}\cdot(f^e_{GDP_j,t-1}-\underline{\hat{\gamma}_j}_{GDP})+\hat{\gamma}_3 e_{j,t-1}+u_{j,t} \quad (16.5)$$

with $u_{j,t} = \hat{\rho}_j u_{j,t-1} + \varepsilon_{j,t}$. Index j refers to the country, t to the time period. Equation (16.5) presents a regression with country-specific coefficients and a country-specific AR(1) error term, which corrects for serial correlation. Choosing the estimation method of seemingly unrelated regressions is supposed to take account of a possible correlation of errors across countries during the Asian crisis.

Parallel to the above delineated regression, Prati and Sbracia perform a Wald test of equality of parameters across countries. This test shows that coefficients $\hat{\gamma}_1$ and $\hat{\gamma}_2$ can be constrained to be the same across countries. Prati and Sbracia stick to this restriction, yet, they point out that this condition is not necessary to derive statistically significant coefficients. For the restricted parameters, they find that coefficient γ_1 is negative and significant at the one percent level, whereas γ_2 is positive and significant at the one percent level. Similarly, $\gamma_{3,j}$ is positive and highly significant (at 1%), except for Hong Kong where this coefficient takes on a negative value and is significant only at the ten percent level. Prati and Sbracia additionally point out that the two coefficients γ_1 and γ_2, which are of most interest, even for the unrestricted case take on negative respectively positive values at the five respectively one percent level of confidence.

Summing up the results, the estimation by Prati and Sbracia confirms the predictions derived theoretically. First, they find that, indeed, higher expected GDP growth diminishes exchange rate pressure. Secondly, estimation results indicate that uncertainty about GDP growth has an additional impact on exchange rate pressure, which is moreover contingent on the expected level of GDP growth. Whenever expected GDP growth is above the threshold estimated for the individual countries, a higher variance in GDP growth forecasts tends to increase exchange rate pressure, but reduces pressure on the parity if expected GDP growth is below the country-specific threshold. From these results, it can be inferred that the main force lying underneath fundamental uncertainty is either a change in the precision of public information, so that the whole market is less sure about economic fundamentals, or uncertainty is due to a change in the precision of private information with the "direct" effect of precision changes in private signals dominating the "indirect" effect.

Additionally to this benchmark regression, Prati and Sbracia try to confirm their initial results concerning the influence of uncertainty on exchange rate pressure by conducting several different forms of sensitivity analyses. In this respect, they use alternative measures of exchange rate pressure and find that the general results do not change. Furthermore, they also re-estimate equation (16.5) for the pre-crisis period, i.e. for the time of January 1995 to July 1997. This approach deserves special emphasis, since it might be suspected that the actual breakdown of the fixed-rate systems during the Asian crisis is the major source of fundamental uncertainty, hence dominating the effects in the regression over the whole period. However, Prati and Sbracia succeed in showing that this is not the case. Rather, even in the pre-crisis sample, uncertainty strongly influences exchange rate pressure. Note, though, that due to the dramatic reduction of observations, $\hat{\underline{\gamma}}$, $\hat{\gamma}_3$ and $\hat{\rho}_j$ had to be restricted to be the same across countries in order to decrease the number of degrees of freedom, so that only intercepts were allowed to be country-specific. This procedure is equivalent to testing panel data with fixed effects (Hsiao, 1986). For all measures of exchange rate pressure, they can show that the effect of uncertainty (γ_2) is positive and statistically significant, while the negative effect of higher expected fundamentals (γ_1) is also confirmed.

Finally, concerning sensitivity analysis, Prati and Sbracia also control for the fact that threshold values $\underline{\gamma}_j$ might be varying over time, for instance as speculators revise their economic outlook during the crisis. In order to do so, they estimate the threshold parameters recursively. Although it can be found that estimated thresholds tend to decline during the crisis before stabilizing below their pre-crisis levels in 1998, Prati and Sbracia show that allowing for time variations does not change the estimates for $\hat{\gamma}_1$ and $\hat{\gamma}_2$. Hence, revising earlier forecasts concerning the development of GDP growth on the part of speculators obviously does not change the effects of uncertainty on exchange rate pressure.

Overall, the empirical testing by Prati and Sbracia confirms the results derived from theoretical considerations. Hence, it can be stated that uncertainty among traders concerning economic fundamentals influences their behavior quite seriously. Whenever fundamentals are commonly believed to deteriorate, this can be expected to increase speculative pressure on the fixed exchange rate. Additionally, it has been confirmed that the effects of a growing uncertainty among individual economic forecasts are contingent on the "market sentiment". Hence, increasing the precision of information cannot generally be found to have a strictly positive or strictly negative influence on the incidence of a currency crisis. Instead, the effects are shown to be truly sensitive to what is generally believed by the market.

16.2 The Mexican Peso Crisis 1994–95 - Descriptive Evidence

This section is dedicated to giving descriptive evidence of the influence of private and public information and its usage by the respective authorities during the currency crisis of 1994–95 in Mexico. Instead of trying to confirm the theoretical predictions derived from Chaps. 9 and 10 by using empirical data at the time of the crisis, we will rather give proof by studying reports and articles on speculators' behavior and governmental decisions concerning information policy during the crisis. In this respect, we will concentrate on two questions: first, is the sudden collapse of the Mexican economy consistent with our theory, and second, can the informational policy conducted by the Mexican government and central bank during the onset of the crisis be explained by our predictions from theory?

In order to find answers to these two issues, we will first of all delineate the venue of the Mexican crisis 1994–95. It is important to understand Mexico's economic development during the late 1980s and the first years of the 1990s in order to see the interrelations with the events at the end of 1994. In depicting the events chronologically, we will put special emphasis on the conduct of information dissemination by the Mexican authorities as well as on information disclosures by politicians and economists to the international audience. Later on, we will scrutinize whether, and if so, in which way the onset of the currency crisis can be explained by the theory. Additionally, we will analyze if the authorities in trying to prevent a crisis behaved as predicted from our model of Chap. 10.

16.2.1 The Venue of the Mexican Crisis

The historical events which finally led to the crisis in the middle of the 1990s have been analyzed extensively by several economists. One of the most interesting descriptions and evaluations of the fundamental situation in Mexico during these years stems from Dornbusch and Werner (1994), written only months before the onset of the crisis. What is noteworthy is that their report is one of the few critical assessments of the Mexican economy that closes with a serious warning for the Mexican government.

As Dornbusch and Werner (1994) point out, Mexico had been a textbook example of financial stability and growth from the mid-1950s to the 1970s. This stability, however, ended when Mexico became insolvent in 1982. Preceding this first currency crisis had been an increase in oil prices in the 1970s, which raised Mexico's revenues from oil exports and sparked off highly expansionary policies. Additionally, government borrowing increased, the fixed currency became overvalued and finally a capital flight started, which, together with the increasing debt burden due to rising U.S. interest rates, led to the collapse of the economy.

However, after the complete breakdown in 1982, the Mexican economy recovered swiftly. As many economists at the time pointed out (Lustig, 1995), this easy recovery has been mostly the consequence of a comprehensive reform program. The main features of the reform concerned *i*) a fundamental opening of the country towards international competition, *ii*) privatization and deregulation, *iii*) fixing the exchange rate against the U.S. $ and using it as a nominal anchor, and *iv*) the so-called Pacto, an agreement between government, labor unions and the private sector to guide the development of prices, wages and the exchange rate.

Concerning the first aspect, Dornbusch and Werner (1994) emphasize the importance of the trade reform, which strongly reduced tariffs, particularly those of consumer goods, and the so-called Brady plan. The Brady plan of 1990 marked a turning point in Mexico's external financing, since, after the complete abolition of capital controls in 1989, it shifted international attention towards reform and modernization efforts implemented by the Mexican government. By reducing interest and principal payments through the Brady plan, Mexico's ability to service external debt had been strongly improved, which strengthened investors' confidence into the country. Additionally, Mexico benefited from large reductions in world interest rates, which both alleviated the debt burden and let large amounts of international capital flow into Mexico. However, the foreign capital invested in the Mexican money market and stocks was highly liquid.

The second bullet point of the reform program was concerned with privatization of state-owned enterprises. Closing unprofitable and selling profitable firms not only helped reducing the budget deficit, but moreover drew foreign attention to interesting investment opportunities in Mexico, thereby fuelling the reform process. In particular the privatization of banks led to the "rediscovery" of Mexico by the international capital market (Lustig, 1995). By consolidating the budget deficit, the Mexican government additionally aimed at reducing inflation, improving confidence in the currency and subsequently lowering interest rates. At the end of 1992, Mexico had reached fiscal balance and inflation was reduced to single digits. This restrictive fiscal policy also gave support for stabilizing the exchange rate, which had been fixed since 1988, the third point of the reform package. Between 1988 and 1994, Mexico changed its exchange rate system several times, from a completely fixed parity over a preannounced rate of devaluation to a band with sliding ceiling. Until autumn 1993, the Peso exchange rate was extremely stable, remaining in the lower half of the band (Obstfeld and Rogoff, 1995).

The last reform aspect, the Pacto, was one of the key elements. Within this agreement, labor unions promised to limit wage increases, the business sector agreed to keep down price inflation and the government guaranteed to limit public sector price increases and to stabilize the exchange rate. Initially, these agreements ran for 2 months only. However, they were extended to 6 and 12 months, and finally were renewed every year.

Concerning the success of the reforms, Edwards (1997) states that a significant difference had arisen between Mexico's achievements in terms of reform policies and in terms of economic results. Although political achievements were sometimes even spectacular, economic outcomes remained rather modest. The real growth rate averaged 2.8 percent between 1988 and 1994. Productivity growth was near zero and private savings were decreasing, while, on the positive side, inflation was strongly diminished from the double digit levels during the 1980s. Also, capital inflows into the country remained to be strong until the beginning of 1994.

What is important for interpreting the onset of the crisis in the light of our informational analysis, is that the economic situation in Mexico at the beginning of the 1990s was highly praised by economists, financial experts, academics and the media in general. With only very few exceptions, the Mexican reforms were seen as a major success, with Mexico's development representing a miracle among the group of emerging countries. The facts that economic growth was still low and the current account deficit was increasing, were mostly neglected by commentators. Even if the lack of fundamental growth was taken into account, it was argued that positive results were "around the corner" (Calvo, Mendoza, Rogers and Rose, 1996). As Edwards (1997) puts it, the "Mexican miracle was invented by these institutions" (i.e. the media, financial analysts, economists etc.). One of the few economists to argue against this common trend of praising Mexican reform efforts was Rudiger Dornbusch. As early as 1992, he claimed that Mexico's most urgent problem was its overvalued exchange rate. He elaborated on this point in his paper with Werner (1994), and linked the real overvaluation to both the Pacto-agreements and the steady flow of international capital into the country. However, there was a large dissent about this point in the community. Whereas some observers did not believe the fixed exchange rate to be overvalued, others claimed that due to the surge in capital inflows, Mexico experienced an "equilibrium-appreciation", which was fully justified by fundamentals. A more modest view admitted that although Mexico had a growth problem, this was only transitory and would be solved automatically over time (Gil-Diaz, 1997). Dornbusch and Werner were among the few who clearly saw a critical real overvaluation of the peso, which they feared to be no temporary phenomenon but rather a serious long-lasting problem: "[...] overvaluation is one of the gravest policy errors along the way. Overvaluation stops growth and, more often than not, ends in a speculative siege on the exchange rate and ultimately currency realignment" (Dornbusch and Werner, 1994). The real appreciation of the Peso exchange rate clearly started with the successful disinflation policy, conducted mostly through the Pacto-agreement. Using the exchange rate as nominal anchor while reducing inflation would certainly be accompanied by a substantial real appreciation of the currency. This point was indisputable among economists (Calvo, 1994). Also, they agreed on the fact that due to trade liberalization, the Brady plan and the resulting surge in capital inflows, Mexico was enabled to finance very large current account deficits. These deficits were aggravated by the fact that the private sector increasingly began to replace government borrowing on the capital markets. However, there was no agreement on the sustainability of the rising current account deficit. During 1991–93, capital was flowing into Mexico at levels exceeding 7 percent of GDP, which, in hindsight, can be seen to be clearly not sustainable in the long run and not consistent with the "equilibrium-rate" theory proposed by several economists at the time. In order to give an overview of the confusingly large number of different views that economists, financial analysts and market commentators held at the beginning of the 1990s, consider the following collection of statements as taken from Edwards (1997):

The IMF praised Mexico's reform efforts, even until only a few months before the crisis hit the economy in December 1994. In a letter to the U.S. Secretary of the Treasury in March 1994, IMF Director Michael Camdessus spoke highly of the Mexican government's fundamentally sound economic policy. In October 1994, the IMF's *World Economic Outlook* predicted that although growth had been low, it would pick up speed rapidly. The World Bank, in contrast, spoke with two voices. In a document released at the 1993 Annual Meeting, the World Bank stated that the reform process in Mexico was mature and appeared to be consolidated. In a publication in November 1994, a month before the crisis, the World Bank publicly argued that the winner of the presidential election, Ernesto Zedillo, would enable a rapid improvement of the economy, so that economic growth should reach its highest level in five years. Moreover, the report announced the anticipation of post election stability. However, in 1993 an article in *Trend in Developing Economies* remarked that, among other facts, the recent slowdown in Mexican growth was due to a real exchange rate appreciation. At another point, the World Bank even warned of the non-sustainability of Mexican policies. Even as early as November 1992, the bank had noted that the opening of the capital account exposed Mexico to a large risk resulting from the volatility of short-term capital movements, which might need to be adjusted to through higher interest rates or a depreciation of the Peso. Investment bankers and fund managers were generally very enthusiastic concerning the Mexican prospects. In this respect, JP Morgan as late as October 1994 and the Swiss Bank Corporation even in December 1994 urged a credit rating upgrade for Mexico. An analysis by Edwards (1997) of the *Emerging Markets Investor* in November/December 1994 indicates that out of twenty analyses released by major institutions at the time, twelve dismissed the possibility of a devaluation. The general optimism among financial analysts is mirrored by the fact that *Euromoney* raised the country risk ranking for Mexico between March and September 1994. Among the group of economists, Dornbusch in November 1992 argued that the daily rate of devaluation for the Peso should be tripled in order to prevent a major crisis. The Mexican central bank argued that, although the capital account was in deficit, there was nothing to worry about, since, first of all, the exchange rate band might deal with eventual disequilibria. Secondly, productivity was expected to surge in no time, and thirdly, fundamentals would remain healthy. The Under Secretary of Finance in 1994 emphasized that an appreciation process in the real exchange rate was nothing but natural following the reform efforts. The Governor of the Mexican central bank argued in an interview with the *Economist* in January 1994 that the current account deficit was associated with an inflow of foreign funds rather than expansionary domestic policy, and hence presented no problem.

Thus, during 1992–94, large uncertainties prevailed over the question of whether the Peso appreciation was only a temporary ("equilibrium") phenomenon or a non-equilibrium real overvaluation. Things became worse in 1994. Not only was the economic situation aggravated by political distress of several forms, but also uncertainty among analysts shifted from economically related aspects to questions referring to political strategy.

At the end of 1993, the market on average was still enthusiastic about Mexico, notwithstanding the slow growth in productivity and the increasing current account deficit. However, in contrast to the conducted modernization policy, the Chiapas uprising on January 1st 1994 reminded the world that Mexico remained to be a country with social problems and inequalities. Several newspapers commented on this fact by pointing out that the Mexican people still had to benefit from the reforms (Edwards, 1997). Following these political uncertainties, the exchange rate rose to the upper bound in February. Surprisingly, international reserves held by the Mexican central bank did not fall, and inflow of direct foreign investment did not recede. The Mexican capital markets did not even react to the Fed's decision to tighten U.S. monetary policy in February 1994, which was taken as a sign of fundamental stability.

However, the climate changed abruptly with the assassination of Luis Donaldo Colosio, the presidential candidate of the ruling party PRI on March 23rd, 1994. This time, investors reacted in panic and strongly reduced their exposures in Mexico. In order to secure the Peso parity, the Mexican authorities intervened, thereby losing almost $10 billion of international reserves: reserves fell from $26 billion to $18 billion almost overnight (Lustig, 1995). Moreover, Peso denominated interest rates were rapidly increasing. Yet, the financial community swiftly regained its faith in Mexico, after the U.S. government decided on March 24th to extend a $6 billion swap facility to Mexico. The Financial Times, on March 25th, reflected the confidence in Mexico by printing the following front page: "Even with Mexico's dependence on foreign capital to cover a current account deficit of over Dollars 20bn, a crisis is eminently avoidable". On March 28th, the Financial Times claimed that a "sense of calm returned to Mexico" (Edwards, 1997). Ernesto Zedillo was made the new PRI's presidential candidate and proclaimed to continue Mexico's reform path.

Contrary to the regaining faith by the media, though, Mexico was experiencing ever larger difficulties rolling over its maturing Peso denominated debt (Cetes). The financial community moreover seemed to have been wide aware of this fact. In April 1994, JP Morgan publicly stated that the Mexican government would have to weigh the trade-off between rising interest rates and devaluing the fixed exchange rate in order to solve its problems. Quite generally, during the first half of 1994 concerns grew among international analysts concerning Mexico's external situation. In the spring meeting of the Brookings Institution Economics Panel, apart from Dornbusch and Werner also Calvo argued that the Mexican exchange rate system was at risk due to lack of credibility (Calvo, 1994). Stanley Fischer expressed doubts as well referring to the sustainability of Mexico's external situation. Moreover, several members of the Federal Reserve Bank of New York argued that a devaluation of the Peso should not be ruled out. However, there were also comments stating the opposite view: on May 2nd, 1994, the U.S. Under Secretary of the Treasury emphasized in a memorandum that Mexico's exchange rate policy was still sustainable (Edwards, 1997).

Between April and October 1994, the Mexican central bank did not disclose any changes in the position of its international reserves to the public. The exchange rate, however, rose with the ceiling band. Additionally, it was observed that the central bank increasingly replaced peso-denominated debt (Cetes) with dollar-denominated Tesobonos, thereby changing the composition of money. Again, these facts were discussed in the media as well as in financial circles. During the course of the year 1994, it became clear to financial observers that the Mexican authorities obviously withheld information on money market aggregates and on data of international reserves. In June 1994, the IMF mission returned to Washington after only two weeks in Mexico, complaining that it did not obtain any data from the Bank of Mexico on the recent development of international reserves. The level of international reserves was timely revealed for the third time in 1994 only as late as on the first of November. Several investors also commented on the lack of readily available and reliable information (Edwards and Savastano, 1998). Yet, risk measures as publicly announced by different financial institutions at the time indicate that, the lack of information notwithstanding, the market's perception of the situation in Mexico remained stable until December.[5]

In August 1994, Ernesto Zedillo was elected president, the Pacto was renewed and the exchange rate system maintained. These decisions surprised many of the market observers, who had hoped for a possibility of changing the currency system (Sachs, Tornell and Velasco 1996a,b). Investors became increasingly nervous after the assassination of another politician in September 1994. Following this incident, the Mexican authorities intensified the substitution of Tesobonos for Cetes. Although on October 21st the Mexican central bank announced the level of international reserve holdings to be at \$17.12 billion, many analysts believed this number to be too high. Following the announcement of disappointing third quarter earnings by several Mexican corporations, the peso weakened further. At the end of November 1994, international reserves in the hand of the central bank had decreased to \$12.5

[5] A calculation of risk premia for the year of 1994 by Edwards (1997) comes to the same conclusion.

billion, with short term public debt in excess of $27 billion. Hence, reserves were clearly insufficient to back short term domestic debt, and a major financial crisis loomed.

In November 1994, the media spread the rumor that although part of the government had already agreed on a devaluation of the Peso, the full decision did not get through. On December 1st, the new administration under President Zedillo took office. Reserves were suspected to continue their declining trend, although the Mexican central bank did not disclose any new figures. On December 5th, the U.S. Secretary of the Treasury was informed from institutional analysts' calculations that Mexico's international reserves must be close to only $10 billion. In contrast to the concern among officials in the United States, however, the private sector in Mexico seemed to be rather unaware of the fast decline of reserves during November and December. Yet, as Edwards (1997) points out, analysts should have had enough information to calculate the necessary figures and get an idea of the country's international reserve position. Obviously, however, financial market participants preferred to be seduced by the still positive information given by Mexican policy makers (Frankel and Schmukler, 1996).

Due to the vanishing reserves, Mexican authorities decided on widening the exchange rate band on December 20th, in order to allow for a devaluation of 15 percent. Yet, this change in policy was not accompanied by a supporting program, and hence did not appear very promising to solve the current problems. Investors started to flee the country in disbelief. As a result, the Mexican central bank lost $4 billion of reserves in one day, and eventually the fixed Peso exchange rate had to be abandoned.[6]

16.2.2 Combining the Observations with Theoretical Results

Summing up the observations relevant for testing our theoretical predictions we can state the following facts: First, until very late in the onset of the crisis, market participants generally believed Mexican fundamentals to be sound. Although some critical voices made themselves heard, and even though belief slightly faltered following political troubles in 1994, the market remained optimistic towards the economic development in Mexico until around November/December 1994. Secondly, if the individual market participants' statements concerning the development in Mexico can be taken to reflect their private information about the fundamental state, we can see that from the beginning of the 1990s, most obviously from 1992 on, private information was characterized by large uncertainties. Following from the description of different statements by international institutions such as IMF and World Bank, but also by individual financial analysts, economists and politicians, we moreover find that private uncertainty increased over time. Whereas in 1992 and 1993 dissent prevailed mostly over the question whether the increasing current account deficit was sustainable and therefore whether the appreciation of the

[6] See also Camdessus (1995).

real exchange rate was following an equilibrium trend or appeared to be a sign of a long-run overvaluation, private uncertainty in 1994 comprised even more aspects. Uncertainty predominated over political aspects as for instance the economic course of the new government, elected at the end of 1994, but also about the informational policy conducted by both the old and the new government. However, uncertainty in private information seemed to have decreased during the second half of 1994, in particular in November and December. During these months, market observers gradually agreed on the fact that the current account deficit was unsustainable and that the fixed exchange rate peg was not sufficiently backed by international reserves. Thirdly, concerning the dissemination of public information, we can conclude that during the course of 1994, parallel to the deterioration of fundamentals (diminishing international reserves, increasing interest rates, increasing current account deficit, etc.), the Mexican authorities consciously and deliberately decided on disseminating very imprecise public information, respectively almost no public information. The best evidence is given by the often stated complaint that information about the development of international reserves was disclosed only three times in 1994. During the last third of the year 1994, hardly any timely information about money market aggregates was available to market participants.

Using these "stylized facts" from the Mexican crisis 1993–94, we can try to verify the predictions from our theory in the light of the peso turmoil. In this respect, let us first analyze the question concerning the onset of the crisis. From theory we know that whenever market participants have complete information about economic fundamentals, both a crisis and a period of tranquillity are possible, if the fundamental state of the economy is not extremely bad (in which case there will always be a devaluation of the currency) or extremely good (so that stability of the peg always prevails). When this multiple equilibria model holds, in order to coordinate on one of the two possible actions of either attacking or not-attacking the fixed peg, speculators need to experience a sunspot event. As stated in earlier parts of this book, such sunspots need not be related to an economic background at all. For the case of the Mexican crisis, a typical sunspot event might have been the political turmoil following the assassination of politicians. However, if public information is sufficiently noisy compared to private information, theory predicts a unique equilibrium, where the fixed parity will successfully be attacked if fundamentals are below a certain threshold, but where the peg will be maintained for fundamentals sufficiently strong above this threshold.

Our observations from the Mexican currency crisis quite clearly substantiate the theoretical mechanism leading to a unique equilibrium. Note, that there is evidence not only in favor of this model, but also evidence against the multiple equilibria model. Let us start with this second point. As indicated above, the beginning of the 1990's in retrospect can be characterized as a self-fulfilling expectation equilibrium for Mexico. Beliefs concerning the results from reform were so tremendously optimistic that this enthusiasm actually generated the "Mexican miracle". Despite the divergence between policy actions and economic results, as stated by Edwards (1997), market participants believed in the miracle, which helped to generate an asset price boom and reassured the believers in the miracle. Following from this fact, one might expect the economy to be in a multiple equilibria situation with speculators having coordinated on the "tranquillity"-equilibrium. However, one would have expected the economy to switch to the "attack"-equilibrium as soon as an adverse sunspot event occurred. Indeed, such a sunspot event did take place in the form of several political turmoils during the course of 1994. However, speculators obviously did not react to these grave moments of political instability, although the possible gains from a speculative attack on the fixed exchange rate must have been perceived to be quite large. This observation clearly speaks against the multiple equilibria theory. Note, that our interpretation is in contrast to the modelling by Sachs, Tornell and Velasco (1996b,c) and Cole and Kehoe (1996), which explains the Mexican currency crisis as a self-fulfilling panic. However, they assume that the sunspot event was given as the government's decision to devalue the fixed parity on December 20th, 1994. Before this point in time, they cannot find evidence for a strong expectation of devaluation,[7] so that only the event on December 20th remains as a possible sunspot, coordinating speculators' decisions towards an attack.

What speaks for the unique equilibrium theory to hold on the other hand, is that the observed onset of the crisis in Mexico quite nicely follows the predictions from this model. Even if the multiple equilibria case were to hold during 1990-1993, due to very confuse private beliefs concerning the fundamental situation in Mexico, private information became more precise at the end of 1994. Traders more and more suspected the fixed exchange rate to be unsustainable. Additionally, the Mexican authorities disseminated increasingly imprecise public information during the latter half of 1994. This ratio of very imprecise public information to improving precision of private information set the stage for a unique equilibrium to hold. The observation that the fixed exchange rate finally was abandoned, can then be attributed to the fact that indeed the fundamental state of the economy was sufficiently bad: international reserves were vanishing, interest rates increasing, growth was sluggish and the current account deficit increasing to unsustainable levels.

All these facts therefore can be seen as a tendency for the model with unique equilibrium to hold. Moreover, it might be suspected that the crisis was inefficient, since, as several economists point out, Mexico was not insolvent but it was merely illiquid (DeLong, DeLong and Robinson, 1996). This prediction also follows from theory: if we take the multiple equilibria case to hold until about 1993-94, fundamentals obviously were not weak enough to justify a speculative attack during this time, i.e. $\theta \in [0, 1]$ in terms of the no-

[7] They use the interest rate differential between Cetes and Tesobonos as an indicator of expected devaluation and show that this spread rose after the assassination in March 1994, fell after the election and remained constant until November 1994.

tation of Chap. 9. During 1994, fundamentals did not deteriorate sharply, but rather followed their modest declining trend, while public information became increasingly imprecise. Hence, switching to the unique equilibrium case led to a devaluation due to the fundamental index lying in the interval $[0, \theta^*]$. In our earlier analysis this has been characterized as the "inefficient" crisis interval, since a crisis could have been prevented if only a large enough proportion of traders had decided not to attack the currency.

After finding evidence for the hypothesis that the Mexican crisis 1994-95 indeed followed the theory of a unique equilibrium, we would like to analyze whether the Mexican authorities behaved as predicted from theory of Chap. 10 in trying to prevent a speculative attack. Again, we find support for our theoretical results. We know that for a vulnerable parity the central bank or government should commit to disseminating very precise public information and very imprecise private information whenever the market generally believes fundamentals to be strong. The opposite combination of information policy is optimal in order to minimize the probability of a currency crisis, if the market sentiment concerning economic fundamentals is rather bad.

From the above delineation of the Mexican crisis we find that the financial community was very optimistic, even enthusiastic towards the developments in Mexico until around March 1994. Up to this point, even adverse political incidents did not destroy the generally positive belief concerning the success of the reform efforts and the fundamental development. Although there is no clear proof of it, we can conjecture from the missing complaints about governmental information dissemination at the time, that information about the necessary parameters has been disclosed timely and sufficiently precisely until spring 1994. Hence, the authorities can be suspected to indeed have committed to a policy of disseminating rather precise public information as long as fundamentals were generally believed to be sound. At the same time, however, individual perceptions of the fundamental state largely deviated from this common mean. The situation changed during the course of 1994. Approximately from summer/autumn 1994 on, the market sentiment concerning economic fundamentals steadily became worse. Whereas in earlier months the media still had praised economic reforms, from this time on it increasingly commented on the growing pressure on the fixed parity and the possible unsustainability of Mexico's external position. Parallel to this development, there was increasing complaint about the lack of timely information about important economic parameters, as for instance international reserves and monetary aggregates. Hence, there is proof of the authorities consciously committing to a policy of disseminating very imprecise public information. This policy, however, is exactly the one that the theoretical model of Chap. 10 would have suggested for the given state of the economy in order to minimize the danger of a speculative attack.

Summing up the results from the explanatory analysis, we can state that there is clear evidence that increasing uncertainty in public information set the stage for a unique equilibrium model to hold for the Mexican currency crisis in 1994–95. Additionally, we find that the onset of the crisis was characterized by policy measurements, which follow closely the theoretical prescriptions for minimizing the attack probability. Hence, although we did not make use of empirical data from the Mexican Peso crisis 1994–95, there is overwhelming evidence from the literature that informational aspects played a major role in triggering the collapse of the fixed parity in December 1994. Even though our analysis is only based on "soft facts" and cannot be taken as hard and exact proof of the influence of information on the onset of the crisis, the descriptive evaluation of this section may be a useful basis for empirically testing the impact of uncertainty and information dissemination in the way of Prati and Sbracia, as delineated in the previous section.

Part VI

Concluding Thoughts

Assessing the role of information disclosures in currency crises only recently became possible through the advanced employment of game-theoretic methods in financial market models. One of the most up-to-date explanations of currency crises by Morris and Shin (1998) applies the global games approach to a second-generation crisis model with self-fulfilling beliefs. By introducing noisy private information about economic fundamentals, not only a unique equilibrium is derived, contrary to the multiple equilibria outcome of earlier second-generation work. Also, the model comes much closer to reality than typical first- and second-generation approaches, since speculators on foreign exchange markets can certainly be seen to base their decisions on incomplete information about the underlying economic state, rather than complete knowledge.

Due to the uniqueness of equilibrium, the model by Morris and Shin (1998) as well as its various extensions permits analyzing the influence of different parameters on the event of a currency crisis. In this book, we investigate into the role of information dissemination in the onset of a crisis. Additionally to private information, we also take into account the disclosure of public information, i.e. information which is publicly announced and therefore becomes common knowledge for all market participants. The "common" character notwithstanding, public information may nonetheless be quite noisy. It might be imprecise, for instance, since economic data is often published preliminary, with some numbers still missing, or based on faulty economic concepts, so that a biased picture of the economy results.

Regarding the influence of private and public information on the event of a currency crisis, it has often been argued that in fixed rate regimes, central bank and government should commit to a high degree of transparency about economic fundamentals in order to prevent speculators from attacking the fixed parity. Whereas this view is confirmed by models taking into account only private information, we find that when allowing for both private and public information, transparency is not always suited for diminishing the danger of a currency crisis. Rather, the analyzed models demonstrate that private and public information might have opposite effects on the onset of a crisis. Additionally, we come to the conclusion that the informational impact is contingent on the fundamental state commonly expected by the market: whenever the market sentiment is optimistic towards the development of economic fundamentals, increasing the precision of public information will decrease the probability that a currency crisis is going to occur. More precise private information will then raise the danger of a crisis. The opposite holds if the market is pessimistic concerning the fundamental state of the economy. In this case, disclosing more precise public information will increase the probability of a crisis and disseminating more precise private information will reduce it.

Based on these results, advice can be given to central bank and government for the optimal choice of informational policy design in order to prevent speculative attacks. Particularly in cases where the fixed parity is highly overvalued and therefore vulnerable to an attack, the central bank should be very careful in selecting the optimal policy regime. Again, it can be found that the optimal policy combination is contingent on the commonly expected fundamental state. Whenever the market is pessimistic towards the economic development, the central bank should commit to disseminating private information of maximal precision, while at the same time maximizing fundamental risk by disclosing public information of minimal precision. If, in contrast, the market takes an optimistic view concerning the economic state, the central bank instead should support this view by "locking-in" the good state through public disclosures of maximal precision, while disseminating private information of lowest possible precision.

Apart from giving policy advice on how to prevent currency crises, employing the global games approach permits to investigate into even more complex structures on foreign exchange markets. In this respect, the book analyzes whether a "large" trader's influence on the market, particularly his suspected ability to make the market more aggressive towards an attack on the peg, is contingent on his informational position relative to the mass of "small" speculators. In contrast to earlier analyses on this topic, taking into account noisy private and public information demonstrated that the Soroses of the world do not necessarily trigger currency crises that could have been avoided otherwise. Rather, both their size and their potential informational advantage might have a positive as well as a negative effect on the probability of an attack. Due to the strong emphasis of coordination behavior in the global games approach, we find that a well-informed large trader will generally strengthen the market belief concerning the sustainability of the fixed parity. Hence, he will increase the probability of a crisis, whenever the market takes an already pessimistic view concerning the economic development. In contrast, he will diminish the danger of a crisis, if the market sentiment is very optimistic.

A very recent approach in financial economics tries to combine the global games method on solving for crisis equilibria with a dynamic setting. Market participants' behavior in this type of model does not only display strategic complementarities, as characteristic of financial crisis situations, but also backward- and forward-looking behavior. Again, this is a step towards a more realistic modelling of today's increasingly complex markets. Concerning the influence of information, the model concludes that by using the signalling effect following his actions, especially a large trader might have an incentive to make clear his informational position in order to magnify his impact on the market.

Due to the combination of game-theoretic methods with a macroeconomic setting, the recent currency crisis models as delineated in this book allow testing of various sorts. Experimental evidence has been found for the behavior of agents when endowed with noisy information. As predicted by theory, agents' optimal strategies in a laboratory situation indeed converge towards a unique equilibrium, which substantiates the theoretical results. Following from the up-to-datedness of the analyzed topic, only very few empirical tests have been conducted on the influence of information during the currency crises of the last years. One of the first analyses on data from the Asian crisis 1997–98, however, demonstrates that informational uncertainty can explain a large part of the speculative pressure on the fixed exchange rate, which might finally lead to the abandonment of the peg.

Summing up, we have to state that the employment of the global games approach in currency crisis models combines both the fundamentals-based explanatory power of first-generation crisis models as well as the expectations-based reasoning of second-generation models. Against this background, the book aimed at analyzing the role of information dissemination in currency crisis situations. In the age of easy, fast and relatively cheap information gathering, processing and disseminating, we think that this is and will be one of the most important channels of influencing the economy, both for central bank and government as well as for market participants. Investigations into the influence of information and disclosures on financial markets therefore remain an important task.

Expansionary work on informational aspects in currency crisis models, complementary to the analyses presented in this book, should be expected to start from either of the two main forces driving the results: the game-theoretic explanation of the market-microstructure, or the macroeconomic setting of fixed exchange rate regimes. As concerns the first point, a refined modelling of the information structure on the market should be desirable. The models examined in this book differentiate between only two types of information: private and public. Certainly, this is a very rough and inaccurate distinction and may be disputable. However, it displays very interesting insights into the interactions of large numbers of participants on complex markets. Nevertheless, in order to explain today's markets, an even finer structure of information is required.

Concerning the macroeconomic setting, several aspects might be worthwhile considering. One of the most urgently called-for issues is the analysis of financial contagion between crisis countries. A similar aspect refers to the interaction between banking and currency crises, which played an increasingly prominent role during financial crises of the recent past, for instance in Asia 1997–98. Introducing macroeconomic problems of these types into the global games approach of currency crisis models might be a fruitful effort for future research.

References

1. Aizenman J (1999) Capital controls and financial crises. Mimeo
2. Allen F, Gale D (1997) Optimal Financial Crises. Wharton Financial Institutions Center, Working Paper 97-01
3. Allen F, Gale D (2002) Optimal Currency Crises. In: Goodhart C, Illing G (eds) Financial Crises, Contagion, and the Lender of Last Resort. Oxford University Press, Oxford
4. Aumann R (1976) Agreeing to Disagree. Annals of Statistic 4:1236–1239
5. Avery C, Zemsky P (1998) Multidimensional Uncertainty and Herd Behavior in Financial Markets. American Economic Review 88(4):724–748
6. Banerjee A (1993) A Simple Model of Herd Behavior. Quarterly Journal of Economics 107(3):797–817
7. Barro R, Gordon D (1983) A Positive Theory of Monetary Policy in a Natural Rate Model. Journal of Political Economy 91:589–610
8. Berg A, Patillo C (1999) Are Currency Crises Predictable? A Test. Journal of International Money and Finance 18:561–586
9. Bhattacharya U, Weller P (1997) The advantage of hiding one's hand: Speculation and central bank intervention in the foreign exchange market. Journal of Monetary Economics 39:251–277
10. Bikhchandani S, Hirshleifer D, Welch I (1992) A Theory of Fashion, Custom, and Cultural Change as Informational Cascades. Journal of Political Economy 100(5):992–1026
11. Bikhchandani S, Hirshleifer D, Welch I (1998) Learning from the Behaviour of Others: Conformity, Fads and Informational Cascades. Journal of Economics Perspectives 12:151–170
12. Binmore K, Rubinstein A, Wolinsky A (1986) The Nash bargaining solution in economic modelling. Rand Journal of Economics 17:176–188
13. Binmore K (1992) Fun and Games. DC Heath and Company, Lexington.
14. Blanchard O, Fischer S (1996) Lectures on Macroeconomics. MIT Press, Cambridge (Mass)
15. Blanco H, Garber P (1986) Recurrent Devaluation and Speculative Attacks on the Mexican Peso. Journal of Political Economy 94:148–166
16. Brandenburger A (1992) Knowledge and Equilibrium in Games. Journal of Economic Perspectives 6(4):83–101

17. Brandenburger A, Dekel E (1993) Hierarchies of Beliefs and Common Knowledge. Journal of Economic Theory 59:189–198
18. Brunner A, Krahnen JP (2001) Corporate debt restructuring: Evidence on lender coordination in financial distress. CFS Working Paper 04/01
19. Brunnermeier M (2001) Asset Pricing under Asymmetric Information: Bubbles, Crashes, Technical Analysis and Herding. Oxford University Press, Oxford
20. Bulow J, Geanakoplos J, Klemperer, P (1985) Multimarket Oligopoly: Strategic Substitutes and Complements. Journal of Political Economy 93:488–511
21. Burdzy K, Frankel D, Pauzner A (2001) Fast Equilibrium Selection by Rational Players Living in a Changing World. Econometrica 69(1):163–190
22. Cabrales A, Nagel R, Armenter R (2000) Equilibrium Selection Through Incomplete Information in Coordination Games: An Experimental Study. Mimeo
23. Calvo G (1988) Servicing the Public Debt: The Role of Expectations. American Economic Review 78:1411–1428
24. Calvo G (1994) Comments on Dornbusch and Werner. Brookings Papers on Economic Activity 1:298–309
25. Calvo G, Mendoza E, Rogers J, Rose A (1996) Foreword: Speculative Attacks in Emerging Markets: What has Mexico Taught Us? A Symposium. Journal of International Economics 41:219–222
26. Camdessus M (1995) Drawing Lessons from the Mexican Crisis: Preventing and Resolving Financial Crises - the Role of the IMF. IMF Speeches 95/8
27. Carlsson H, van Damme E (1993) Global Games and Equilibrium Selection. Econometrica 61:989–1018
28. Carlsson H, Ganslandt M (1998) Noisy equilibrium selection in coordination games. Economics Letters 60:23–34
29. Chamley C, Gale D (1994) Information revelation and strategic delay in a model of investment. Econometrica 62(5):1065–1085
30. Chan K, Chiu S (2002) The role of (non-) transparency in a currency crisis model. European Economic Review 46:397–416
31. Chang E, Pinegar M, Schachter B (1997) Interday variations in volume, variance and participation of large speculators. Journal of Banking and Finance 21:797–810
32. Chari V, Kehoe P (2000) Financial Crises as Herds. Federal Reserve Bank of Minneapolis Working Paper 600
33. Cole H, Kehoe T (1996) A self-fulfilling model of Mexico's 1994-1995 debt crisis. Journal of International Economics 41:309–330
34. Cooper R (1999) Coordination Games. Complementarities and Macroeconomics. Cambridge University Press, Cambridge
35. Corsetti G, Dasgupta A, Morris S, Shin HS (2001) Does One Soros Make A Difference? A Theory of Currency Crises with Large and Small Traders. Cowles Foundation Discussion Paper 1273, Yale University
36. Corsetti G, Pesenti P, Roubini N (2001) The Role of Large Players in Currency Crises. NBER Working Paper 8303
37. Cukierman A, Meltzer A (1986) A Theory of Ambiguity, Credibility, and Inflation under Discretion and Asymmetric Information. Econometrica 54(5):1099–1128
38. Cumby R, van Wijnbergen S (1989) Financial Policy and Speculative Runs with a Crawling Peg. Journal of International Economics 27:111–127
39. Daniel B (2000) The Timing of Exchange Rate Collapse. Journal of International Money and Finance 19:765–784

40. Dasgupta A (2000) Social Learning with Payoff Complementarities. Mimeo.
41. Dasgupta A (2001) Coordination, Learning and Delay. Mimeo
42. DeLong B, DeLong C, Robinson S (1996) In Defense of Mexico's Rescue. Foreign Affairs 75
43. Dönges J, Heinemann F (2000) Competition for Order Flow as a Coordination Game. Mimeo
44. Dornbusch R, Werner A (1994) Mexico: Stabilization, Reform, and No Growth. Brookings Papers on Economic Activity 1:253–297
45. Edwards S (1997) The Mexican Peso Crisis: How Much Did We Know? When Did We Know It? NBER Working Paper 6334
46. Edwards S, Savastano M (1998) The Morning After: The Mexican Peso In The Aftermath Of The 1994 Currency Crisis. NBER Working Paper 6516
47. Eichengreen B, Rose A, Wyplosz C (1994) Speculative Attacks on Pegged Exchange Rates: An Empirical Exploration with Special Reference to the European Monetary System. NBER Working Paper 4898
48. Eichengreen B, Rose A, Wyplosz C (1996) Contagious Currency Crises. CEPR Discussion Papers 1453
49. Faust J, Svensson L (2000) Transparency and Credibility: Monetary Policy with Unobservable Goals. International Economic Review 42(2):369–398
50. Financial Stability Forum (FSF) (2000) Report of the Market Dynamics Study Group of the FSF Working Group on Highly Leveraged Institutions. http://www.fsforum.org/Reports/RepHLI.html
51. Fischer S (1994) Comments on Dornbusch and Werner. Brookings Papers on Economic Activity 1:304–309
52. Flood R, Garber P (1984) Collapsing Exchange-Rate Regimes: Some Linear Examples. Journal of International Economics 17:1–13
53. Flood R, Garber P, Kramer C (1996) Collapsing exchange rate regimes: Another linear example. Journal of International Economics 41:223–234
54. Flood R, Marion N (1996) Speculative Attacks: Fundamentals and Self-Fulfilling Prophecies. NBER Working Paper 5789
55. Flood R, Marion N (1997) Policy Implications of Second-Generation Crisis Models. IMF Staff Papers 9:10–17
56. Flood R, Marion N (1998) Perspectives on the Recent Currency Crisis Literature. NBER Working Paper 6380
57. Frankel J, Schmukler S (1996) Country Fund Discounts, Asymmetric Information and the Mexican Crisis of 1994: Did Local Residents Turn Pessimistic Before International Investors? NBER Working Paper 5714
58. Frankel D, Morris S, Pauzner A (2000) Equilibrium Selection in Global Games with Strategic Complementarities. Mimeo
59. Friedman M (1979) The Information Value of Observing Monetary Policy Deliberations. Journal of Economic Dynamics and Control 1:383–393
60. Fung W, Hsieh D, Tsatsaronis K (2000) Do Hedge Funds Disrupt Emerging Markets? Brookings-Wharton Papers on Financial Services
61. Galambos J (1995) Advanced Probability Theory. Marcel Dekker, New York
62. Gale D (1996) What have we learned from social learning? European Economic Review 40:617–628
63. Geanakoplos J (1992) Common Knowledge. Journal of Economic Perspectives 6(4):53–82
64. Gibbons R (1992) A Primer in Game Theory. Prentice Hall, London

65. Gil-Diaz F (1997) The Origin of Mexico's 1994 Financial Crisis. The Cato Journal 17(3)
66. Goldberg L (1994) Predicting Exchange Rate Crises: Mexico Revisited. NBER Working Paper 2702
67. Goldfajn I, Valdés R (1997) Are Currency Crises Predictable? IMF Working Paper 159
68. Goldstein I (2000) Interdependent Banking and Currency Crises in a Model of Self-Fulfilling Beliefs. Mimeo
69. Goldstein I, Pauzner A (2000) Demand Deposit Contracts and the Probability of Bank Runs. Mimeo
70. Gourieroux C, Monfort A (1997) Time series and dynamic models. Cambridge University Press, Cambridge
71. Greene W (2000) Econometric Analysis. Prentice-Hall, New Jersey
72. Gul F, Lundhom R (1995) Endogenous timing and the Clustering of Agents' Decisions. Journal of Political Economy 103:1039–1066
73. Hamilton J (1994) Time Series Analysis. Princeton University Press, Princeton
74. Harsanyi J (1973) Games with Randomly Disturbed Payoffs: A New Rationale for Mixed-Strategy Equilibrium Points. International Journal of Game Theory 2:235–250
75. Harsanyi J, Selten R (1988) A General Theory of Equilibrium Selection in Games. MIT Press, Cambridge (Mass)
76. Hartigan J (1983) Bayes Theory. Springer, Berlin Heidelberg New York
77. Heinemann F (1995) Rationalisierbare Erwartungen. Physica, Heidelberg
78. Heinemann F, Illing G (1999) Speculative Attacks: Unique Sunspot Equilibrium and Transparency. Frankfurter Volkswirtschaftliche Diskussionsbeiträge, University of Frankfurt/Main 97. Forthcoming in Journal of International Economics
79. Heinemann F (2000) Unique Equilibrium in a Model of Self-Fulfilling Currency Attacks: Comment. American Economic Review 90(1):316–318
80. Heinemann F, Nagel R, Ockenfels P (2001) Speculative Attacks and Financial Architecture: Experimental Analysis of Coordination Games with Public and Private Information. Mimeo
81. Heinemann F, Metz C (2002) Optimal Risk Taking and Information Policy to Avoid Currency and Liquidity Crises. University of Kassel Discussion Paper 31/02
82. Hellwig C (2000) Public Information, Private Information and the Multiplicity of Equilibria in Coordination Games. Forthcoming in Journal of Economic Theory
83. Hirshleifer J, Riley J (1992) The Analytics of Uncertainty and Information. Cambridge University Press, Cambridge
84. Holler M, Illing G (1996) Einführung in die Spieltheorie. Springer, Berlin Heidelberg New York
85. Hsiao C (1986) Analysis of Panel Data. Cambridge University Press, Cambridge
86. Hubert F, Schäfer D (2001) Coordination Failure with Multiple-Source Lending. Forthcoming in Journal of Institutional and Theoretical Economics.
87. Illing G (1998) International Capital Markets and Central Bank Sovereignity: Comment. Journal of Institutional and Theoretical Economics 154(1):287–290
88. Isard P (1995) Exchange Rate Economics. Cambridge University Press, Cambridge

89. Jeanne O (1996) Would a Tobin-tax have saved the EMS? Scandinavian Journal of Economics 98:503–520
90. Jeanne O (1997) Are currency crises self-fulfilling? A test. Journal of International Economics 43:263–286
91. Jeanne O (1999) Currency Crises: A Perspective on Recent Theoretical Developments. CEPR Working Paper 2170
92. Jeanne O, Masson P (2000) Currency crises, sunspots and Markov-switching regimes. Journal of International Economics 50:327–350
93. Jensen H (2001) Optimal Degrees of Transparency in Monetary Policymaking. CEPR Discussion Paper Series 2689
94. Kaminsky G, Lizando S, Reinhart C (1997) Leading Indicators of Currency Crises. Mimeo
95. Kaminsky G, Reinhart C (1999) The Twin Crises: The Causes of Banking and Balance-of-Payments Problems. American Economic Review 89(3):473–500
96. Kim J, Wei S-J (1997) The Big Players In The Foreign Exchange Market: Do They Trade on Information Or Noise? NBER Working Paper 6256
97. Krugman P (1979) A Model of Balance-of-Payment Crises. Journal of Money, Credit and Banking 11:311–325
98. Krugman P (1997) Are Currency Crises Self-Fulfilling? NBER Macroeconomics Annual: 345-378. MIT-Press, Cambridge (Mass)
99. Krugman P, Obstfeld M (2000) International Economics. Theory and Policy. Addison-Wesley, New York
100. Kydland F, Prescott E (1977) Rules Rather than Discretion: The Inconsistency of Optimal Plans. Journal of Political Economy 85:473–491
101. Lawrence D (1999) The Economic Value of Information. Springer, Berlin Heidelberg New York
102. Lee IH (1993) On the convergence of informational cascades. Journal of Economic Theory 61(2):395–411
103. Levine D, Pesendorfer W (1995) When Are Agents Negligible? American Economic Review 85(5):1160–1170
104. Lustig N (1995) The Mexican Peso Crisis: the Foreseeable and the Surprise. Brookings Discussion Papers in International Economics 114
105. Lux T (1995) Herd Behaviour, Bubbles and Crashes. Economic Journal 105:881–896
106. Lyons R (2001) The Microstructure Approach to Exchange Rates. MIT Press, Cambridge (Mass)
107. Marshall D (2002) Financial crises and coordination failure: A comment. Journal of Banking and Finance 26:547–555
108. Menkhoff L, Michaelis J (1995a) Ist die Tobin-Steuer tatsächlich 'tot'? Review of Economics 46:34–54
109. Menkhoff L, Michaelis J (1995b) Steuern zur Begrenzung unerwünschter Währungsspekulation. AUSSENWIRTSCHAFT 50:443–462
110. Metz C (2002a) Private and Public Information in Self-Fulfilling Currency Crises. Journal of Economics 76(1):65-85
111. Metz C (2002b) Currency Crises - The Role of Large Traders. University of Kassel Discussion Paper 28/02
112. Milgrom P (1981) Good news and bad news: representation theorems and applications. Bell Journal of Economics 12:380–391
113. Milgrom P, Roberts J (1990) Rationalizability, Learning, and Equilibrium in Games with Strategic Complementarities. Econometrica 58(6):1255–1277

114. Milgrom P, Roberts J (1994) Comparing Equilibria. American Economic Review 84(3):441–459
115. Monderer D, Shapley L (1996) Potential Games. Games and Economic Behavior 14:124–143
116. Morris S (1995) The Common Prior Assumption in Economic Theory. Economics and Philosophy 11:227–253
117. Morris S, Shin HS (1998) Unique Equilibrium in a Model of Self-Fulfilling Currency Attacks. American Economic Review 88:587–597
118. Morris S, Shin HS (1999a) Coordination Risk and the Price of Debt. Mimeo
119. Morris S, Shin HS (1999b) Rethinking Multiple Equilibria. NBER Macroeconomic Annual: 139–161. MIT-Press, Cambridge (Mass)
120. Morris S, Shin HS (1999c) A Theory of the Onset of Currency Attacks. In: Agenor P-R, Miller M, Vines D, Weber A (eds) The Asian Financial Crisis. Cambridge University Press, Cambridge
121. Morris S, Shin HS (2000) Global Games: Theory and Applications. Forthcoming in Dewatripont M, Hansen L, Turnovsky S (eds) Advances in Economics and Econometrics, the Eighth World Congress of the Econometric Society. Cambridge University Press, Cambridge
122. Morris S, Shin HS (2001) The CNBC Effect: Welfare Effects of Public Information. Mimeo
123. Myerson R (1999) Nash Equilibrium and the History of Economic Theory. Journal of Economic Literature 37:1067–1082
124. Nagel R (1995) Unraveling in Guessing Games: An Experimental Study. American Economic Review 85:1313–1326
125. Obstfeld M (1986) Rational and Self-Fulfilling Balance-of-Payments Crises. American Economic Review 76:72–81
126. Obstfeld M (1994) The Logic of Currency Crises. Cahiers Economiques et Monetaires 43:189–213
127. Obstfeld M (1995) International Currency Experience: New Lessons and Lessons Relearned. Brookings Papers on Economic Activity 1:119–196
128. Obstfeld M, Rogoff K (1995) The Mirage of Fixed Exchange Rates. Journal of Economic Perspectives 9(4):73–96
129. Obstfeld M (1996) Models of Currency Crises with Self-Fulfilling Features. European Economic Review 40:1037–1047
130. O'Hara M (1997) Market Microstructure Theory. Blackwell, Cambridge Oxford
131. Popper H, Montgomery J (2001) Information sharing and central bank intervention in the foreign exchange market. Journal of International Economics 55:295–316
132. Prati A, Sbracia M (2001) Currency Crises and Uncertainty About Fundamentals. Mimeo
133. Rasmusen E (1995) Games and Information. An Introduction to Game Theory. Blackwell, Cambridge Oxford
134. Rose A, Svensson L (1994) European Exchange Rate Credibility before the Fall. European Economic Review 38(6):1185–1216
135. Rubinstein A (1989) The Electronic Mail Game: Strategic Behaviour under 'Almost Common Knowledge'. American Economic Review 79(3):385–391
136. Sachs J, Tornell A, Velasco A (1996a) Financial Crises in Emerging Markets: The Lessons from 1995. Brookings Papers on Economic Activity 16:147–215
137. Sachs J, Tornell A, Velasco A (1996b) The Mexican Peso Crisis: Sudden Death Or Death Foretold? NBER Working Paper 5563

138. Sachs J, Tornell A, Velasco A (1996c) The Collapse of the Mexican Peso: What Have We Learned? Economic Policy: A European Forum 22:15–63
139. Salant S, Henderson D (1978) Market Anticipation of Government Policy and the Price of Gold. Journal of Political Economy 86:627–648
140. Sbracia M, Zaghini A (2001) Expectation and Information in Second Generation Currency Crises Models. Economic Modelling 18:203–222
141. Scharfstein D, Stein J (1990) Herd Behaviour and Investment. American Economic Review 80:465–479
142. Selten R (1975) Reexamination of the Perfectness Concept for Equilibrium Points in Extensive Games. International Journal of Game Theory 4:25–55
143. Shiller R (1995) Conversation, Information and Herd Behavior. AEA Papers and Proceedings 85(2):181–185
144. Shin HS (1993) Logical Structure of Common Knowledge. Journal of Economic Theory 1:1–13
145. Stahl D, Wilson P (1994) Experimental Evidence on Players' Models of Other Players. Journal of Economic Behaviour and Organization 25:309–327
146. Van Damme E (1991) Stability and Perfection of Nash Equilibria. Springer, Berlin Heidelbeg New York
147. Vives X (1993) How fast do rational agents learn? Review of Economic Studies 60:329–347
148. Vives X (1996) Social learning and rational expectations. European Economic Review 40:589–601
149. Von Neumann J, Morgenstern, O (1974) Theory of Games and Economic Behavior. Princeton University Press, Princeton
150. Welch I (1992) Sequential Scales, Learning, and Cascades. Journal of Finance 47:695–732
151. Weymark D (1998) A General Approach to Measuring Exchange Market Pressure. Oxford Economic Papers 50:106–121
152. Willman A (1987) Speculative Attacks on the Currency with Uncertain Monetary Policy Reactions. Economics Letters 25:75–78
153. Willman A (1988) The Collapse of the Fixed Exchange Rate Regime with Sticky Wages and Imperfect Substitutability between Domestic and Foreign Bonds. European Economic Review 32:1817–1838

Lecture Notes in Economics and Mathematical Systems

For information about Vols. 1–434
please contact your bookseller or Springer-Verlag

Vol. 435: L. Chen, Interest Rate Dynamics, Derivatives Pricing, and Risk Management. XII, 149 pages. 1996.

Vol. 436: M. Klemisch-Ahlert, Bargaining in Economic and Ethical Environments. IX, 155 pages. 1996.

Vol. 437: C. Jordan, Batching and Scheduling. IX, 178 pages. 1996.

Vol. 438: A. Villar, General Equilibrium with Increasing Returns. XIII, 164 pages. 1996.

Vol. 439: M. Zenner, Learning to Become Rational. VII, 201 pages. 1996.

Vol. 440: W. Ryll, Litigation and Settlement in a Game with Incomplete Information. VIII, 174 pages. 1996.

Vol. 441: H. Dawid, Adaptive Learning by Genetic Algorithms. IX, 166 pages.1996.

Vol. 442: L. Corchón, Theories of Imperfectly Competitive Markets. XIII, 163 pages. 1996.

Vol. 443: G. Lang, On Overlapping Generations Models with Productive Capital. X, 98 pages. 1996.

Vol. 444: S. Jørgensen, G. Zaccour (Eds.), Dynamic Competitive Analysis in Marketing. X, 285 pages. 1996.

Vol. 445: A. H. Christer, S. Osaki, L. C. Thomas (Eds.), Stochastic Modelling in Innovative Manufactoring. X, 361 pages. 1997.

Vol. 446: G. Dhaene, Encompassing. X, 160 pages. 1997.

Vol. 447: A. Artale, Rings in Auctions. X, 172 pages. 1997.

Vol. 448: G. Fandel, T. Gal (Eds.), Multiple Criteria Decision Making. XII, 678 pages. 1997.

Vol. 449: F. Fang, M. Sanglier (Eds.), Complexity and Self-Organization in Social and Economic Systems. IX, 317 pages, 1997.

Vol. 450: P. M. Pardalos, D. W. Hearn, W. W. Hager, (Eds.), Network Optimization. VIII, 485 pages, 1997.

Vol. 451: M. Salge, Rational Bubbles. Theoretical Basis, Economic Relevance, and Empirical Evidence with a Special Emphasis on the German Stock Market.IX, 265 pages. 1997.

Vol. 452: P. Gritzmann, R. Horst, E. Sachs, R. Tichatschke (Eds.), Recent Advances in Optimization. VIII, 379 pages. 1997.

Vol. 453: A. S. Tangian, J. Gruber (Eds.), Constructing Scalar-Valued Objective Functions. VIII, 298 pages. 1997.

Vol. 454: H.-M. Krolzig, Markov-Switching Vector Autoregressions. XIV, 358 pages. 1997.

Vol. 455: R. Caballero, F. Ruiz, R. E. Steuer (Eds.), Advances in Multiple Objective and Goal Programming. VIII, 391 pages. 1997.

Vol. 456: R. Conte, R. Hegselmann, P. Terna (Eds.), Simulating Social Phenomena. VIII, 536 pages. 1997.

Vol. 457: C. Hsu, Volume and the Nonlinear Dynamics of Stock Returns. VIII, 133 pages. 1998.

Vol. 458: K. Marti, P. Kall (Eds.), Stochastic Programming Methods and Technical Applications. X, 437 pages. 1998.

Vol. 459: H. K. Ryu, D. J. Slottje, Measuring Trends in U.S. Income Inequality. XI, 195 pages. 1998.

Vol. 460: B. Fleischmann, J. A. E. E. van Nunen, M. G. Speranza, P. Stähly, Advances in Distribution Logistic. XI, 535 pages. 1998.

Vol. 461: U. Schmidt, Axiomatic Utility Theory under Risk. XV, 201 pages. 1998.

Vol. 462: L. von Auer, Dynamic Preferences, Choice Mechanisms, and Welfare. XII, 226 pages. 1998.

Vol. 463: G. Abraham-Frois (Ed.), Non-Linear Dynamics and Endogenous Cycles. VI, 204 pages. 1998.

Vol. 464: A. Aulin, The Impact of Science on Economic Growth and its Cycles. IX, 204 pages. 1998.

Vol. 465: T. J. Stewart, R. C. van den Honert (Eds.), Trends in Multicriteria Decision Making. X, 448 pages. 1998.

Vol. 466: A. Sadrieh, The Alternating Double Auction Market. VII, 350 pages. 1998.

Vol. 467: H. Hennig-Schmidt, Bargaining in a Video Experiment. Determinants of Boundedly Rational Behavior. XII, 221 pages. 1999.

Vol. 468: A. Ziegler, A Game Theory Analysis of Options. XIV, 145 pages. 1999.

Vol. 469: M. P. Vogel, Environmental Kuznets Curves. XIII, 197 pages. 1999.

Vol. 470: M. Ammann, Pricing Derivative Credit Risk. XII, 228 pages. 1999.

Vol. 471: N. H. M. Wilson (Ed.), Computer-Aided Transit Scheduling. XI, 444 pages. 1999.

Vol. 472: J.-R. Tyran, Money Illusion and Strategic Complementarity as Causes of Monetary Non-Neutrality. X, 228 pages. 1999.

Vol. 473: S. Helber, Performance Analysis of Flow Lines with Non-Linear Flow of Material. IX, 280 pages. 1999.

Vol. 474: U. Schwalbe, The Core of Economies with Asymmetric Information. IX, 141 pages. 1999.

Vol. 475: L. Kaas, Dynamic Macroeconomics with Imperfect Competition. XI, 155 pages. 1999.

Vol. 476: R. Demel, Fiscal Policy, Public Debt and the Term Structure of Interest Rates. X, 279 pages. 1999.

Vol. 477: M. Théra, R. Tichatschke (Eds.), Ill-posed Variational Problems and Regularization Techniques. VIII, 274 pages. 1999.

Vol. 478: S. Hartmann, Project Scheduling under Limited Resources. XII, 221 pages. 1999.

Vol. 479: L. v. Thadden, Money, Inflation, and Capital Formation. IX, 192 pages. 1999.

Vol. 480: M. Grazia Speranza, P. Stähly (Eds.), New Trends in Distribution Logistics. X, 336 pages. 1999.

Vol. 481: V. H. Nguyen, J. J. Strodiot, P. Tossings (Eds.). Optimation. IX, 498 pages. 2000.

Vol. 482: W. B. Zhang, A Theory of International Trade. XI, 192 pages. 2000.

Vol. 483: M. Königstein, Equity, Efficiency and Evolutionary Stability in Bargaining Games with Joint Production. XII, 197 pages. 2000.

Vol. 484: D. D. Gatti, M. Gallegati, A. Kirman, Interaction and Market Structure. VI, 298 pages. 2000.

Vol. 485: A. Garnaev, Search Games and Other Applications of Game Theory. VIII, 145 pages. 2000.

Vol. 486: M. Neugart, Nonlinear Labor Market Dynamics. X, 175 pages. 2000.

Vol. 487: Y. Y. Haimes, R. E. Steuer (Eds.), Research and Practice in Multiple Criteria Decision Making. XVII, 553 pages. 2000.

Vol. 488: B. Schmolck, Ommitted Variable Tests and Dynamic Specification. X, 144 pages. 2000.

Vol. 489: T. Steger, Transitional Dynamics and Economic Growth in Developing Countries. VIII, 151 pages. 2000.

Vol. 490: S. Minner, Strategic Safety Stocks in Supply Chains. XI, 214 pages. 2000.

Vol. 491: M. Ehrgott, Multicriteria Optimization. VIII, 242 pages. 2000.

Vol. 492: T. Phan Huy, Constraint Propagation in Flexible Manufacturing. IX, 258 pages. 2000.

Vol. 493: J. Zhu, Modular Pricing of Options. X, 170 pages. 2000.

Vol. 494: D. Franzen, Design of Master Agreements for OTC Derivatives. VIII, 175 pages. 2001.

Vol. 495: I Konnov, Combined Relaxation Methods for Variational Inequalities. XI, 181 pages. 2001.

Vol. 496: P. Weiß, Unemployment in Open Economies. XII, 226 pages. 2001.

Vol. 497: J. Inkmann, Conditional Moment Estimation of Nonlinear Equation Systems. VIII, 214 pages. 2001.

Vol. 498: M. Reutter, A Macroeconomic Model of West German Unemployment. X, 125 pages. 2001.

Vol. 499: A. Casajus, Focal Points in Framed Games. XI, 131 pages. 2001.

Vol. 500: F. Nardini, Technical Progress and Economic Growth. XVII, 191 pages. 2001.

Vol. 501: M. Fleischmann, Quantitative Models for Reverse Logistics. XI, 181 pages. 2001.

Vol. 502: N. Hadjisavvas, J. E. Martínez-Legaz, J.-P. Penot (Eds.), Generalized Convexity and Generalized Monotonicity. IX, 410 pages. 2001.

Vol. 503: A. Kirman, J.-B. Zimmermann (Eds.), Economics with Heterogenous Interacting Agents. VII, 343 pages. 2001.

Vol. 504: P.-Y. Moix (Ed.),The Measurement of Market Risk. XI, 272 pages. 2001.

Vol. 505: S. Voß, J. R. Daduna (Eds.), Computer-Aided Scheduling of Public Transport. XI, 466 pages. 2001.

Vol. 506: B. P. Kellerhals, Financial Pricing Models i Continuous Time and Kalman Filtering. XIV, 247 pages 2001.

Vol. 507: M. Koksalan, S. Zionts, Multiple Criteria Decisio Making in the New Millenium. XII, 481 pages. 2001.

Vol. 508: K. Neumann, C. Schwindt, J. Zimmermann, Projec Scheduling with Time Windows and Scarce Resources. X 335 pages. 2002.

Vol. 509: D. Hornung, Investment, R&D, and Long-Ru Growth. XVI, 194 pages. 2002.

Vol. 510: A. S. Tangian, Constructing and Applyin Objective Functions. XII, 582 pages. 2002.

Vol. 511: M. Külpmann, Stock Market Overreaction an Fundamental Valuation. IX, 198 pages. 2002.

Vol. 512: W.-B. Zhang, An Economic Theory of Cities.X 220 pages. 2002.

Vol. 513: K. Marti, Stochastic Optimization Techniques VIII, 364 pages. 2002.

Vol. 514: S. Wang, Y. Xia, Portfolio and Asset Pricing. XII 200 pages. 2002.

Vol. 515: G. Heisig, Planning Stability in Material Require ments Planning System. XII, 264 pages. 2002.

Vol. 516: B. Schmid, Pricing Credit Linked Financial In struments. X, 246 pages. 2002.

Vol. 517: H. I. Meinhardt, Cooperative Decision Making i Common Pool Situations. VIII, 205 pages. 2002.

Vol. 518: S. Napel, Bilateral Bargaining. VIII, 188 pages 2002.

Vol. 519: A. Klose, G. Speranza, L. N. Van Wassenhov (Eds.), Quantitative Approaches to Distribution Logistic and Supply Chain Management. XIII, 421 pages. 2002.

Vol. 520: B. Glaser, Efficiency versus Sustainability i Dynamic Decision Making. IX, 252 pages. 2002.

Vol. 521: R. Cowan, N. Jonard (Eds.), Heterogenous Agents Interactions and Economic Performance. XIV, 339 pages 2003.

Vol. 522: C. Neff, Corporate Finance, Innovation, an Strategic Competition. IX, 218 pages. 2003.

Vol. 523: W.-B. Zhang, A Theory of Interregional Dynamics XI, 231 pages. 2003.

Vol. 524: M. Frölich, Programme Evaluation and Treatmen Choise. VIII, 191 pages. 2003.

Vol. 525:S. Spinler, Capacity Reservation for Capital Intensive Technologies. XVI, 139 pages. 2003.

Vol. 526: C. F. Daganzo, A Theory of Supply Chains. VIII 123 pages. 2003.

Vol. 527: C. E. Metz, Information Dissemination in Currency Crises. XI, 231 pages. 2003.

GPSR Compliance

The European Union's (EU) General Product Safety Regulation (GPSR) is a set of rules that requires consumer products to be safe and our obligations to ensure this.

If you have any concerns about our products, you can contact us on ProductSafety@springernature.com

In case Publisher is established outside the EU, the EU authorized representative is:

Springer Nature Customer Service Center GmbH
Europaplatz 3
69115 Heidelberg, Germany

Batch number: 10844675

Printed by Printforce, the Netherlands